MAKING A
PERFORMANCE

Making a Performance: Devising Histories and Contemporary Practices
traces innovations in devised performance from early theatrical
experiments in the twentieth century to the radical performances of
the twenty-first century.

This introduction to the theory, history and practice of devised
performance explores how performance-makers have built on the
experimental aesthetic traditions of the past. It looks to companies as
diverse as Australia's Legs on the Wall, Britain's Forced Entertainment and the USA-based Goat Island to show how contemporary
practitioners challenge orthodoxies to develop new theatrical languages.

Designed to be accessible to both scholars and practitioners, this
study offers clear, practical examples of concepts and ideas that have
shaped some of the most vibrant and experimental practices in
contemporary performance.

Emma Govan, Helen Nicholson and **Katie Normington** are practitioners in different forms of devised theatre and lecture in drama at
Royal Holloway, University of London.

MAKING A PERFORMANCE

Devising Histories and Contemporary Practices

EMMA GOVAN,
HELEN NICHOLSON,
KATIE NORMINGTON

Routledge
Taylor & Francis Group

LONDON AND NEW YORK

First published 2007
by Routledge
2 Park Square, Milton Park, Abingdon, Oxon OX14 4RN

Simultaneously published in the USA and Canada
by Routledge
270 Madison Ave, New York, NY 10016

Routledge is an imprint of the Taylor & Francis Group, an informa business

© 2007 Emma Govan, Helen Nicholson and Katie Normington

Typeset in Minion by
Florence Production Ltd, Stoodleigh, Devon
Printed and bound in Great Britain by
MPG Books Ltd, Bodmin, Cornwall

British Library Cataloguing in Publication Data
A catalogue record for this book is available from the British Library

Library of Congress Cataloging in Publication Data
Govan, Emma.
Making a performance: devising histories and contemporary practices/
Emma Govan, Helen Nicholson, Katie Normington.
p. cm.
Includes bibliographical references and index.
1. Experimental theater – History – 20th century. 2. Experimental
theater – History – 21st century. I. Nicholson, Helen, 1958–
II. Normington, Katie, 1964– III. Title.
PN2193.E86G68 2007
792.02′2 – dc22

ISBN10: 0–415–28652–2 (hbk)
ISBN10: 0–415–28653–0 (pbk)
ISBN10: 0–203–94695–2 (ebk)

ISBN13: 978–0–415–28652–7 (hbk)
ISBN13: 978–0–415–28653–4 (pbk)
ISBN13: 978–0–203–94695–4 (ebk)

CONTENTS

ILLUSTRATIONS

FIGURES

TABLES

ACKNOWLEDGEMENTS

We should like to thank all those who have contributed to the process of writing this book. We are especially grateful to Blast Theory, Mark Brodzinski, Gob Squad, Ben Harrison, IOU Theatre, Rona Lee, Lone Twin, Clive Mendus, Simon Purins, Reckless Sleepers, RIFCO, Talia Rodgers, Third Angel, Tim Spicer, David Thurlby, Mole Wetherell and Libby Worth for their generous support and advice. We are indebted to the insights of colleagues in the Department of Drama and Theatre at Royal Holloway, University of London and to the creativity of students we have taught on courses in devised performance.

Introduction

ONE

THE ART OF DEVISING

The theatre reproduces life. *The art of theatre* invents life.
Howard Barker (Barker 2005: 6)

Often associated with the innovative and experimental, devised performances have frequently marked both the restrictions and possibilities of theatre as a mode of cultural production. The practice of devising has been instrumental in enabling theatre-makers to develop artistically satisfying ways of working by stretching the limits of established practices and reshaping their creative processes. By questioning orthodoxies, devised performance has set new challenges for both audiences and performers and has thereby made a significant and enduring contribution to the contemporary theatrical landscape. This book offers an investigation into the practices, processes and principles of devising performance that have shaped and continue to inform this energetic aspect of theatre.

Devised performance occupies a distinct place in contemporary arts practice and has a history of exceeding traditional theatrical boundaries. The success of companies as diverse and innovative as Australia's Legs on the Wall, Britain's Forced Entertainment and the US-based Goat Island, to name but three of the best known, has ensured a loyal following among audiences eager to witness challenging new practice. Supported by the imaginative programming of international arts festivals and a burgeoning university and college sector that is keen to encourage drama students to recognise the aesthetic, political and artistic potential of theatre-making, devised performance has achieved popularity on an unprecedented scale. In Britain, the 2005 productions of DV8's *Just for Show* at the National Theatre in London and Frantic Assembly's site-specific piece *Dirty Wonderland* shown at the Brighton Festival sold out within days or even minutes. Devised performance, always associated with the counter-cultural fringe, is becoming increasingly commercially successful and entering the mainstream.

The appeal of devising performance for practitioners lies in its pliability and porousness. The invented tradition of devised performance has, of course, no single aesthetic or ideological objective; its strategies and methods are indebted to a wide range of cultural fields including political and community theatres, physical theatre, performance and live art. Theoretically, innovative practitioners have gained insights from cognate research in various disciplines including psychology, sociology and anthropology as well as theatre and performance studies. Practice has been informed by this inter-disciplinarity, and enriched by dialogue and cross-fertilisation between practices and practitioners. Devised performance is closely connected to the context and moment of production, and new practices have been invented to extend contemporary notions of what performance might be. Devising has, therefore, the flexibility to enable theatre-makers to address matters of personal concern, to interrogate topical issues, and to extend the aesthetics and reception of performance.

What is devising?

It is useful to begin with definitions, even when they are unreliable and constantly in flux. Devising is widely regarded as a process of generating a performative or theatrical event, often but not always in collaboration with others. It is interesting that, in the USA, this aspect of theatre-making is often described as 'collaborative creation' or, in the European tradition, as the product of 'creative collectives', both terms that emphasise group interactivity in the process of making a performance. 'Devised theatre' or 'devised performance' is sometimes used as a collective noun to indicate that it is an original piece of work developed by a company or sometimes by solo performers, but it would be misleading to suggest that this umbrella term signifies any particular dramatic genre or a specific style of performance.

Recent definitions of devising performance indicate both its historical roots and the shifting applications of the term. In the first book published with an explicit focus on the subject, Alison Oddey's *Devising Theatre: A Practical and Theoretical Handbook* (1994), devising is described in terms that emphasise the oppositional intentions of artists and how their aspirations were translated into creative processes and affected collaborations:

> Devised work is a response and a reaction to the playwright–director relations, to text-based theatre, and to naturalism, and challenges the prevailing ideology of one person's text under another person's direction. Devised theatre is concerned with the collective creation of art (not the single vision of the playwright), and it is here that the emphasis has shifted from the writer to the creative artist.
>
> (Oddey 1994: 4)

In this description Oddey maintains the view that devising rejects more 'writerly' forms of theatre such as naturalism in favour of dramatic styles that are more visual and physical. In the process Oddey accepts that text-led theatre inevitably represents the sole vision of the playwright, a way of thinking about mainstream theatre that implies that it is still hierarchical in structure and dominated by naturalism. This vision of devising as alternative, oppositional and democratic recalls its avant-garde and radical histories, but by the early 1990s, as Oddey acknowledges, this particular form of idealism was already beginning to wane:

> In the 1970s devising companies chose artistic democracy in favour of the hierarchical structures of power linked to text-based theatre, and yet within the last twenty years or so there has been a move from this standpoint in response to an ever-changing economic and artistic climate. In the cultural climate of the 1990s, the term 'devising' has less radical implications, placing greater emphasis on skill sharing, specific roles, increasing division of responsibilities . . . and more hierarchical groups structures.
>
> (Oddey 1994: 9)

It is interesting to note that economic need, as well as artistic vision, is held accountable for changing working practices. This recognises that bringing together diverse creativities and different specialist skills presents rich artistic opportunities. This may involve actors, directors, choreographers and writers working together. This form of collaboration also supports the commercial viability of companies where they employ specialised freelance practitioners on a project-by-project basis to support their core teams rather than offering expensive permanent contracts. In educational contexts, by contrast, where devising is a regular requirement of examinations in school and college drama, undifferentiated patterns of work in which all participants share similar responsibilities for the production are still often encouraged (Neelands and Dobson 2000; Lamden 2000).

In their 2006 study of devising performance, Deirdre Heddon and Jane Milling question whether devising was ever non-hierarchical and democratic. Despite rhetoric to the contrary, they point to directors such as Judith Malina and Julian Beck, Richard Schechner, Elizabeth LeCompte, Tim Etchells and Hilary Westlake, all of whom have led ensembles in the process of devising performance (Heddon and Milling 2006: 5). Although sceptical of the rhetoric of equality and equity that has sometimes accompanied accounts of devising, Heddon and Milling maintain that one of the distinguishing features of devising is collaboratively produced performance text. As they point out, the generic term 'devising' describes 'a mode of work in which no script – neither play-text nor performance score – exists prior to the work's creation by the company' (Heddon and Milling 2006: 3).

Although breaking the authority of the written text is not generally held to be a political ideal by contemporary theatre-makers, and many no longer prefer to work outside the mainstream, the practice of generating, shaping and editing new material into an original performance remains a central dynamic of devised performance. Contemporary devisers are also likely to have an expectation that the work will be performed by those involved in the devising process, at least in the first production. The British company Forced Entertainment provides a good example of how the balance between authorship and performance is negotiated. Tim Etchells, the artistic director, consistently rejects the concept of an authentic authorial voice in his work, arguing that writing for performance is often 'about collecting, sifting and using bits of other people's stuff' rather than an expression of a coherent voice or 'self' (Etchells 1999: 101). When the company was approached by someone wanting to stage its show *Speak Bitterness* (1996), however, it was, in the words of John Deeney, 'unconvinced that it could be performed by other people' (Deeney 1998: 28). This suggests an approach that, while questioning the authority and authenticity of textual construction, values the creative collaboration of theatre-makers in the devising process. This builds a language of performance that uniquely suits the actors' particular identities, strengths and abilities.

Since its inception in the early twentieth century, devising performance has thrown a spotlight on the creative process. Although this has been variously theorised and articulated at different times, twentieth- and twenty-first-century practitioners have focussed on discovering experimental creative processes and provoking the development of new theories and modes of practice. While rejecting the idea that there is an overarching theory of devising that might be applied to all contexts, Heddon and Milling suggest that it might be 'best understood as a set of strategies' (Heddon and Milling 2006: 2). Although the material for devised performances may be generated through spontaneous improvisation, the processes of working are also likely to include an eclectic and experimental mix of playing, editing, rehearsing, researching, designing, writing, scoring, choreographing, discussion and debate.

If devising is most accurately described in the plural – as *processes* of experimentation and sets of creative *strategies* – rather than a single methodology, it defies neat definition or categorisation. New practices have arisen from a combination of creative conversations and dissatisfaction with how current modes of practice address contemporary climates. This book examines the plurality of strategies and approaches used by devisers past and present, not with an intention of establishing an overarching vision of what devising is, nor to recommend specific ways of working, but to explore how and why changes have taken place, why experimentations with practice have occurred, and what this means for contemporary performance-makers.

From theatre to performance?

Informed practitioners have consistently extended their creative processes by drawing on the influences and legacies of their antecedents, enabling them to break with tradition and generate new and innovative performances. This interest in reconceptualising creative practices is particularly evident in devising, which has experimented with the limits and potential of theatre and performance. The different inflections associated with the terms 'theatre' and 'performance' might be observed across a wide range of artistic practices, marking an uneasy and incomplete paradigm shift in both theory and practice.

One way to explore innovations in devising is to consider how distinctions between theatre and performance have impacted on both critics and practitioners. On the one hand, some cultural critics have argued that theatre is limited by its association with commercialism and consumerism, and that its highly codified theatre practices and intimidating buildings restrict its potential to question contemporary social values. Baz Kershaw, for example, argues that theatre is a 'disciplinary system' and 'system of cultural production' that encourages audiences' passive acceptance of the status quo (Kershaw 1999: 31–32). In this configuration, theatre is associated with artificiality and showiness, and consequently remote from the more pressing concerns of daily existence. On the other hand, performance is generally seen to be wider and more eclectic in scope, extending not only to theatrical performances that take place in and outside theatre buildings, but also to the performative aspects of everyday life. Building on insights from anthropology, in the emergent field of performance studies scholars have turned their attention to celebrations, ritual, sport and other forms of paratheatrical activities.

Debates about theatre and performance turn on how far each is regarded as potentially radical – in aesthetic form, in content and in the means and methods of production – and it is partly for this reason that they are significant to this book about devising. Practitioners as well as cultural commentators have shown an interest in stretching the boundaries of representation. In terms of artistic practice, Janelle Reinelt has argued that the term 'performance' became associated with the avant-garde and anti-theatre, particularly in the 1960s and 1970s, when it was used to denote a rejection of mimetic representation and the authority of the written script (Reinelt 2002: 02). In this conceptualisation, devised performance shows practitioners' interest in exploring physicality before textuality, and in experimental ways of working that emphasise the creative freedom and spontaneity of both performers and spectators. This approach draws attention to the actual experiences of performers and audiences in the moment of performance where conventional boundaries between them are broken down. Theatre, by contrast, is concerned with representational space rather than everyday places, in creating imaginary characters and fictional worlds. The Canadian theorist Josette Féral has, however, argued that theatricality, as well as performance, has radical potential. By framing the tensions between reality and fiction, she argues that theatre emphasises the aesthetic distance between performers and audiences, and in so doing invites them to see and imagine the world differently. Féral recognises the creative and socially constructive qualities of theatricality, suggesting that it is in the gaps between the artistic symbolism of theatre and lived experience that new insights are glimpsed: 'the duality of a gaze, a perception or a word that recognises this gap between reality and fiction where theatre takes place' (Féral 2002: 11).

Although theatre and performance have been characterised as separate sites of struggle, there has been, of course, much productive dialogue between these two related modes of cultural practice. Not only do practitioners move between making performances in theatres as well as in everyday spaces, but both terms have also been used metaphorically in the social sciences, linguistics and philosophy to analyse human existence and the social structures of everyday life. The concept of performativity, drawing on phenomenology, has been particularly widely applied to theories of identity, human action and behaviour. Used to explain how human subjectivity is constructed, theories of performativity suggest that social identities are sustained and re-imagined through the self-conscious patterning of behaviour and unconscious repetition of performative gestures and acts. Although these metaphors are differently theorised and often complex in their application, the cross-fertilisation between theatre and performance, theatricality and performativity that has been generated by engagement with the social sciences has raised awareness of the cultural significance and complexity of live performance and performative events beyond the confines of conventional theatre.

One of the recurring themes, evident in the various and disparate histories that have impacted on contemporary devised performance, is practitioners' commitment to developing conceptual, embodied and often political understandings of performance-making. For the purposes of this book, we have recognised that theatre and performance are often interwoven, and that contemporary devisers have interrogated both modes of culture practice, not as fixed and stable categories, but as sites of experimentation that are continually in play.

Paradigms, practices and processes: the scope of the book

This study represents an attempt to capture some of the ephemeral moments of devised performance in order to reflect on its effects, effectiveness and efficacy. Jill Dolan has written evocatively of public performance as 'poised . . . between appearance and disappearance' in which memories are distorted, accounts partisan and for which surviving documentation may be scant (Dolan 2005: 8). In this book we have drawn on written accounts of practice, our experiences as audience members, recorded documentation of performance and interviews with practitioners. This process is, of course, highly selective and consequently it has not been our intention to present a thorough survey of contemporary practices, nor is this study a systematic history of all the twists and turns of devised performance. Rather, we hope to shed light on some of the movements and concepts that have informed devising, marking some of the major paradigm shifts and changing practices evident in the varied and highly complex strategies that constitute devised performance.

Theatre is always responsive to the artistic, cultural and intellectual climates in which it takes place, but devised performance has particularly asserted its inventiveness through the interplay between the conceptual and the formal. The twentieth-century antecedents of contemporary practitioners – such as the avant-garde Dadaist performers of the 1920s; those who staged the counter-cultural 'Happenings' of the 1960s; members of the politically radical Workers' Theatre Movements in the 1920s and 1930s; those engaged in the civil rights movements of the 1960s and 1970s – transformed the cultural landscape by demonstrating how artists' beliefs and values and forms of performance are interdependent and mutually sustaining. Part One of this book, Genealogies and Histories, historicises devised performance and maps the contours of these radical and alternative traditions. It is not our intention to imply that there is an artistic canon of devised performances, nor to suggest that there is an established canon of artistic practices. These three chapters offer an example of the interplay between the conceptual, the ideological and the formal by exploring how distinctions between art and life were blurred and challenged by early devisers. In turn, the opening section addresses the visual and conceptual experiments of the avant-garde, the rise of interest in the psychology, physiology and creativity of the actor, and the ideological motives of politically radical theatre-makers in the twentieth century. Part One of the book is structured around some of the concepts, interests and practices that emerge from early innovations in devised performance. In its three chapters it charts the counter-cultural movements that set the scene for future experiments in devising. Taken together, Part One frames subsequent discussions of practices and performances that have occurred more recently.

Parts Two, Three and Four offer an analysis of different conceptual models of devising, illustrated by the practice of recent and contemporary performance-makers. Part Two examines how experiments in narrative have become a central element of devising. The fragmentation of narrative, and an implied rejection of the coherent linear narratives often associated with more conventionally scripted plays, is a source of inspiration for practitioners seeking to provoke new ways of seeing. By experimenting with how narrative might be shaped performatively, practitioners have altered perceptions by representing narratives as multiple, open and unstable. Rather than offering a comprehensive account of how narrative is understood, in this section we have focussed on three specific areas of practice – autobiographical narratives, community narratives and adaptation of fictional narratives – each of which is illustrative of particular performance paradigms and different ways of working.

Part Three examines the ways in which practitioners have made inventive use of space and place. With a history of experimentation with performance in environments and places outside theatre spaces, devised performance has often sought to challenge cultural expectations about the relationships between audiences and performers. This section takes discourses of place and space as a starting point, exploring how they have been configured and reconfigured in different contexts and settings in order to challenge and unfix contemporary notions of what might constitute theatre and performance. The fourth section develops earlier discussions about the expanded role and physicality of the creative performer, and finally we examine how notions of role, cultural identities and physicality are challenged when practitioners enter into dialogue with fast-changing multimedia technologies.

Choosing examples to illustrate the ideas within this book is highly contentious and has been problematic. Devising is traditionally sensitive to context and audience and for this reason we have selected practices from a range of settings, including, for example, an analysis of performative walks, work that takes place in hotel rooms and on the street, as well as performance that is designed for more conventional theatre spaces. This selection of material is also intended to question paradigm shifts from theatre to performance, and to show how different practitioners have interpreted this development. Another means by which we organised and selected material was to consider the political motivations, aesthetic concerns and artistic backgrounds of different devisers and devising companies, and we have given examples of work created by practitioners who might identify themselves with related movements in the visual arts, in dance and physical theatre, multimedia performance and in community arts. Although each mode of performance has its own history, theories and traditions to which we cannot do justice in a study of this length, we have chosen to include such diverse examples in order to illustrate the inspiring proliferation of forms and styles that might be recognised as devised performance. Inevitably, however, in our desire to recognise the expansiveness and inclusivity of devised performance, the choices we have made have been constrained by our own geographical location and ability to witness live performance, and by what is publicly available as records of practice. Of course this process of researching devised performance is very selective and often subjective; published accounts of practice indicate the level of critical interest in the work; reviews are dependent on the tastes of the press and recordings of practice tend to be generated by companies that have effective publicity machines. The examples of practice we have chosen reflect both the circulation of ideas and the discontinuities inherent in disparate artistic movements and we intend that the structure of the book supports an understanding that the development of devised performance has not been linear or compartmentalised but reflective of artists and practitioners in dialogue with each other. It is our intention that readers will be able to recognise the practices and paradigms we have chosen here in the work of a range of companies. We hope that our observations about contemporary performance and its antecedents might furnish readers with theoretical lenses through which to view other examples of devised performance, perhaps including their own creative practices.

Although this book is primarily concerned with artistic endeavour, the notion of the laboratory is at its heart. It seeks to examine the reformulation of elements of performance practice by devised performance-makers and to note the developments that have, consequently, expanded the language of performance. Rather than closing the work down to a synthesised narrative of history, we hope that this exposition of contextualised practice will enable readers to trace agents of change and artistic response and thus open up the discussion of experimental practice. Devising performance has been concerned not only with testing and redefining the conceptual limits of art, but also with using the art of devising to question the artfulness of living.

PART ONE

Genealogies and Histories

INTRODUCTION: PERFORMANCE AND THE ART OF LIVING

Western art actually has two avant-garde histories: one of artlike art and the other of lifelike art. They've been lumped together as parts of a succession of movements fervently committed to innovation, but they represent fundamentally contrasting philosophies of reality ... artlike art holds that art is separate from life and everything else, whereas lifelike art holds that art is connected to life and everything else. In other words, there is art at the service of art and art at the service of life. The maker of artlike art tends to be a specialist; the maker of lifelike art, a generalist.

(Kaprow 1993: 201)

Performing the avant-garde

Devised performance is often seen to be innovative in its negotiation of cultural conventions. Although variously inflected and differently motivated, the performance practices that are investigated and documented in this book share an aspiration to break with tradition, to find new working methods and to challenge audiences through their inventive use of theatre form. Contemporary devised performance does not constitute a coherent movement or a distinct cultural ambition, and consequently there is no single or continuous history that can account for the richness of its influences and artistic practices. Nonetheless, however radical it may appear, no artistic endeavour is developed without cultural conversation, or dissent and affiliations, and this section marks an attempt to explore some of the contours of history that might be traced in the contemporary cultural landscape of devised performance.

Because of their emphasis on artistic innovation, the practices of the historical avant-garde of the early twentieth century and the neo-avant-garde of the 1960s and 1970s provide an appropriate touchstone for this discussion of the genealogy of devised performance. Contemporary devised theatre practitioners are indebted to avant-garde artists, whose radical questioning of the role of the arts in society led to a critical re-evaluation of the European artistic tradition. The modernist avant-garde grew up in a particularly turbulent period of European history around the First World War, and generally signalled a move away from the élitist values that had become associated with Romanticism. The avant-garde specifically challenged the Romanticist view that artists have specialised imaginative powers, described by Coleridge (among others) as poetic genius. Modernists sought to renew and redefine Romanticist notions of authenticity and originality by examining what artists bring to aesthetic encounters and how spectators enter into dialogue with artistic representations of reality. This led avant-garde artists to question the social values attributed to art, and their work was intended to demonstrate how the art object had become commodified.

The term 'avant-garde' does not, however, refer to a fixed or static set of values. As Andrew Benjamin points out, the modernist avant-garde 'implies movement. The movement within it questions the possibility of art itself' (Benjamin 1991: 99). Peter Bürger provides a theoretical reading of the avant-garde which has become an important point of reference for further analyses. He claims that the two periods of aesthetic invention (the historical avant-garde of the early twentieth century and the neo-avant-garde of the 1960s and 1970s) were each characterised by an intention to reconnect art and life. It is the connectivity between art and life, however differently inflected and interpreted, that provides the conceptual lens for this section through which the interrelated histories of devised performance will be viewed.

Bürger insists that the radicalism of the historical avant-garde lay in its ability to transform everyday life by enabling people to recognise the oppressive patternings of daily existence. This process was, he argues, regarded as a precursor to both personal liberation and social change. Bürger claims that the central characteristic of this eclectic movement was that artistic practice and the art of living became mutually embedded:

> Art was not to be simply destroyed, but transferred to the praxis of life where it would be transformed, albeit in a changed form.
>
> (Bürger 1984: 49)

Avant-garde artists working within this idealistic movement frequently wanted to shock their audiences into an engagement with personal and social 'truths' as they saw them, and used the practices of art itself to facilitate shifts in the audience's perspective. Avant-garde practice, therefore, was not just about probing the conventions of artistic practice, but also challenging and changing the practices of everyday life.

Bürger's narrative of the avant-garde has been critiqued by Hal Foster among others for conflating its many different theories and practices into one homogenous discourse, and for his interpretation of the early years of the movement as more politically radical than the later neo-avant-garde period. Foster charts the shift in thinking between the historical avant-garde of the early twentieth century (spanning Dadaism, surrealism, expressionism, and constructivism) and the counter-cultural movement of the later period. The avant-garde of the mid-twentieth century, Foster suggests, was concerned with producing new aesthetic experiences which, unlike the historical avant-garde, sought not to destroy artistic institutions but to extend them by challenging the boundaries of art and non-art. Foster claims that Bürger failed to recognise the radical potential of mimesis (the imitation of life in artistic form) in his analysis of the avant-garde, observing that the avant-garde attacked 'languages, institutions, and structures of meaning, expectation and reception' (Foster 2001: 16). He specifically cites how everyday practices and objects were framed as if they were art objects in order to prompt social critique and radical questioning. It is possible, Foster suggests, to read the avant-garde subversion of established practice as performative in that it is a productive force which initiates new languages and modes of reception. The relationship between art, mimesis and non-art in the performative practices of the avant-garde provides the basis for discussion in the first chapter in this section. There were various artistic movements in the early and mid-twentieth century that might have served to illustrate the relationship between art and non-art, including the theatrical experiments of Oskar Schlemmer in the Bauhaus. The choice of Dadaism and the counter-cultural 'Happenings' of the 1960s is intended to demonstrate how the interrelationships and conversations between artists led to new performative activities, although there were many other productive connections between artists and theories of the everyday that might have been traced.

The avant-garde's concern with blurring the boundaries between life and art led to performances that invited both actors and audiences to participate spontaneously in the event. The idea of the creative performer, which was developed during the period of the avant-garde, remains a significant aspect of contemporary devised performance, and this will be discussed in the second chapter of this section. Emphasising the creativity of performers in the process of theatre-making not only reflected a commitment to breaking the authority of directors and, in some instances, to challenging the authorial voice of the playwright, it also signalled a new interest in the power of spontaneity and improvisation. It was a way of thinking about human subjectivity which drew inspiration from the newly emergent field of psychology, where freedom of expression and self-exploration was considered both personally and socially enriching. This led to theatrical experiments that aimed to liberate individuals through unleashing their 'natural' creativity in rehearsal and devising processes. This legacy has led to practices where performers use their own experiences – social, physical and psychological – to create performance texts.

The third chapter extends the idea of the avant-garde to theatre as political activism. In the social upheaval that followed the First World War and the Bolshevik revolution in Russia, political activists devised performances that acted as a means of communication and mobilisation. In his study of the avant-garde, David Graver categorises this aspect of the movement as 'partisan art' in which dissent from mainstream culture became harnessed to organised political action, and theatre was used to serve revolutionary objectives (Graver 1995: 13). Writing in 1920, Erwin Piscator stated that 'any artistic intention must be subordinated to the revolutionary purpose of the whole' (quoted in Bradby *et al.* 1980: 168). Following Piscator's dictum many radical theatre companies tried to live, as well as work, according to their political ideals, particularly during the period of the 1960s and 1970s, where idealistic experiments with collective living aimed to integrate life and art-making as a practical cultural politics. Devised theatre-making chimed particularly well with left-wing idealism in that it fostered ways of working in which ideas and practices were (in theory at least) discussed democratically and shared understandings reached.

The final chapter in this section maps the paradigm shifts that led to performance practices being harnessed to social efficacy, and considers how and why devised theatre became a potent weapon in the armoury of the politically committed.

One of the outstanding legacies of the period lies not so much in the artistic product, but in the process of working – on the expanded role of the audience, the development of collaborative ways of making theatre, on the rehearsal process, on ensemble acting and actor training. Taken together, this selective tradition marks different ways to practise and theorise the elision of life and art that was furthered by avant-gardism and related political movements. Because artistic creativity thrives on dialogue, there are inevitably areas of overlap within the narratives woven in the three chapters in this section. Each offers a different perspective and identifies some of the antecedents of the cultural strategies associated with devised performance, albeit long after the specific political and cultural impulses of twentieth-century practitioners had been questioned and redefined.

TWO

BUT IS IT ART?

Art and Non-Art

Relationships between the arts and everyday life became subject to radical scrutiny in the period of the historical avant-garde. Sceptical of the ways in which the high arts, and specifically the visual arts, had been commodified and rarefied by the capitalist market, the challenge to the bourgeois cultural institutions in the period during and immediately following the First World War was led by the Dadaists. This movement began in the politically neutral zone of Zurich in Switzerland and quickly spread to Paris, Barcelona and New York. The Dadaist project was to expose the uselessness of art, not by rejecting art itself but by removing the frame that separated and elevated the work of art from everyday life. Their practice was intentionally controversial, designed to provoke audiences into questioning both the values of the arts and contemporary social values. The spontaneity and playfulness that characterised Dadaism was re-imagined and reconfigured in the later, neo-avant-garde period, where it became associated with 'Happenings' as part of the permissive and counter-cultural performance practices of the 1960s and 1970s. This chapter will examine these two specific historical moments as illustrative of aesthetic experiments that sought to challenge perceptions of both art and the everyday.

Walter Benjamin commented that 'Dadaists attached much less importance to the sales value of their work than its uselessness for contemplative immersion' (Benjamin 1999: 231). In Dadaist performance, the cabaret format was particularly popular because it easily accommodated topical issues and had, therefore, a spontaneity that worked against the idea that art objects should be enduring and revered. In the visual arts, Dadaists rejected oil paintings in favour of work that was equally anti-commodity in its immediate, throwaway nature.

Whatever the medium of artistic expression, Dadaist work consistently sought to shock audiences into recognising how they had uncritically accepted the conventions of society. When modernists presented a mimetic representation of reality, therefore, they did so in order to offer a social critique of the world as they saw it. Hal Foster argues that 'the avant-garde mimes the degraded world of capitalist modernity in order not to embrace but to mock it' (Foster 2001: 16). He also suggests that Dada's attack on the formal conventions of culture was utopian in proposing 'not what can be so much as what *cannot* be' (Foster 2001: 16). The exposition of the uselessness of art, rather than following a particular political agenda, lies at the heart of the Dada project. Rather than seeking to create art, Dadaists sought to make 'anti-art' or 'anti-performance' that marked their dissatisfaction with the art market and their nihilistic vision of the world acquired by living through the atrocities of the First World War. Anti-art was not, therefore, a coherent set of practices but rather a motto for invention, signalling what the 1960s' art critic Hans Richter characterised as a 'new artistic ethic' (Richter 1997: 9).

This chapter shares the aims of cultural theorist Renato Poggioli who, writing in the 1960s, examined 'the avant-garde art not under its species as art but through what it reveals, inside and outside of art itself' (Poggioli 1968: 4). The examples are intended, therefore, to serve as models of avant-garde practice that indicate innovation in artistic form. Three aspects of innovation will be examined: first the use of 'ready-mades', secondly the use of chance, and thirdly the newly configured relationship between performers and audiences.

The art of the everyday

The art of the everyday was newly conceptualised by Marcel Duchamp (1887–1968), a key Dadaist innovator whose work in Europe and North America has influenced many conceptual artists. Duchamp famously asked, 'Can one make works which are not works of "art"?', and he saw beauty in mass-manufactured items and machines rather than in more conventional artworks. Duchamp is celebrated for his 'ready-mades', in which he reframed everyday objects as works of art in order to trouble the nineteenth-century idea that art is defined according to specific aesthetic principles. One of his most famous ready-mades was a piece entitled *Fountain*, which was actually a mass-produced urinal inscribed with the signature R. Mutt. *Fountain* was shown in a New York Gallery in 1917, and its exhibition in the gallery space invited viewers to reconsider their ideas about what constituted art. Art critic Hans Richter comments on the playfulness of this performative gesture:

> The urinal says that 'art is a trick' . . . Duchamp set up Reality, as represented by his ready-mades. His purpose was to administer a strong purgative to an age riddled with lies.
>
> (Richter 1997: 90)

Both Duchamp's humour and his seriousness of purpose imbued his work with ready-mades. The impulse behind his conceptual artworks was the belief that everyday objects can be viewed as artworks because the active agent in making a work is not the artist, but the audience's perception. He was pleased, for example, when visitors did not notice two ready-mades that had been placed in the entrance hall of a gallery exhibition as it demonstrated that works of art have no special 'aura'.

The notion of the 'aura' of an artwork is a complex one in relation to ready-mades. In his essay 'The Work of Art in the Age of Mechanical Reproduction' (1935), the Marxist critic Walter Benjamin suggests that the special 'aura' associated with original works of art was the product of history and ideology rather than any intrinsic quality of the artwork itself. He argues that the invention of mimetic machinery that could reproduce works of art (he cites cameras as an example) would strip away the mystery and mystique associated with artworks. Benjamin regards mimetic technology as potentially liberating because, by showing the detail of everyday objects in mass reproduction, the ideological patterning that ruled people's lives might be amplified and exposed. The Dadaists, as Benjamin points out approvingly, were similarly intent on 'a relentless destruction of the aura of their own creations' (Benjamin 1999: 231). For the Dadaists, however, the 'aura' of originality, although resisted, remained an important signifier of authorship. Duchamp's biographer Calvin Tomkins explains how Dadaists transferred the discourse of originality from the intrinsic value of the art object to the creative mind of the artist:

> Only by giving it a title and an artist's signature could it attain the odd and endlessly provocative status of a readymade, a work of art created not by the hand or skill but by the mind and decision of the artist.
>
> (Tomkins 1997: 157)

In this sleight of hand, Dadaists retained for themselves qualities of creative individuality which recalled and adapted earlier aesthetic traditions.

The principles of the ready-made were applied to Dadaist perform-ance practice. Tristan Tzara, a key experimenter in the field, also sought to blur everyday life with the fictional realm of performance. His performance on 22 January 1920 entitled *La Crise du Change* was staged at a venue in Paris that contained scenery that had been abandoned by an amateur theatre company. Tzara and his collab-orators employed the ready-made setting of half-salon, half-forest they found as a miscellaneous backdrop to their performance. This inappropriate setting served to 'make strange' the activity on stage, and they hoped this juxtaposition would unsettle the audience. As part of the programme, which included music, readings and the exhibition of painting, it was announced that Tzara, the Dada leader, would be performing one of his works. When Tzara came on stage he read from a found text, the transcript of an address that had recently been given to the French parliament. This was accompanied by the ringing of many bells. This cacophonous bell-ringing served to undercut the Kantian perspective that great art required contemplation, and mem-bers of the audience – who had thought they would be attending a cultural afternoon – were outraged. The piece apparently challenged the authority and authenticity of performance because that which was framed as Tzara's 'own work' was, in fact, merely a repetition of a speech by a politician. Nevertheless, the effectiveness of this performative intervention relied on Tzara's 'authentic' presence (his 'aura' in Benjamin's terms) as Dada leader. In referring to this work he showed that he was aware of the necessary ambiguity of his aesthetic statement: 'All I wanted to convey was simply that my presence on stage, the sight of my face and my movements ought to satisfy people's curiosity' (quoted in Melzer 1976: 7).

The principles applied to the ready-made offered an ironic comment on the idealisation of the art object, and implied a radical questioning of the Enlightenment perspective that great art is to be recognised and revered through aesthetic contemplation. This had the effect of drawing attention to what philosopher Jacques Derrida described as 'a discourse on the frame' that places meaning on works of art and invites spectators to question the limits of art and non-art (Derrida 1987: 45).

Taking chances

Related to the cultural experimentation of the ready-mades was the concept of chance, which became one of the guiding principles of Dadaist performance practice. Like the framing of a ready-made item, chance problematises the idea that great art is dependent on the skill of the artist. Furthermore, it also complexifies the relationship between everyday life and the artwork as the creative impulse is taken from a 'real' source rather than from the imagination. Tzara's recipe for a Dadaist poem provides a good illustration of the process of making art in this way:

> Take one newspaper. Take one pair of scissors. Choose from that newspaper an article of the length desired for the poem you intend to write. Cut out the article. Next cut out with care each of the words forming that article. Next put them in a bag. Mix gently. Take out one by one each excision in the order they fall from the bag. Copy carefully. The poem will resemble you. *Voilà*, there you are, an infinitely original poet of seductive sensibility.
>
> (quoted in Poggioli 1968: 190)

The phrase 'the poem will resemble you' warrants further analysis. As chance determines the shape of the poem, the poet's skills and craft are apparently relinquished to the immediacy and spontaneity of form. This is an important element in Dadaist practice; rather than the poet making the poem, the poem seems to create the poet. Ironically invoking Romanticist idealisation of poetic genius, Tzara uses the metaphor and practice of chance to challenge the perception that 'seductive sensibility' is the authentic product of the artist.

Influenced by their Dadaist predecessors, chance became an important component of the performance practices of the composer John Cage and choreographer Merce Cunningham, whose long-term collaboration began in 1942 and continued until Cage's death in 1992. Cunningham used the principle of chance throughout his work, mostly in terms of composition, and he literally worked with dice as a means of structuring performance work. Chance was used to plot movement, decide the running order for a sequence of movement pieces, identify how many dancers may take part in a performance or to decide which piece of recorded music to play to accompany a pre-rehearsed piece. Cage perceived music in everyday sounds such as radio static or traffic noise. In terms reminiscent of Dadaism, he found music in the immediate environment and reframed it as art. Cage advised that there was 'one way to write music: study Duchamp', and his work included ready-made instruments such as beer bottles and flowerpots (quoted in Goldberg 1995: 124).

Cage spoke of 'non-intentional music', a term he used to suggest the element of chance in framing any aural landscape as music. A celebrated example of Cage's non-intentional music was 4′33″, first performed in 1952. For this performance, David Tudor, a concert pianist, moved his arms silently three times while sitting at a piano for four minutes and thirty-three seconds. The concept of the piece was that the audience would become attuned to the noises within the auditorium and that these would constitute the music.

Cage's commitment to framing everyday and 'real' interactions as artwork married well with Cunningham whose work was exploring the dance vocabulary embodied in everyday gestures. For *Symphonie pour un homme seul,* choreographed for a Festival of the Creative Arts at Brandeis University in 1952, Cunningham employed the kind of methodology that Cage had been using in music. In this work, alongside steps lifted from social dances and those he had invented himself, Cunningham utilised non-dance movements. He explained this process as the integration of art and non-art:

> It occurred to me that dancers could do the gestures they did ordinarily. These were accepted as movement in daily life, why not on stage?'
> (quoted in Goldberg 1995: 124)

On one level this approach was based on a pragmatic decision because it facilitated Cunningham's work with untrained dancers. By rejecting skills acquired through the conservatoire tradition of training, Cunningham opened up new possibilities for a language of movement based on walking, standing and running. Conceptually, this challenged the conventions of performance practice which separates artistic movement from the everyday.

In 1948 Cage and Cunningham visited Black Mountain College, Asheville, North Carolina, a radical educational establishment founded in 1933, and it was here that Cage conceived of an event which became influential in the development of neo-avant-garde performance work. Black Mountain College was envisaged as a democratic, co-educational learning environment where students and faculty lived and worked together, with everyone taking on domestic duties and responsibilities on the college farm. The arts were central to this progressive education, and improvised performances often explored the relationship between the communality of everyday life and art. Precipitated by Cage's reading of Artaud's *The Theatre and Its Double*, an untitled performance event took place which was inspired by Artaud's description of 'l'événements' or 'Happenings'. The event at Black Mountain College appears to have been organically generated. People brought their particular interests to the work and the happening itself was structured around chance interactions according to real-time events. Cage read a text on the relation between Zen Buddhism and music which he punctuated with pauses. By turning dials, he also performed a 'composition with a radio' while Rauschenberg played old records on a hand-wound gramophone and David Tudor played the piano. Tudor went on to work with two buckets, pouring water from one to the other, an action which was juxtaposed against the simultaneous reading of poetry by Charles Olsen and Mary Caroline Richards who had been planted in the audience. White-on-white paintings by Robert Rauschenberg hung overhead as a false ceiling and images were projected firstly onto the ceiling and then down the walls.

The creative focus for Cage was the spectators, who were required to make their own meanings from what they saw. Drawing from Zen, Cage observed that 'art should not be different [from] life but an action within life. Like all of life, with its accidents and chances and variety and disorder and only momentary beauties' (quoted in Goldberg 1995: 126). Cage's work offers an important illustration of the ways in which the aesthetic of chance drew attention to the activity of spectatorship as well as the practice of making art, implying that each is an inherently creative process.

From audience to player

Cage encouraged the students on his composition course at The New School for Social Research in New York to use elements such as chance, non-intentional actions, montage and audience interaction in their experimentations in practice. One of Cage's students was Allan Kaprow, an artist who has been recognised as being instrumental in developing the 'Happening' as a new mode of performance which gained momentum in the 1960s and 1970s. Allan Kaprow was influenced by the Black Mountain College event and was inspired to develop the spontaneous and interactive qualities of the work further. Like Dadaist art, there were no formal conventions for the Happening, and the blurring boundaries between art and life was related to a spontaneous and improvisatory aesthetic of non-art, as Kaprow advocates:

> *The line between the Happening and daily life should be kept as fluid and perhaps as indistinct as possible.* The reciprocation between the handmade and the readymade will be at its maximum power this way.
>
> (Kaprow 1993: 62, italics in original)

Kaprow particularly argues for composition which is 'artless' and for the employment of non-professional performers in order to work against a polished artistic aesthetic. Happenings experimented with the relationship between audience and performer and worked towards a situation where there was 'no separation of audience and play' and in which the audience became players (Kaprow 1993: 17). Neo-avant-garde Happenings were staged as participatory experiences, and the process of interaction was placed at the centre of the work. Drawing on the work of the philosopher John Dewey, Kaprow promoted the idea that art that was 'not separate from experience' and Happenings were produced in the moment with *all* participants – both 'performers' and 'spectators' – involved in shaping the encounter.

The conceit of the Happening, which was set up by a professional practitioner such as Kaprow, served to frame the event. In reflecting on the qualities of this methodology, Lebel, the French theorist of Happenings, notes:

> The Happening interpolates actual experience directly into a mythical context. The Happening is not content merely with interpreting life; it takes part in its development within reality. This postulates a deep link between the actual and the hallucinatory, between real and imaginary.
>
> (quoted in Sandford 1995: 271)

The deep link between the actual and the hallucinatory can be seen to relate the blurring of the fictional world of the play space, with its fantastical settings, to the real interactions that the participant undergoes. This is unlike the conventional drama where the separation between audience and performer is most often clearly marked.

It is possible that those who took part in Happenings were not acting as they would in their everyday lives, and they used the space of performance to explore other modes of behaviour. 'Authenticity' is a problematic concept in that the contrived settings of Happenings may have served to disorientate participants, prompting ways of interacting that were unfamiliar or otherwise different. Furthermore, as social anthropologist Victor Turner has pointed out, a performance event is often a liminal space in which normal social conventions are suspended. In this context, although Happenings did not necessarily have an explicit political agenda, their investigation of the everyday can be seen as counter-cultural because it put participants in touch with alternative ways of being. Foster, however, is less convinced about the political efficacy of Happenings. He argues that the Happenings of the neo-avant-garde reduced the ready-made from an anti-élitist statement to a stylistic innovation. Kaprow himself acknowledged the difference in intent between his work and that of the Dadaists:

> Nonart is often confused with antiart . . . which in Dada time and even earlier was nonart aggressively (and wittily) intruded into the arts world to jar conventional values and provoke positive esthetic and/or ethical responses . . . Nonart has no such intent.
>
> (Kaprow 1993: 99)

Kaprow regarded the participatory experience of Happenings as a means whereby they might be connected with the 'natural processes beyond society', and thereby maintained a mystical aspect to the work (Kaprow 1993: xv). This connection to the 'natural' was often reflected in the choice of environment for the work. Kaprow's *Eat* (1964), for example, was an environment created within the caves in the Bronx, a 'wild' place at the edge of the urban jungle of New York.

Kaprow's *18 Happenings in 6 Parts* (1959) and *Calling* (1965) are good examples of the ways in which Happenings actively positioned participants to execute the desired action. Kaprow's invitations to the work stated that 'you will become part of the Happenings; you will simultaneously experience them', and so the sense of agency was introduced before the work even began (Goldberg 1995: 128).Through this process Happenings theatricalised the audience and they became their own spectacle as they observed each other within the event. The object of performance, in such a situation, can be seen to be the participants themselves. By 1965 *Calling* was designated for performers only and any sense of an audience was removed. Richard Schechner describes the richness and significance of the place of performance on Kaprow's later Happenings, and cites *Calling* as an example of a work which literally took place on the streets of New York City. People were required to wait at street corners in order to be incorporated into the event and other participants were those who came across the work as it traversed the city. The outline devised by Kaprow for the first part of the event was as follows:

FOR EACH OF THEM

A car pulls up, someone calls a name [the names used are those of the participants], the person gets in, they drive off.

During the trip, the person is wrapped in aluminium foil. The car is parked at a meter somewhere, is left there, locked; the silver person sitting motionless in the back seat.

Someone unlocks the car, drives off. The foil is removed from the person; he or she is wrapped in cloth or tied into a laundry bag. The car stops, the person is dumped at a public garage and the car goes away.

At the garage, a waiting auto starts up, the person is picked up from the concrete pavement, is hauled into the car, is taken to the information booth at Grand Central Station. The person is propped up against it and left.

The person calls out names, and hears the others brought there also call. They call out for some time. Then they work loose from their wrappings and leave the train station.

They telephone certain numbers. The phone rings and rings. Finally, it is answered, a name asked for, and immediately the other end clicks off.

(quoted in Sandford 1995: 195)

These notes acted as an outline for action. There were briefing meetings for participants but the actual profile of the Happening could not be finalised until the event itself on Saturday 21 August 1965, as it was intended that chance encounters would serve to shape the work. So, for example, heavy traffic meant that the three cars did not arrive at Grand Central Station at the same time. Individual participants obviously affected the tone of the work, through the way in which they called each other's names, for example. As Michael Kirby points out in his study of acting and not-acting, the emotions felt during such a performance are recognisably those of the performers themselves (quoted in Sandford 1995: 3–15).

Influences and legacies

Abandoning the discipline of the fictional frame and blurring boundaries of art and life certainly raises many ethical issues, particularly about the actor–audience relationship. Interacting with a 'real' performance rather than witnessing an artistic event from outside the safety of the 'fourth wall' brings a different quality to the encounter with the artwork that may cause audience members to feel vulnerable. Although such work announces that it is seeking to engage with 'real' life by blurring the boundaries with art, it might be justly criticised on the grounds that it is another example of art for art's sake rather than offering an experience that illuminates the spectators. Poggioli suggests that there is an élitist ethic within aesthetic avant-garde practice which does not want to engage with the everyday life of the masses. He argues that the 'avant-garde is by nature solitary and aristocratic; it loves the initiated and the ivory tower' (Poggioli 1968: 39). In this sense, the works discussed in this chapter may speak only to an audience which shares a particular artistic and cultural vocabulary.

Certainly experimental work enters into a dialogue with both the work of the practitioners' contemporaries and their antecedents. Although this chapter has traced formal innovation from the avant-garde to the neo-avant-garde, it is important to restate, as with all paradigm shifts, that the negotiation of mimesis has not been a straightforward evolution, but a contextual response which bears traces of that which has come before.

The influence of Dadaism and the neo-avant-garde Happenings on contemporary devised performance is conceptual as well as formal. These innovative practitioners questioned the ways in which art is received and understood, and paved the way for further creative investigations into how the practices of everyday life might be framed in, and as, performance. As part of the process of making the 'lifelike art' to which Kaprow refers in the quotation that introduced this section, practitioners recognised the performative qualities of site, space and place. These experimentations with everyday settings have not only impacted on the aesthetic of devised performance, but have illustrated the significance of audience interaction with, and participation in, the processes of performance.

THREE

THE CREATIVE
PERFORMER

The processes of devising rely on the creativity of performers, and practitioners throughout the twentieth century tested methods of working that both reflected and challenged contemporary intellectual and cultural views of selfhood and performance. The concept of the creative actor was, as Philip Auslander points out, integral to the 'problematic of the self' that entered the popular imagination in the early twentieth century and that has continued to be revised thereafter (Auslander 1997: 29). This chapter will explore the ways in which performers came to be regarded as central to the devising process.

The emphasis on the 'presence' of the actor in performance, and the rhetoric of truthfulness, honesty and authenticity that have now become commonplace descriptions of good performance, owe their genesis to the discipline of psychology that was entering the popular imagination at the beginning of the twentieth century. The Russian director Stanislavsk, working at the end of the nineteenth century, was among the first to acknowledge his debt to psychological thought, citing the French psychologist Theodule Ribot in the development of his rehearsal method. As Philip Auslander has observed in his study of acting, although twentieth-century practitioners theorised the relationship between subjectivity, creativity and performance in different ways, practitioners as apparently diverse as Brecht, Grotowski and Artaud all stressed the significance of the actors' self in performance-making (Auslander 1997: 38). Within the fields of dance, practitioners such as Mary Wigman, Martha Graham, Doris Humphrey and later proponents such as Anna Halprin also explored the use of the self within performance. This way of working introduced a new vocabulary in performer training; as noted in the previous chapter, the language of 'trust', 'sincerity', 'authenticity', 'intuition', and so on, brought the values of psychoanalysis into the rehearsal room. Selfhood has been variously and complexly theorised, and this chapter will explore approaches to performing that were motivated by concepts of subjectivity that frequently elided the psychology of the actor and dancer with the processes of making performance.

The natural performer: creativity and self-knowledge

The development of the creative performer drew inspiration from theories of selfhood and creativity that brought a new focus on the interior world of the individual. As the works of psychological thinkers including Freud and Jung became widely available, performing increasingly focussed on self-exploration and self-expression. For practitioners working with different traditions of the avant-garde there was frequently a utopianism to this creative impulse; it was assumed that freedom from repression would be found inwardly, as a psychological state of well-being, rather than externally in people's social or material circumstances. Parisian Dadaists, for example, shared the Surrealists' belief that freeing the imagination and releasing the unconscious through spontaneous creative practice was both socially advantageous and personally liberating. Based on the principle that better people make better societies, it was assumed that stripping away layers of socialisation would enable people to recognise the truth of their repression. Nowhere was this seen more clearly than in the 'natural' dances of Isadora Duncan, performed in the early 1900s.

The idealisation of the creative individual was responsive to the mood of the times, in which traditional values associated with Christianity and patriotism were subject to radical scrutiny by artists and intellectuals scarred by the horrors of trench warfare in the First World War. If adhering to values of duty and honour had led to such wholesale slaughter, trusting one's own instincts provided a more optimistic alternative than following the heroism of 'great men', whether they were in the arts or from other sectors of society. Tzara's Dadaist manifesto of 1918 explicitly acknowledges the devastation of the First World War, and he follows this way of thinking by linking redemption not to Christianity, but to liberation through individual independence and creative freedom:

> The principle: love thy neighbour is a hypocrisy. 'Know thyself' is utopian but more acceptable, for it embraces wickedness. No pity. After

the carnage we still retain the hope of purified mankind . . . . Dada was born of a need for independence, a distrust towards unity. Those who are with us preserve their freedom.

(quoted in Harrison and Wood 1992: 249–250)

Although Tzara's aesthetic strategies were specific to Dadaism, his belief in the redemptive powers of creativity and artistic practice were not unique to this specific movement. As Raymond Williams points out, the centrality of individual authenticity (being 'true' to yourself) and personal choice in the early modernist period provided the basis for the contemporary culture of individualism in the West (Williams 1992: 86–88). In terms of theatre, this way of thinking about subjectivity had the effect of placing the performer as both subject and object of the creative process.

Within this context, the idea that creativity liberated the individual was brought to practical theatre-making through the application of games and other playful activities and improvisation into the devising and rehearsal process. Interest in the newly emergent field of developmental psychology introduced the idea that playfulness was a natural activity, and led to the belief that play would restore actors to the state of innocence found in childhood but suppressed by layers of adult socialisation. The spontaneity of play was particularly valued as an effective way for performers to access their unconscious minds and their innate and childlike creativity. A good example of this way of thinking about the link between childhood play and artistic creativity is found in the work of Jacques Copeau, a French director working in the 1920s:

It is through play, in which children imitate more or less consciously all human activities and sentiments, which is for them a natural path towards artistic expression and for us a living repertoire of the reactions of the most authentic kind.

(Copeau, quoted in Rudlin 2000: 55)

This interest in self-expression in the modernist period accepted a specific vision of human subjectivity. Not only did this assume that selfhood is innate, natural and essential, it also rested on the belief that mind and body might be re-integrated through the depth of self-knowledge gained through artistic practice. This is signalled by the rhetoric of 'authenticity' and 'sincerity', suggesting that creative play enables performers to 'know' themselves more fully.

The naturalness of play was emphasised by anthropologists Johan Huizinga and Caroline Loizos, whose work theorised the functionality of play in human behaviour, cultural organisations and animal development. Huizinga's publication *Homo Ludens: A Study of The Play Element in Culture* (1938) made a case for play in primates as an aesthetic ritual, and Loizos (1969) stressed that the playful activity of all primates derives from their mimetic observations of life. Developmental theories of play, often based on psychoanalysis and anthropology, have had an important and abiding influence on theatre-makers and performance theorists. Studies of different forms of play – imaginary play, role play, representational play, physical play – have appealed to devisers because they emphasise process and improvisation rather than textual analysis and technique.

This interest in the processes of play was thought to be not only beneficial for individuals but also socially advantageous, and the playful drama workshop has been seen to enable actors and dancers to come closer to their own inner natures, in a space where they are thought to be less encumbered by the alienating effects of society.

The sacred performer

One of the most influential figures in the rise of the creative performer was Jerzy Grotowski, a Polish director working professionally from 1959 until his death in 1999. Although Grotowski's work followed many different phases, it offers consistent insights into the integration of life and art through the programme of psychophysical training he developed for and with actors. Influenced by the methods of Russian theatre directors Stanislavsky and Meyerhold, Grotowski required actors at his Laboratory Theatre to undertake a process of self-exploration and physical training in order to strengthen their creativity. Grotowski was not, however, interested in mimetic representation of everyday life and his disciplined approach to actor training was orientated towards the spontaneous revelation of higher spiritual truths.

Acting, for Grotowski, was an act of self-sacrifice, a state of being which he described as 'secular holiness'. In his book, *Towards a Poor Theatre*, he explained the connection between the psychic and the theatrical, the actor and the audience:

> I speak about holiness as an unbeliever. I mean a 'secular holiness'. If the actor, by setting himself a challenge publicly challenges others, and through excess, profanation and outrageous sacrifice reveals himself

by casting off his everyday mask, he makes it possible for the spectator
to undertake a similar process of self-penetration. If he does not exhibit
his body, but annihilates it, burns it, frees it from every resistance to
any psychic impulse, then he does not sell his body, but sacrifices it.

(Grotowski 1975: 34)

By using a spiritual vocabulary to describe his aesthetic practice,
Grotowski demonstrates his commitment to self-knowledge as a means
of attaining a healthy psyche. Through 'peeling off the life mask',
theatre would enable each person to 'struggle with one's own truth'
(Grotowski 1975: 21). The secularised sanctity of the actor was,
therefore, the spiritual medium through which inner truths of both the
individual and the human condition might be realised.

Athough Grotowksi's actor training was primarily based on intro-
spection, his work was designed to highlight the encounter between the
creative actor and the audience in the moment of performance.
Influenced by Artaud's vision of a poetic theatre that transcended
'discursive reason and psychology', Grotowski emphasised the act
of personal transformation at the heart of this aesthetic exchange.
His interest in myth and the mystical led him to focus increasingly
on paratheatrical and ritual performance as a means of engaging *all*
participants in the healing powers of psychophysical activity. As
Richard Schechner notes, consistent with his view of the virtues of a
'natural' human subjectivity, these paratheatrical events often took
place in pastoral settings in which it was expected that participants
would experience the purity and goodness of nature rather than the
artificiality of socialisation (Schechner 1988: 211). Anyone who was
willing to engage in self-exploration was welcomed, and at the height
of their popularity in the early 1970s several thousand people would
meet to participate in communal activities such as ritual dance,
spontaneous movement and chanting which were designed to release
the individual participants' creativity. This model of interactive performance was also to be found within the San Francisco Dancers'
Workshop founded by Anna and Lawrence Halprin. In this context the
motivation was explicitly political; Halprin's 1960s' platforms stressed
the importance of collaboration and the civil rights movement by
emphasising the importance of multiracial practice.

Grotowki's vision of the creative actor has been widely assimilated
to practice in devised performance; his influence is described by
Schechner as operating 'the way a rock dropped into a pond causes
concentric waves to expand onwards in ever-widening circles'

(Schechner 1997a: xxvii). Grotowski's admiration for Artaud's non-literary poetic theatre and his holistic approach to creativity within actor training led many practitioners to reject the dramatic script in favour of more spontaneous and improvisatory performance practices. Schechner cites Grotowski's influence on the work of practitioners such as Eugenio Barba, Nicolás Nunez, Joseph Chaikin and Peter Brook and companies like Gardzienice, The Wooster Group and his own Performance Group. Each of these practitioners re-evaluated the spiritual dimensions of Grotowski's psychophysical training in different ways, and innovative practice was developed that built on his radical vision of the creative performer.

Collaborative performances and liberated actors

Grotowski's work raises questions about the significance of collaboration and the role of the director within devised performance. While it is clear that Grotowski's rehearsal system foregrounded the creative actor, what is less clear is the degree to which his work fostered collaboration within an ensemble. Actor Zbigniew Cynkntis describes his working processes with Grotowski at the Laboratory Theatre in the 1960s in the following terms:

> Everything that we did that was any good was not even made by Grotowski, but was born between me and Grotowski.
> (Zbigniew Cynkntis, quoted in Kumiega 1985: 51)

By contrast, actor Stanislaw Scierski's description of the devising process challenges the perception that the creative process was shared equally:

> The progress of the collective search was in Grotowski's hands. He helped the 'studies' to develop, respecting our right to take risks; he selected them; very often he inspired them . . . it must be stressed that many 'studies' were improvisational in nature . . . From the 'studies' which we had presented to Grotowski, and from those he created with us from the outset – he built a new structure. For those parts, which were not based on text but were obviously in need of them he made suggestions, in collaboration with us.
> (Kumiega 1985: 89–90)

Although Grotowski was adamant that his processes fostered collaboration, Richard Schechner rightly points out that after Grotowski left the group in the 1970s, they were unable to create any further original performance work (Schechner 1997c: 116–117).

Grotowksi's vision that freedom from social repression would be found inwardly, in the actor's psyche, was shared by Julian Beck and Judith Malina, co-founders of Living Theatre in New York in 1951. Beck and Malina developed a poetics of performance that was built on the premise that breaking down the barrier between reason and instinct would also dissolve the division between art and life. Beck was attracted to Artaud's comparison of theatre to the plague which, in Artaud's words, 'upsets our sensual tranquillity, releases our repressed subconscious, drives us to a kind of potential rebellion' (quoted in Beck 1986: 19). The processes of collaboration developed by the company aimed to release participants' 'repressed subconscious' and thereby develop the individual's creativity.

In common with Grotowski's paratheatre and Kaprow's Happenings, Living Theatre extended its desire for personal liberation by inviting members of the public to take part in performance events. In 1964 it formulated the idea of 'Free Theatre' which created 'a situation in which performers and public were to be given the taste of freedom' through 'improvisation unchained' (Beck 1986: 83). This approach was realised in Living Theatre's first collectively devised piece, *Mysteries and Smaller Pieces*, which was developed during its period in Paris in 1964. The performance largely consisted of a series of exercises designed to release the actors' inner creativity, described as 'non-fictional acting' by Judith Malina (quoted in Tytell 1997: 200). The final section of the *Mysteries* was a direct response to Artaud's *The Theatre and the Plague*, and this was the only sequence where the actors worked with theatrical illusion. Beck described the collective creation of the *Mysteries* in terms which support his idea that creativity is close to a mystical experience:

A group of people come together. There is no author to rest on who wrests the creative impulse from you. Destruction of the superstructure of the mind. Then reality comes. We sit around for months talking, absorbing, discarding, making an atmosphere in which we not only inspire each other but in which each one feels free to say whatever he or she wants to say. Big swamp jungle, a landscape of concepts, souls, sounds, movements, theories, fronds of poetry, wildness, wilderness, wandering. Then you gather and arrange . . . . At the end no one knows who was really responsible for what, the individual ego drifts into darkness, everyone has greater personal satisfaction than the satisfaction of the lonely 'I'.

(Beck 1986: 85)

Collaboration, therefore, was created randomly between individuals rather than as a rehearsed ensemble. Spectators were encouraged to participate in the performative experience by taking part in the drama exercises or joining the pile of corpses left by the plague.

Perhaps the most notorious example of audience participation was Living Theatre's production *Paradise Now*, first performed in 1968. This piece dramatised Beck's idea that sexual repression was the cause of social oppression, and that creative freedom will only be found by the sexually liberated. Tytell describes how audience members were encouraged to 'speak out about sexual taboos, to undress, and to join the "body pile", a gathering of onstage actors and audience groping for each other' (Tytell 1997: 228). This way of working, designed to unleash the spontaneous creative energy Beck regarded as necessary for individual and social freedom, brought Living Theatre into conflict with civil authorities.

Although spectators were invited to participate in Living Theatre performances, collaborations were based on a vision of the power of the creative actor that was highly individualised; the intention was to promote inner psychological freedom rather than ensemble perform-ances. The first practitioner in North America in the neo-avant-garde who developed a more systematic and theorised approach to collaboration was Joseph Chaikin. Chaikin's experience as an actor in Living Theatre informed his work with Open Theatre, which he established in 1963. It was with Beck and Malina that Chaikin encountered ideas about the creative actor that were to influence his later work. Open Theatre's aims were set out in a programme note from the opening performances:

> (1) to create a situation in which the actors can play together with a sensitivity to one another required of an ensemble, (2) to explore the specific powers that only the live theatre possesses, (3) to concentrate on a theatre of abstraction and illusion (as opposed to a theatre of behavioural or psychological motivation), (4) to discover ways in which the artist can find his expression without money as the determining factor.
>
> (quoted in Hulton 2000: 163)

These ideas are central to Chaikin's work: the emphasis on the creativity of the actor's self, the establishment of an ensemble, and the explora-tion of abstract themes. The concept of the actor's 'presence' united

Chaikin's theatrical aesthetic, an idea that he explored in his book, *The Presence of the Actor*, first published in 1972.

The Presence of the Actor documents Chaikin's thoughts, experiences and struggles with Open Theatre. Chaikin's work places collaboration between actors at the centre of the creative process, and the company generated material together through improvisation which was then shaped and scripted by a dramaturg or playwright. Chaikin's reasons for collaboration were somewhat different from the spontaneity of Living Theatre in the same period, and he was critical of practice that relied solely on a post-Freudian belief in psychic conditioning. He commented ruefully that:

> If we all stay with our hang-ups, and we define ourselves completely in relation to them and get all excited in our work when we find a repressive release for them, we haven't got very far . . . What's less clear is the way we're controlled by the givens of society.
>
> (Chaikin 1972: 83)

Chaikin's interest in social conditioning led him to study the work of Brecht, whose ideas of *Verfremdungseffekt*, he believed, had been misinterpreted by North American theatre practitioners of the time as indicating a lack of emotional involvement. Chaikin recognised that, on the contrary, performers in Brecht's theatre had an emotional commitment to the play as a whole. Chaikin's theories of the ensemble reflect the dual influences of Brecht's analytical approach to the ensemble, and more individualised theories of subjectivity and creativity inherited from Grotowski and Living Theatre. In other words, he explored both the 'inner' world of the actor, an Artaudian, ceremonial, ritualistic mode, and the 'outer' world of society which was influenced by Brecht (Pasolli 1970: 105). Chaikin described the work of an ensemble as 'a process of collaboration' which developed from empathetic support between actors rather than competition, and a technical ability to generate a shared dynamic and rhythm between actors in performance. In practice, of course, this synthesis of minds and bodies was often difficult to achieve.

Chaikin reflected on the difficulties of building an ensemble of creative actors in relation to his production of *The Serpent* (1968), which had a particularly troubled rehearsal period. Grotowski visited Chaikin's company in 1967, and the physical rigour that resulted can be seen in *The Serpent*, but the performance comprised elements that were clearly derived from a Chaikin-led process. Discussion and improvisation formed the basis of the devising process. Sometimes the stimulus was taken directly from the story of Genesis in the Bible; at other moments it involved an exploration of the self, described by Chaikin as 'projecting ourselves into images and questions' (Pasolli 1970: 116). One strategy that was used in the process of collaborative story-building was the 'emblem'. For this the actors utilised words, sounds and movement to communicate with each other and, from this workshop, they would identify moments which served as emblems for the whole story. Once an emblem was found the actors engaged in 'jamming', a phrase borrowed from jazz music improvisation. Jamming comprised an actor creating an 'extended study', through playing with the words, sound or movement of the emblem; following rhythms; transposing the whole emblem to movement or pure sound (Chaikin 1972: 116). In *The Serpent*, Christopher Innes notes, this exercise became transposed into the production, which used repeated emblematic 'locked actions' to suggest negative images of contemporary society through the biblical story of the Fall of Man (Innes 1993b: 178). The construction of the piece was Brechtian with six episodes charting the degradation of humanity, while the scenes of liberation showed the release from psychological and sexual repression that involved spontaneous interaction with the audience.

The process of creating *The Serpent* highlighted some of the difficulties in creating devised pieces. Rehearsals began with Chaikin collaborating with a number of writers. Eventually Claude van Itallie, who had not been present during the first three months of workshops, undertook the scripting process. Although he was sensitive to the collaboratively created material there was a sense that 'what had once belonged to the troupe in common looked at the time of opening very like van Itallie's property' (Pasolli 1970: 121).

The problem of how collaborations work in practice, and how companies that are committed to fostering the creativity of the performer manage divisions of labour required for theatrical production, are recurring issues for devising companies. A good example of the ways in which processes of collaboration have changed over time is offered by Ariane Mnouchkine at the Théâtre du Soleil, whose work became synonymous with the term 'collection creative'. The group was established in 1964 as a workers' cooperative, and at some points there were up to sixty members each earning a similar wage. The organisation of the company also challenged the role of the specialist and instead of actors, or technicians, every company member participated in all avenues of work (Williams 1999: 31; Féral 1989b: 98). In early interviews director Mnouchkine emphatically endorsed the benefits of collective creation in terms of the development of each individual:

> We want to eliminate all hierarchy, to make sure that each person can develop and contribute his or her best. When great plays are performed, the same people always take the major roles.
>
> (Williams 1999: 59–60)

She also defended devised work as providing the best framework through which to mirror the organisation of a workers' cooperative (Williams 1999: 22). Much of the company's early work was collectively created, but since the mid-seventies the company has worked with established texts, and more latterly with texts written by the feminist writer Hélène Cixous. The transition to pre-existing play texts was made to sharpen the political acuity of its work, but the company's interest in the creative actor is retained through an emphasis on improvisation during the rehearsal preparation (Williams 1999: xvii). Mnouchkine's long-term assistant Sophie Moscoso has identified the difference between these two forms of improvisation:

> Collective creation is a theatre without a text – little groups of actors create scenes, invent their text . . . Improvisational work is a work of research. In this case, even if you have a text, there is improvisational work. That is, you improvise with the text.
>
> (Féral 1989b: 106)

Moscoso explains that the second form of improvisation, the one that the company still uses, is a way of discovering the origin of the text.

The shift in focus from collectively devised work to rehearsal strategies that rely on improvisation is indicative of the changing role of the creative actor in these companies. Both Mnouchkine and Chaikin, like Grotowksi, have frequently worked from existing dramatic texts or with contemporary playwrights, but the concept of a creative actor responsible for making part of the performance has remained central to their work.

Legacies and influences

The legacy of the different performative experiments in the neo-avant-garde has resulted in establishing the place of the performer at the heart of the devising process. This initiated new collaborative practices and new visual and physical languages of performance that enabled actors to explore their experiences and feelings as part of the process of generating material. Although the quasi-mystical tone of these visions of acting may have been eroded, the commitment of performers to break down superficial barriers between art and life, mind and body continues to resonate in contemporary devised performance. The rise of the creative actor marks, as Elinor Fuchs has pointed out, the desire to fuse the 'long struggle in Western metaphysics between body and mind, action and reflection' (Fuchs 1996: 69).

FOUR

ART, POLITICS AND ACTIVISM

Theatre, as the most public of the arts, is second cousin to politics.
Raphael Samuel (1994: 28)

The performance practices documented so far in this section are all concerned with making connections between art and life. The provocative anarchism of Dadaism challenged the pretensions of art, Happenings provided a focus for redefining the role of the 'non-artists' in performance, and the counter-cultural performance of the neo-avant-garde sought to inspire personal liberation through shared acts of creativity. Taken together, they present compelling reconceptualisations of the role of art in society. Kaprow comments that avant-garde movements 'all focussed in one way or another on the primacy of the irrational and/or the unconscious . . . . the idea of art as an act rather than an aesthetics was implicit by 1909 and explicit by 1946' (Sandford 1995: 219). Interwoven with the avant-gardists' interest in the healing powers of the unconscious there was, however, more overtly political and materialist theatre in which radical performance was used as a tool of social mobilisation and as a medium of communication.

Activism plays an important part in the history of twentieth-century Western theatre, spanning the workers' theatre movements of the 1920s and 1930s, the counter-cultural and civil rights movements of the 1960s and 1970s. As collective political movements began to fracture at the end of the 1970s, community-based theatre became a significant force for social change and activist agendas based on shared identities became increasingly evident during the 1970s and 1980s. Although many political theatre-makers were sceptical about the élitism of the aesthetic avant-garde which was often seen to be isolated from society, it would be wrong to suggest that political activists were completely distinct from the avant-gardists. Practitioners are often in dialogue with each other, and companies such as Living Theatre, Open Theatre and The San Francisco Dancers' Workshop becoming increasingly politicised during the Free Speech Movement of the 1960s. Recipro-cally, activist theatre groups such as the San Francisco Mime Troupe and The Bread and Puppet Theatre drew inspiration from the experimental practices of the neo-avant-garde. Despite their different interests, both movements shared a concern with building practice from a strong conceptual basis, and the work they developed offered opportunities for non-artists to participate in performances that took place outside conventional theatre spaces.

Among companies whose primary agenda was political mobilisation there was, however, a scepticism about using the term 'avant-garde' to describe their performance practices. In their critical history, *Devising Performance* (2006), Deirdre Heddon and Jane Milling point out that the terms 'avant-garde' and 'radical' were the subject of rigorous debate among experimental theatre-makers. At stake was how far devising companies had maintained their position outside of the mainstream, or whether they had become, in the words of Ronnie Davis of the San Francisco Mime Troupe in 1975, 'an extension or a deviation from the bourgeois theatre, and . . . closely aligned with the aesthetic avant-garde' (Davis 1975: 67). As Heddon and Milling suggest, Davis recognises a relationship between the entertainment industry and devised theatre that was to grow steadily closer from the 1980s onwards, pointing out that contemporary devising companies similarly place themselves outside mainstream theatre practice, 'although the idea of the fringe or margins has greatly changed' (Heddon and Milling 2006: 225).

For those on the political left whose primary concern is political activism and social change, theatre is only useful as a vehicle if it convinces, challenges or inspires the audience in particular ways. Jan Cohen-Cruz has argued that efficacy always depends on a number of factors: 'people already engaged or engageable with specific issues, aesthetic strategies that are compelling to desired audiences, strong alliances with political or community organisations, sufficient material support, and synchronicity with the energy of the times' (Cohen-Cruz 2002: 95). For successive generations of theatre activists, this continual need to find new ways to engage audiences led to an inventive range of aesthetic strategies which has been revised and reinvented as part of a process of cultural renewal. As Brecht was well aware, radical performance always builds on past methods and experiences as well as articulating with present-day issues:

> Methods become exhausted; stimuli no longer work. New problems appear and demand new methods. Reality changes; in order to represent it, modes of representation must change. Nothing comes of nothing; the new comes from the old, but that is why it is new.
>
> (Brecht 1974: 51)

This chapter charts some of the methods of performance that have been devised to address the concerns of activist theatre-makers, and whose legacy of participatory practices and inventive use of space continues to be felt in performances devised for specific communities and places.

A workers' theatre

The social purpose of theatre was newly configured in the resurgence of activism following the international political events of the 1920s and 1930s, and specifically linked to the political left as a result of the Great Depression, the General Strike in the UK, the Wall Street Crash, the aftermath of the Bolshevik revolution in Russia. As Raphael Samuel has pointed out, the 1920s and 1930s introduced a 'whole new epoch in the socialist imagination' in which politically engaged theatre began to make a social impact (Samuel *et al.* 1985: xix). Members of the Communist Party in the newly established USSR were among the first to recognise the potential ideological role of theatre in the class struggle, and the influence of the workers' theatre movements established in the Soviet Union during this period spread internationally.

Particularly significant to the development of activist theatre was the Blue Blouses, founded in Moscow in 1923 by the journalist Boris Yuzhanin. The Blue Blouses touring theatre company aimed to make news and revolutionary propaganda accessible to an illiterate populace. These 'living newspapers' were also a medium of education, and included topics on health and farming as well as more overt political messages. Performing in the open air, in factories and workers' clubs, these performers adopted the blue smocks worn by factory workers in order to indicate solidarity with them. In their collectively written document 'Simple Advice to Participants' (1925), they identified a political relationship between their theatre-making and everyday life:

Organisation of Everyday Life: Not a photograph but a construction – BB not only shows our way of life like a mirror but influences the brain of the spectator with all scenic means and prepares him for the perception of new social conditions.

(Drain 1995: 182)

The Blue Blouses' political objective was to use theatre to demonstrate social 'reality' to audiences, and thus further the spread of revolutionary ideas. For this, they aimed to break the theatrical illusion of naturalism which they associated with the bourgeois attitudes of pre-Revolutionary Russia, and they experimented with social realism as a tool of dramatic expression. Borrowing from the traditions of popular entertainment, the players used forms such as popular song, acrobatics, burlesque and vaudeville which they turned to political use. They also celebrated an urban and industrialised culture in their performances, and Meyerhold's interest in the mechanical was integral to this project. Advice offered to performers in 1925 about the pace of performance shows their indebtedness to a newly industrialised political economy:

Tempo/Speed: The BB members must learn to work with industrial tempo, the parade march, a definite beat. The leading role belongs to the accompanist. All little numbers, the satirical pieces and sketches (feuilleton) use medium speed, and at the finale the speed increases again, ending on a high note.

(Drain 1995: 182)

The idea that a theatre might be built from the players' experiences of industrial life, using acting techniques which built on machine movements, was seen as genuinely revolutionary. By using these theatrical languages, theatre activists acquired relationships between performer and audience that were dynamic and interactive, intended not only as an act of resistance, but also as a means of raising political consciousness and galvanising the masses to political action.

The British Workers' Theatre Movement (WTM) was founded in 1926 and followed its Soviet comrades by regarding industry as a force for workers' power. Rather than seeking to ameliorate the effects of industry by replacing them with visions of pastoral beauty, the communist theatre-makers' performance practices were resolutely urban, working-class and populist. The WTM had been deeply influenced by dramatic practices emerging from the young Soviet Union and from Weimar Germany, in particular propagandist forms such as those developed by the Blue Blouses and the Red Megaphones in Germany. Names of British theatre companies affiliated to the WTM reflect this influence – Hackney Red Radio, Deptford Red Blouses, Lewisham Red Players – and this allegiance was also mirrored in the propagandist theatre forms they adopted. Ness Edwards, whose tract *The Workers' Theatre* (1930) was particularly influential in the development of the British movement, summed up the political objective:

> *The Workers' Drama is an agitational force.* It is propaganda by a dramatisation of facts ... The object of the workers' drama is to organise the working class for the conquest of power, to justify this conquest of power, and arouse the feelings of the workers to intensify this struggle.
>
> (quoted in Samuel *et al.* 1985: 195)

'Agit-prop' theatre was devised for the sole purpose of political agitation and propaganda and quickly travelled from 1920s' Soviet Union to the rest of Europe, arriving in New York in 1930. Members of the British WTM were drawn to agit-prop's use of short, improvisational sketches to convey unambiguous political messages. At their first national conference in 1932, a statement was issued about the politics of form. It described naturalism as 'greatly hindering the portrayal of the class struggle in dramatic form' and argued that agit-prop was able to 'give a much more flexible and dynamic picture of society' (quoted in Samuel *et al.* 1985: 101–102).

As a tool of social mobilisation, the living newspaper provided the desired balance between factual information and political comment which appealed to activist theatre-makers. The Federal Theater, working in 1930s' New York, offered its analysis of social problems arising from the agricultural depression in the form of a living newspaper called *Triple-A Ploughed Under*, which was staged in 1936. *Triple-A* comprised twenty-six short scenes, using characteristic living newspaper devices such as radio announcements, cartoon-style characters, projected diagrams and various forms of direct address through loud speakers and mass recitation. The piece conveyed the salient points of news about the drought in 1934, and also made political comment about the inadequacy of the government response and the effects of its policies on victims of the drought. This touring production ran for eighty-five performances. For communist theatre-makers, the technical simplicity of agit-prop, of which the living newspaper was a specific form, was both a practical necessity and a political statement.

Without the technical trappings of bourgeois theatre (curtains appear to have incited particular irritation), the clarity and topicality of the political message would not be obscured. This approach led Tom Thomas, a central figure in the British WTM, to call for a 'propertyless theatre for the propertyless classes', where culture would exist not only behind the closed doors of bourgeois theatre buildings, but also in places where audiences might learn to participate in revolutionary action, such as in the factory, the pub and the street (quoted in Samuel *et al.* 1985: 101–102). It was also a form of theatre that sought to portray the cultural experiences and views of the proletariat in performance, and tackled social issues head on.

Agit-prop made a brief re-appearance in activists' repertoire after the *évenements* of Paris in May 1968; the British company Red Ladder used agit-prop to support industrial disputes, but its effectiveness was waning. Perhaps most notably, their factory-gate performances of the gloriously entitled play *Stick Your Penal Up Your Bonus* were intended to engage Ford workers in political debates about inequities in wages, but it failed to capture their attention. Such failures not only revealed the company's lack of organised political alliance with the Ford workers, it also demonstrated the limitations of agit-prop as a form. Even devotees such as Red Ladder's Richard Seyd had to admit that agit-prop had restrictions because, in his words, 'it provides answers rather than asking questions' (Seyd 1975: 40).

More lasting than propagandist forms of performance was the idea of the theatre collective that developed during the 1930s. Initially founded as socialist cooperatives, collaborative practices led to experiments with collective writing. There had been experiments with collective writing in the Workers' Laboratory Theater in the United States and following this lead, the WTM in Britain recorded the following advice to groups wishing to engage in collective writing in 1932:

> It can have great results, not only in the material produced, but by way of political and technical training. Every member of a group can help in some way . . . . First a theme is chosen, and then every member of the group endeavours to get information about it by talking to the workers it concerns. Then, at a subsequent meeting, the information is collectively discussed, the line of the sketch determined, and, if necessary, it can be left to one or two members to write up.
>
> (Samuel *et al.* 1985: 104)

This advice is clearly addressed to political activists rather than theatre professionals; their process of collective decision-making was primarily a practical expression of socialist principles rather than a prerequisite for making an artistically coherent piece of theatre. It is significant that the process of working was seen as an element of political training, orientated towards becoming well-informed activists rather than creative artists. Ewan MacColl, a member of the Salford Red Megaphones in the early 1930s, said that at the time he 'knew bugger all about theatre. But I knew, or I thought I knew a great deal, about politics' (Samuel et al. 1985: 226). MacColl's description of co-writing a sketch on the bus, rehearsing for half an hour, performing in the marketplace and leaving before the police managed to catch up with them would rather confirm that the company's interests were predominantly political rather than artistic (Samuel et al. 1985: 45–46).

Collectivism, ensemble and all that jazz

One of the legacies of socially committed theatre of the twentieth century is the democratisation of processes of working. It is perhaps this aspect of practice with which devised theatre has become most associated; devised theatre is often characterised by its emphasis on improvisation, on ensemble acting, on collective decision-making and skills-sharing within a non-hierarchical company structure. In part, the development of processes of collaborative working was a political response to the hierarchical structures of established theatre in the first half of the century, which radical theatre-makers found politically restrictive and artistically stifling.

When professionally trained theatre practitioners and political activists began to work together there was marked a change in both sets of practices. A good example is the working partnership that developed between Ewan MacColl (originally a political activist) and Joan Littlewood (a professionally trained performer) which began in 1934 and led to the formation of Theatre Workshop in 1946. Littlewood had learnt her craft at the prestigious Royal Academy of Dramatic Art (RADA), but found the atmosphere of the rehearsal room stultifying, the acting style false and mannered, and the rigid hierarchies of commercial theatre not conducive to innovation and creativity. MacColl, who by 1934 was working with Manchester's Theatre of Action, had found that collaboratively written sketches were both time-consuming and artistically ineffective. What is particularly interesting about the collaboration between MacColl and Littlewood is that they emphasised the process of research, training and education – both artistic and political – as a central part of the theatre companies' work. Littlewood had developed an interest in the working methods of Stanislavsky and Laban while at RADA, and this formed the basis of their investigation into the practices of Meyerhold, Toller, Appia and other European Expressionists. Actors who worked in their companies were expected to research different aspects of theatre history, and to acquire the performance skills and flexibility needed to move quickly from one acting style to another. By the time they came to formulate the philosophy for theatre which inspired Theatre Workshop, Littlewood and MacColl had developed an efficient rehearsal process, based both on their shared knowledge of theatre practice and on their understanding of the political processes of collective decision-making.

The core of Theatre Workshop's process was built on the concept of the ensemble, which united socialist politics with theatre practice. Littlewood had a deep antipathy to the star system of London's commercial theatre, and the idea of the ensemble was in part her artistic response as a director to it. The idea of the ensemble was to create more democratic working relationships in the rehearsal room, in performance and in the company organisation and management. When she temporarily left Theatre Workshop in 1961, Littlewood summed up her idea of the collaborative process:

> My objective in life . . . is to work with other artists – actors, writers, designers, composers – and in collaboration with them, and by means of argument, experimentation and research, to keep the English theatre alive and contemporary. I do not believe in the supremacy of the director, designer, actor or even the writer. It is through collaboration that this knockabout theatre survives and kicks.
>
> (Littlewood 1961: 15–16)

It is important to stress that Theatre Workshop was designed as an ensemble, and there was dissent about how far it lived up to its democratic ideals. Although funds were shared equally among the company, and it was intended that policy decisions would be made collectively, Littlewood and MacColl effectively held the power until MacColl's departure in 1953. Howard Goorney, one of the founder members of Theatre Workshop, explained that although 'all decisions were discussed', the company was 'collective in the sense that you were party to anything that went on', and Littlewood and MacColl would usually 'get their own way' (quoted in Runkel 1987: 45).

In terms of practice, it was the working methods and process of rehearsal that Littlewood used to create an on-stage ensemble that have remained particularly influential. Clive Barker has compared the Theatre Workshop ensemble to the work of a jazz combo, a process which requires more 'rigorous investigation of form, structure and style and greater instrument flexibility and virtuosity' than playing in a symphony orchestra (Barker 2000: 114). In order to achieve this virtuosity, Barker describes a laboratory process of experimentation and improvisation, using games and exercises to develop an awareness of 'time, weight, rhythm, direction and flow' (Barker 2000: 119). As part of the training process, Littlewood expected individual actors to face and overcome their inhibitions, and to learn to trust other ensemble members. Barker described the different roles of actor and director in the process of creating an ensemble:

> The work of the director who acts as coach and trainer of an ensemble is more often concerned with removing obstacles to authenticity than adding to, or refining, what the actor preconceives. Directing is conceived as steering rather than ordering.
>
> (Barker 2000: 122)

This way of working has become hugely influential on actor training and on devised theatre practice, with the codification of games and exercises in books and manuals (including Barker's own) which aim to encourage actors to develop techniques of working collaboratively and creatively, with all the energy and spontaneity of a good jazz band.

It is interesting to note that Julian Beck, founder of Living Theatre in New York in 1951, used the metaphor of jazz to describe collective improvisation. Writing in 1970, Beck stated that collaborative theatre-making was designed to release the 'repressed subconscious', a spontaneous process of self-discovery which he compared to jazz improvisation:

> Jazz. Jazz is the hero, jazz which made an early break into actual improvisation. It was related to the automatic writing of surrealism. Chronologically the improvisatory flights of jazz musicians antedated

the experiments of Dada and Surrealism . . . . Charlie Parker . . . inspired
us, he showed us that by becoming really engaged and then letting go
the great flight of the bird could happen.

(Beck 1986: 80)

Beck's metaphor of individual freedom – 'the great flight of the bird'
– is very different from the 'rigorous investigation of form' used by
Barker to describe and compare the qualities of jazz to the rehearsal
processes of Theatre Workshop. For Beck, jazz symbolised a new
aesthetics of living and he followed the Surrealists in accepting that art,
as the free expression of the subconscious, would be socially redemptive. This differed substantially from the materialism of the workers'
theatre and related activist theatre-makers, and illustrates the philosophical differences and political distinctions between the aesthetic
avant-garde and radical theatre practices of the mid-twentieth century.

The disciplined atmosphere of Theatre Workshop was intended
to enable the creation of a popular theatre, a theatre that would demo-
cratise 'great' plays by performing them in a vibrant and accessible
acting style. Although they worked with new writers including MacColl
himself, Brendan Behan and Shelagh Delaney, there was little collectively devised work in their repertoire – *Oh! What a Lovely War* being
a notable exception. For socialist practitioners such as Littlewood,
MacColl and members of Theatre Workshop, spontaneity and creativity in the process of theatre-making were seen as a means to an end
– developing an energetic, popular and politicised theatre.

Popular theatres and public spaces

Many activist theatre-makers retained an interest in performing in
outside spaces where people gathered. A good example is offered by
the work of the San Francisco Mime Troupe, founded in 1959. The
Mime Troupe had its roots in the San Francisco Actors' Workshop
which was part of the avant-garde theatre movement that performed
in mainstream theatre houses, and was formed when some members
of the Actors' Workshop became politicised by the civil rights
movement. This political journey led them to investigate forms of how
popular entertainment might be combined with political protest and
instruction. Almost from its inception the Mime Troupe became
interested in street performance, a forum that it hoped would reach a
wide and diverse audience. Its street performance required theatrical
forms to capture attention, and the troupe chose to work in highly

visual styles of theatre based on popular genres such as commedia dell'arte, vaudeville and melodrama. These genres were specifically chosen for their wide appeal, but the lively integration of satire and comedy was intended to disrupt the audiences' expectations and awaken their political consciousness. Commedia was a particular favourite, appealing to the Mime Troupe players because it was originally intended for the marketplace or street, and the combination of easily recognisable stock characters, subversive satire, clownery, colourful masks and energetic performance style made it ideally suited to their free open-air performances. There is also an improvisational quality to much popular theatre, which meant that topical political references could be easily introduced to the performance.

One example of how the Mime Troupe used popular entertainment for social efficacy was its first collectively devised show, *A Minstrel Show or Civil Rights in a Cracker Barrel*, first performed in 1964. *A Minstrel Show* followed the formula of the black and white minstrel show, a popular form of local theatre, to expose the racism endemic in United States society. In order to understand how the form might be used effectively, the company undertook a period of research into both the traditions of the minstrel show and the play's political content. In performance, therefore, it was able to subvert the audience's familiarity with the form – a collage of sketches, songs and gags – and challenge their racist attitudes through satire. The Mime Troupe's work was characterised by its fast pace and lively humour, aimed at maximum audience involvement; the company appreciated that unless performances were entertaining, audiences would lose interest and political messages would not be heard. There was some dispute, however, about precisely which audiences their work should reach, and at the end of the 1960s splits occurred between the Marxists, who wished to play exclusively to a working-class audience, and Ronnie Davis, founder of the troupe, who was convinced that college-educated audiences would have more revolutionary impact. After both parties had left the company in 1970, Theodore Shank records Mime Troupe writer Joan Holden's view that it had become increasingly difficult to identify what constituted the working class and, in a redefinition of terms, they focussed their attention on hard-to-reach audiences, 'the people who work for wages, who are not college educated, and who think theatre is not for them' (Shank 2002: 65). The Mime Troupe, whose actors were predominantly from middle-class backgrounds or college-educated themselves, consistently experimented with forms of popular theatre that engaged their target audiences.

Outside the experimental avant-garde, and beyond the immediate political dynamic of agit-prop and popular street performance, there is less evidence for the popularity of collectively devised performance. Although many theatre activists throughout the 1970s organised themselves as collectives, the process of creating devised performances was often abandoned after a fairly brief period of experimentation. Both Gay Sweatshop and the feminist company Monstrous Regiment found the process of creating collectively devised work artistically limiting, favouring collaboration with writers who were either members of the company, or sympathetic to their aims. Gillian Hanna, founder member of Monstrous Regiment, offered an analysis of this process of political thinking:

> One of the questions that came up again and again in the 1970s was the breaking down of the division of labour and the consequent hierarchy of skills . . . Wouldn't it be more democratic to write scripts collectively? If you were working as a collective, how could one voice represent the ideas of the whole? We acknowledged some truth in this, but there were some areas where we recognised it as bunk. Enough of us (and I was one of them) had been through the painful experience of writing shows collectively in other groups to know that the skill of playwriting was one skill we wished to acknowledge. We also knew that women writers had to be found and nourished.
>
> (Hanna 1991: xxxiii)

This way of thinking about artistic collaboration within a theatre collective ensured that playwrights became integral to the actors' dialogue. Monstrous Regiment, among other companies, often developed successful relationships with relatively unknown writers, and its development of one of Caryl Churchill's early plays, *Vinegar Tom*, stands as testament to this process of collaboration and indicates the complexity of the writer's role in politically committed theatre-making.

Legacies and influences

One of the most significant legacies of twentieth-century theatre activists is an awareness of the significance of the context of performance, and a commitment to extending democratic participation in theatre-making through active collaboration with different communities and social groups. Jan Cohen-Cruz has charted the paradigm shift that led theatre activists and the experimental performance-makers of the neo-avant-garde to gravitate towards community-based theatre (Cohen-Cruz 2005). Baz Kershaw similarly recognises the radical potential of this paradigm shift, and makes a persuasive case for community theatre as cultural force for mediating change (Kershaw 1992).

Cohen-Cruz argues that community-based performance follows its more overtly politicised predecessors in its concern for participation, and she notes that professional practitioners frequently become actively involved in the communities with which they work. Dramatising local narratives, and stories which have a particular significance to a specific community group, often forms the bedrock of community-based performances. In making a case for the political efficacy of contemporary community-based theatre, Cohen-Cruz recognises that community-based theatre follows the legacy of the avant-garde and radical theatres of the twentieth century as it is motivated by a belief in the reciprocal relationship between art and life (Cohen-Cruz 2005: 78).

PART TWO

Shaping
Narratives

INTRODUCTION: SHAPING NARRATIVES

Authenticity and performativity

Creating an original performance, as opposed to staging a play, inevitably involves drawing upon personal experience or reframing preexisting material within a collectively designed structure. The selection of these events and moments, and the ordering and retelling of them, involves performance-makers working with narrative devices. Narrative at its most basic level has been defined as 'a perceived sequence of non-randomly connected events' (Toolan 2001: 6). These events can be personal, owned by a group, or invented by writers and thus given the status of fiction.

Raymond Williams notes that the term 'fiction' embodies a duality of meaning in which two clear but contradictory ideas are acknowledged. He recognises that the term covers both imaginative literature and also 'pure (and sometimes deliberately deceptive) invention' (Williams 1983: 134). Williams' observation draws attention to the way in which the term 'fiction' embraces both made-up fantastical stories and the idea of invented and untrue incidents. In other words, this second use of the term shows the disparity between fiction and fact, and in doing this exposes the sense of what is true and authentic and that which is embellished.

This section draws upon two main theoretical threads through which the issue of the authenticity of narrative and the resultant concept of performativity are explored. The first of these ideas is articulated by the critic Louis Renza who uses an examination of autobiographical modes to investigate how memory serves as a filter to later re-express the reality of lived experience as a fiction: 'The content of the narrative set[s] up a screen between the truth of the narrated past and the present of the narrative situation' (Renza 1980: 271). Renza's comments emphasise the difficult relationship between truth and representation and in doing so make the reader aware of the distance between self and the performance of self-identity. It is this notion that the projection of one's self may constitute 'performance' that is fundamental to the concept of performativity, first developed by J.L. Austin in 1955, where he noted that some forms of speech presupposed an action: 'To *say* something is to *do* something' (quoted in Schechner 2002: 110). The idea of performativity thus collapses the boundaries between that which occurs on stage and everyday events, and many of the performance practices outlined in this section continue to challenge these divides.

One of the recurring themes in this section is how contemporary devisers construct theatrical narratives that are explicitly intended to challenge neat distinctions between the fictional and real, between secrets and lies, and between imagination and authenticity. In the chapters which follow, three related critical perspectives illuminate how performance-makers have extended the act of narrative production in ways which trouble and unfix these binaries. Postmodern theories of selfhood are used to challenge the perception that autobiographical performance offers a transparent representation of subjectivity. The acting styles (or 'non-acting' techniques that have been identified within this genre) draw attention to how habitual roles and everyday performative acts contribute to the construction of personal identities. The process of shaping intimate thoughts, feelings and experiences for a witnessing audience inevitably fuses truth and fiction by recognising that the imagination is integral to the narrative of selfhood. The audience is frequently left wondering what is truthful and what is fictional; thus the question of the authenticity of narratives is raised. Theatrical constructions of community narratives similarly recognise the importance of the self-reflexive individual, although the process of devising emphasises how a sense of belonging is built on identification with the narratives of others. These community narratives reflect how a shared story can bind a group together. A phenomenology of community recognises that theatrical meanings applied to all narratives are dependent on time and context, and this raises ethical questions about what is 'real' and what might be imagined. Adapting fiction for the stage is illuminated by a reading of classical narratology, and by the Russian formalists' analysis that the structural origins of narrative offer familiar archetypes which transcend transcultural difference. Although this position maintains the philosophical distinction between fiction and reality, the process of adapting familiar narratives for the stage disturbs the underlying structural features of novels and raises new questions about how fiction is defined and constructed. Taken together, the unfixed qualities of performance invite audiences to recognise the ways in which fiction is contained in reality, and how reality is always implied in fictional or fictionalised narratives.

Performed narratives

The second major theoretical strand explored within this section is expressed through the work of Paul Ricoeur who notes that narratives are not unbiased, but are loaded with ethical and moral signification. They act as a place in which to try out new possibilities and models for living. This notion, though expressed in a different manner, is shared by Lévi-Strauss's analysis of shared stories and myths whereby he notes that two differing groups of participants can be brought together to reach new ground through the sharing of fiction.

A distinctive feature of narratives is that they have a teller and a told. In other words there is a person or group of people responsible for relating the events and another person or group who are the receivers of that material. Within performance events these roles usually distinguish the actors from the spectators, although the sharing of a narrative may attempt to conjoin these groups. Arthur Frank in *The Wounded Storyteller* considers the importance of the relationship between the teller and the audience and identifies the importance of the storyteller's stories as a means of creating a bond between the individual who tells the story and the rest of the community. Within devised performance the use of narrative material raises a number of issues connecting with the creation of the piece. These include the relationship between the audience and the narrative, and the positioning of the company in relation to the chosen material.

The following chapters consider different types of contracts which are made with the audience through theatrical storytelling. Chapter Five considers the way in which audience members are acknowledged as witnesses to the personal testament of the performers of autobiographical performance. Chapter Six examines how the theatrical event might serve to articulate a shared story through participation as well as spectatorship within community theatre. It identifies ways in which community narratives and social history as well as personal archives can provide material from which performances may be constructed. Chapter Seven goes on to explore how the dramatic representation of well-known narratives may serve as a platform for creativity that can be enjoyed by both audience and performers.

Hayden White has commented that 'to raise the question of the nature of narrative is to invite reflection on the very nature of culture and, possibly, even on the nature of humanity itself' (White 1987: 30). The link between narrative and culture is frequently subject to radical questioning in devised performance; narrative shapes experience, tests assumptions and makes connections. The presentation of a shared story offers not only the potential for the establishment of a bond between the audience and performers, but also an opportunity for the spectators to partake of a creative aesthetic that challenges the patterns established by traditional plays. The examples chosen demonstrate how the stage becomes a flexible playground in which epic presentations of place, time and characterisation embrace the audience as collaborators in an imaginative journey.

FIVE

AUTOBIOGRAPHICAL
PERFORMANCE

Drawing on your own experience

Autobiographical narratives are spaces where an individual's private stories are offered up for public consumption. Since its identification as a discrete practice, autobiography, with its reflection on personal experience, has prompted discussion about the relation between fact and fiction, the nature of selfhood and the mechanics of representation. These concerns can also be related to autobiographical performance, which is the subject of this chapter. The contemporary practice of autobiographical performance can be traced back through the Happenings of the 1960s and 1970s where the relationship between art and everyday life was blurred and the focus was not on the skilled performance of a character in a narrative but on participants being 'themselves' in a range of situations.

Issues of self and identity have been central to discussions of performance practice in general but autobiographical performance throws up particular questions in that the selfhood of performers is explicitly foregrounded as they seek to represent themselves. While Stanislavky and Brecht (among many others) have offered up theories of acting which are concerned with how performers may apply their own experiences to the roles they are playing, a discussion of auto-biographical performance demands a consideration of the performance of self rather than the representation of another person. Indeed, this type of performance has even been termed 'non-acting', as it appears to work against a masking role and to communicate with the audience in a direct manner. Non-acting can be understood as functioning in the tradition of the modernist avant-garde in that it is not a mimetic practice that seeks to represent a fictional character, but a reframing of reality that seeks to blur the boundaries of art and life. Furthermore, non-acting can be viewed as a performative practice that frames the everyday in a manner which reflects upon the constitution of identity itself.

Contemporary devisers often explicitly draw on their own experience when creating work for performance and such work can be seen to engage with issues of authenticity, selfhood and reception. Questions of authenticity are raised when fact is blended with fiction; selfhood is addressed as performers present a distinct persona to the audience; and the processes of reception are heightened as they invite the audience into an active relationship with the material. Methodologically, the use of personal interests and narratives as source material leads to a complex creative process that reflects upon real life data to shape a performance piece. As with other autobiographical narratives, autobiographical performance often fuses factual material with fictional elements. The processes of production which bring together truth and fantasy are highlighted by Louis Renza, a postmodern critic who, with reference to the bricolage that may constitute an autobiographical narrative, disputes the idea that the self is a coherent unity which might be called 'authentic'. Rather than viewing autobiography as a direct communication between the essential selves of the author and their audience as earlier commentators on the field had done, Renza foregrounds the process of creation which sits at the heart of the production and reception of autobiographical texts. He notes that the production of autobiography is a result of a reflection upon personal experience that is subjected to the filters of memory and personal editing. Instead of seeing autobiography as a direct reflection of reality or a purely fictional creation, Renza posits that:

> We might say, then, that autobiography is neither fictive nor nonfictive, not even a mixture of the two. We might view it instead as a unique, self-defining mode of self-referential expression.
>
> (Renza 1980: 295)

Renza highlights the way in which an autobiographical text may trouble the binary opposition of truth and fiction through inhabiting a creative space in-between. This blends elements of both factual detail and fictional fantasy around the persona of the performer.

A variety of reasons can be identified for the use of personal experience within contemporary devised work, ranging from ideological impulses to artistic pragmatism. Some devising companies employ personal experience as a vehicle to explore sociopolitical situations. For example, feminist theatre company Common Ground drew on its collective personal experience of the peace camp outside the gates of Greenham Common cruise missile site to develop a production (*The Fence*, 1984) that examined women working together for peace. Such work holds to the feminist principle that the personal is political and employs autobiographical narrative as a means of substantiating an ideological message. Aesthetic concerns may also lead to the application of autobiographical methodology. Thus, as with the modernists, the practice of non-acting may be employed as a strategy to disrupt conventional modes of presentation and reception and encourage a fresh perspective on the relationship between life and art within the performance event. For example, British theatre company Frantic Assembly makes use of the personas of company members within its shows. Company members have used each other's given names within performances and even included sections which made reference to their everyday lives. This strategy encourages audience members to identify with the actual performers, something that may, in turn, heighten their anxiety about the level of personal risk the company members are taking in their highly physicalised performance. In short, the autobiographical element of the work is used as a device to encourage engagement as the audience's awareness of physical and emotional vulnerability in the performance is heightened.

Public witnessing is also a significant element within contemporary autobiographical performance practice. While American sociologist Scott Lasch sees the contemporary confessional mode as evidence of increasing narcissism, trauma studies scholar Shoshana Felman notes that the witnessing of personal testimony has become increasingly important. She argues that large-scale traumas such as the Holocaust can prove to be overwhelming and incomprehensible, yet, through the narration of a personal story, an individual may make sense of it within their own psyche. Within this process the listener has a responsibility to bear witness to the story and as such, '[break] down the isolation imposed by the nature of the event' (quoted in Anderson 2001: 129). Rather than being passive spectators, audiences for autobiographical performance are drawn into a relationship with the performer due to the authentic nature of the material and the fact that the story is being told directly to them. Autobiographical performance acknowledges observers and places an emphasis on sharing intimacies with witnesses.

Autobiographical performance is a distinct mode of working with an emphasis on a self-reflexive, creative methodology which itself has implications for the formal presentation and reception of the work in terms of the framing of intimate content. Those engaged in the practice are concerned with presenting personal material to an audience and, as such, work to fashion narratives from their everyday lives into an artistic product that may be presented within a public arena. In such work tensions arise from the public presentation of thoughts, feelings and behaviours which are conventionally considered personal and confidential. These tensions are explored and even exploited for their theatrical effect. The making, delivery and reception of the work are all shaped by an approach that centres on personal experience. This chapter will consider the implications of fusing fact and fantasy; the performance of self; and the notion of the audience as witnesses.

Secrets and lies

Sheffield-based Third Angel is an example of a devising company which explicitly draws on autobiographical material to develop creative work. The company describes its working practice as follows:

> We are used to making work that borrows stories from our own lives and other people's lives. We're used to making work that strays into the grey area between the truth and fiction, memory and imagination. This is what we do: work that incorporates documentary detail and fiction but doesn't bother to point out which is which.
>
> (Kelly 2000: 49)

Third Angel's inhabitation of the 'grey area' between truth and fiction is exemplified in its piece *Where from Here* (2001) where a description of a room in the fictional story is an actual description of a performer's real bedroom. During rehearsal the company discovered that the rooms they fabricated lacked the detail that they felt was necessary to carry the action of the show. The director noted that they were 'not mundane enough' and so they looked to borrow from everyday life as they perceived that such material would provide an engaging aura of authenticity (Third Angel 2004). In its experimental work, Third Angel has continued to explore possibilities of blending the details of autobiography with fictional narratives.

Class of '76 (1999) is an autobiographical project that caused Third Angel to reflect upon its working processes. The show had its first incarnation as a fifteen-minute piece wherein performer Alexander Kelly presented information about his former classmates from Chuckery Infants' School and what they had become. All the information – such as Lahkir Singh playing football for the world – was fabricated, even some of the names were made up because Kelly could not remember them. This prompted a research process which led to a second version of the piece that sought to present the truth and was witnessed by some of the people that Kelly was discussing. The final development of the work was a version that reflected upon the preceding process. In this piece Kelly introduced himself and his project to the audience and then explained about the making and reception of the work, taking time to reflect upon the role of memory in this process.

Memory is a key aspect in the creation of autobiographical performance. The human memory acts as a filter and, as a consequence, what is remembered may not be the truth but an embroidered version of the real. In *Class of '76* Kelly says of his classmates, 'This is how I remember them', highlighting the potential slippage between how they really were and how they are being represented (Third Angel 2003). Through such comments, the piece foregrounds the possibility of different versions of reality which arise due to different subjectivities. For example, Kelly allows for various perspectives of playground encounters. In other words, Kelly announces himself as a storyteller and actively engages in a mode of self-representation which also allows for the possibility of writing from other subject positions.

The practice of retelling and remembering can also lend a formal structure to the performance work. *Class of '76* was presented as if it were a factual encounter. Kelly often read from a clipboard, and pointed to faces from a class photograph in a manner that seemed to authenticate the information that was being delivered. Sequences within the piece were framed by comments such as 'What else can I remember?', which were then followed by a list of bullet-point memories such as: 'Mr Turner teaching us how to brush our teeth and cutting his tie in half in assembly' (Third Angel 2003). There was no attempt to recreate the action; instead, the emphasis was on the moment of remembering. This relationship between the past and the present indicates the ways in which autobiography is constructed. Renza notes that:

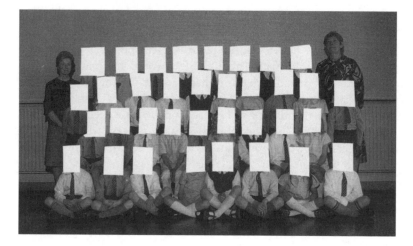

Figure 5.1 Third Angel: *Class of '76*. Projected memories served as the substance for the performance event.

Reproduced by permission of Third Angel.

> The content of the narrative set[s] up a screen between the truth of the narrated past and the present of the narrative situation.
>
> (Renza 1980: 271)

In performance the present of the narrative situation is heightened in a way it might not be on the page as the performers stand in front of the audience and directly announce themselves as storytellers. Thus Kelly presented information directly to the audience in the present moment of performance and acted as a conduit for information about events that happened in the past. The audience was aware that his account of events may have involved a reshaping of facts. Indeed, the company commented that, in question and answer sessions, audience members often asked about what was true, even though Kelly had stated that he was telling the truth (Third Angel 2004). It seems that there is a concern in the minds of the audience to make sense of the narrative and to understand where reality lies.

Renza posits that an autobiographical narrative is always 'an incomplete literary project' in that, although it has a beginning, it has no middle or end (Renza 1980: 295). This complex relationship between the past and present affects the ways in which autobiography is constructed. Kelly notes that *Class of '76* has a sense of 'unfinished business'. He does have all the information about all the people in the photograph and, within the piece itself, there is not time to give a full account of the information he does have (Third Angel 2003). Kelly offers his memories of the people but, as he states to the audience at one point in the piece, 'you might know differently' (Third Angel 2003). The reception of the piece certainly seems to indicate that audience members made personal associations with the material. Discussions of school life provoked laughter as the audience related to the performer's narratives. For example, it seems that many people can relate to a story about a school bully. Presenting authentic detail from the performer's experience opens up personal memories for audience members.

Performing self

Class of '76 is a good example of the practice of non-acting that is often seen in autobiographical performance. Rather than working to present named characters that are distanced from themselves, performers can be seen to be performing themselves – or at least versions of themselves. At the beginning of the piece Kelly introduced himself as a 'large part of Third Angel' and described how he always wanted to be a detective (Third Angel 2003). These are truths about himself. However, the presentation of these facts is framed by an editing process. So, for example, although he also always wanted to be a geologist, such information does not serve the thrust of the creative piece and so is left out. Nigel Charnock, a founder member of British-based physical theatre company DV8 and now maker of his own shows including solo work, describes how this performance of self might be negotiated. He states:

> The shows I do are always about the people that are in the show, not about something separate from them. I don't ask them to play characters – it's always: What would you do? . . . So on stage they are who they are only more heightened: bigger, with the volume turned up a bit.
>
> (Charnock 1996: 31)

This is a common working practice, and performers in autobiographical work are often engaged in presenting heightened versions of themselves. Their identity as 'real people' and as performers is blurred as they do not have a mask of character, yet they are also clearly behaving in a heightened and self-conscious manner. Howell suggests that 'acting [is] pretending to be someone else, and nonacting performance [is] concentrat[ing] on pretending to be yourself' (Howell 1999: 408). Thus autobiographical performance troubles the activity of presenting a role and does not delineate between the authentic person and the creation.

Autobiographical performance heightens an awareness of the complexity of the presentation of self and this is intentionally made explicit to the audience. This may, in turn, prompt the audience to reflect upon the performance of self within everyday life and its codes and conventions. In *The Presentation of Self in Everyday Life*, Erving Goffman discusses the way in which people shape their behaviour in order to suit the social drama they are in and, as such, play out particular roles. American performance artist Laurie Anderson, who has been creating experimental performance work for over twenty years, draws on this role-playing for her performance work. She describes herself as not acting but engaging in different 'talking styles' as happens in everyday life:

> For instance, I've used about eight talking styles today, starting with a phone call about a death in the family and talking with my mother, then screaming at the lawyer in my most efficient, business-like style.
>
> (quoted in Howell 1999: 407)

This conflation between real life and performer is a development of modernist avant-garde practice which Claire MacDonald notes has 'sought to close the gap between art and life' (MacDonald 1995: 191). The self-conscious presentation of self draws attention to the exploration of identity which is often at the heart of autobiographical performance.

The sense of reality in autobiographical performance lends the encounter a certain dynamic. Rather than pretending to be a character, performers are involved in narrating past events directly to an audience. This lends a vibrancy to the relationship between the storyteller and the audience; where actors address audiences directly, audiences become very aware that they are sharing space and a present moment. This demands a particular sense of presence from the performer. Anderson describes the texture of performing as herself. She says, 'You have to be right there and make it happen' (quoted in Howell 1999: 408). Being engaged in the moment is of course key to all performance practice but with autobiographical work this dynamic is heightened as performers seek to make real connections with the audience through the revelation of self. So, for example, like much other autobiographical work, Anderson's performances often involve minimal staging so that the focus is instead on building a real rapport between the performer and the audience members.

Anderson's piece *Happiness* (2002) is one which explicitly engages with the exploration of selfhood and identity – both Anderson's own personal identity and the wider cultural identity of the United States. Anderson has long been a polemicist, producing work that is committed to exploring the contemporary sociopolitical climate, and *Happiness* is her response to the events of the terrorist attacks of 11 September 2001. Autobiographical material has been a key part of the artist's practice and she has developed a performance persona that is 'Laurie Anderson'. In *Happiness*, Anderson emphasised the personal resonances of the political situation and describes the work as her 'most autobiographical to date' (Anderson 2003a). Anderson's studio is a few blocks away from the Twin Towers site and, as such, she had a particular personal perspective on the international events. Anderson states that 'the shock of terrorism propelled me into a different place, (Anderson 2003a). *Happiness* is an intimate account of the personal journey that Anderson undertook and, as such, Anderson appears within the work as both subject and object. As in her other work there was no sense of the presentation of a character on stage; instead Laurie Anderson appeared as herself – or perhaps more correctly – as her*selves*. Anderson wore no overt costume that might suggest character, but instead formal clothing – black trousers and jacket with a white shirt – which can be seen to suggest 'neutrality'. The series of monologues that Anderson shared with the audience focussed on identity and shape-shifting which served to heighten the audience's awareness of the performance of self that took place within the piece. Anderson describes how 'For the past year I've been looking for ways to escape my own perspective by putting myself in weird situations' (Anderson 2003a). Like many artists she carried out experimental work that generated material which she then assembled into a performance piece. *Happiness* is made up of episodic monologues in which Anderson gives account of her experiments in identity and recounts, among other things, her time with an Amish community, her work as a juror and her employment as a McDonald's server.

The McDonald's narrative in particular highlights the issue of everyday performance. Anderson described how her co-workers thought she was German and she did nothing to dispel that idea.

Indeed, she draws on the racial stereotype of German efficiency, stating that 'thinking of myself as German helped' as she endeavoured to meet McDonald's productivity standards (Anderson 2003b). This sense of shifting subjectivities and the exploration of the possibilities within the performance of self can be seen to be at the heart of both Anderson's project in particular and autobiographical performance in general. Heddon notes that:

> experience, then, does not indicate some central core of identity, but seems to constitute subjectivity and, rather than being the reflection of some reality, should be the ground for an analysis of discursive systems.
>
> (Heddon 1998: 52)

Anderson's work, as with that of other autobiographical artists, opens up questions about the constitution of identity and the discursive systems that regulate it. The framed performance of self allows audiences the opportunity to consider how selfhood is created.

The staging of self demands a certain meta-theatricality as the performer demonstrates awareness that they are presenting an artefact for consumption by an audience. While this dynamic was apparent throughout *Happiness*, the closing section of the piece was explicitly self-referential. Anderson directly addressed the audience with the statement: 'It is the end of the play and the actors come out and look at you' (Anderson 2003b). This sequence acknowledged herself as a performer and heightened the audience members' awareness of their role as spectators through the manner in which she returned their gaze.

Audience as witness

The act of witnessing is central to the reception of autobiographical performance. Rather than being passive spectators, members of the audience are acknowledged as active listeners and the authentic nature of the material often draws the audience into an active engagement with the performer. In a review of Laurie Anderson's *Happiness*, Michael Betancourt notes that:

> [Anderson's] stories leave us with the feeling that we have no answer to what we witness, and that simply bearing witness to these horrors through stories is a way of diminishing them.
>
> (Betancourt 2002)

The reality of the material that Anderson is presenting, as well as the intimate way in which she presents it in the first person, commands an active mode of readership. Betancourt identifies this as an act of witnessing.

Theatre is fundamentally predicated on the presence of an audience but the notion of witnessing suggests a different level of engagement. In examining the process of witnessing within performance, scholars have drawn on work within the field of trauma studies which is concerned with the analysis of emotional trauma and memory, and the relationship between these two. As in trauma studies, performance scholars acknowledge the efficacy of personal narratives and recognise the impulse within witnesses to bear testament to the story that has been presented to them. Witnessing is often identified as a response to catastrophe, but the performance scholar Peggy Phelan also notes that:

> Witnessing in the theatre . . . can also help us discover the capacity to respond to the equally treacherous and equally urgent need to witness joy, pleasure, and the profundity of delight we feel in our mortal bodies, flawed minds, imperfect hearts, and impoverished tongues.
>
> (quoted in Etchells 1999: 13)

Witnessing, then, is an invitation to engage in two-way communication and, within devised autobiographical performance, that invitation is usually personal and intimate. Practitioners make the consideration of their audience a core element of their performance-making. Third Angel, for example, describes how it always asks the question 'who are the audience and why are they here?' (Third Angel 2004). In this manner the audience can be seen to be another character within the piece.

The emphasis on witnessing can be seen to shape form as well as content. Direct address to the audience has already been mentioned as being fundamental to autobiographical performance, as it recognises a dialogue between performer and audience within the performance event. Tim Etchells, director of devising ensemble Forced Entertainment, discusses the significance of the 'in-the-same-roomness' of theatre to the work that his company makes. He speaks of the:

> struggle to produce witnesses rather than spectators [which] is present everywhere in the contemporary performance scene . . . an invitation

to be here and now, to feel exactly what it is to be in this place at this time.

(Etchells 1999: 18)

Forced Entertainment is based in Sheffield, UK and many of the performers have collaborated for twenty years, making a range of work from touring theatre pieces to installations. Their show *Speak Bitterness* navigates the concept of witnessing in a particularly challenging manner. The piece was first performed in 1994 and was made up of a litany of confessions both real and fictional. It has since been performed both as a theatre piece and as a six-hour durational work. The performers, dressed in formal suits, lined up behind a long table littered with papers and delivered their admissions directly to the audience – sometimes these were declared in loud voices and other times the confessions were barely audible. Within the theatre piece sections were also left unscripted allowing the performers the opportunity for spontaneous interaction with each other and the audience. The company decided that the audience should be lit throughout the performances in order to allow for eye contact between performers and audience members. It was the performers' desire to make contact with individuals within the auditorium in order to draw them into the performance work.

Etchells asserts that 'For us performance and confession have always gone hand in hand' (Etchells 1999: 219) and thus *Speak Bitterness* can be seen as a logical progression in practice, in that it experiments with the performative elements of confession. This impulse can be seen to arise from an autobiographical mode of working where, as Renza suggests, the orientation is towards what is usually kept secret (Renza 1980: 295). It can also be related to the cultural climate that feeds an interest in autobiographical narratives. Richard Sennett, among other cultural commentators, has suggested that Western society has become increasingly privatised and, in such a climate, critics have observed that access to the stories of others has been maintained through the media. What would have once been witnessed in everyday life is now only accessible as media products, a dynamic which has its apex in TV chat shows where guests present their personal stories for public consumption. Etchells describes how the text of *Speak Bitterness* draws on confessional forms such as chat shows, churches and public trials in order to create a piece where it appears that the desire is to confess to everything. A section of the text reads as follows:

We handcuffed Lee Morris to the railings in the playground and pulled his trousers down. We lived a harsh fast life; we were glad to be alive; we didn't have an opinion on anything except how crazy the world was. We're guilty of attic rooms, power cuts and bombs; we confess to statues, ruins and gameboys.

(Etchells 1999: 186)

The heady mixture of the outrageous and the banal, delivered in a self-reflexive manner that apes the confessional mode offers up a complex negotiation for the audience. MacDonald notes that this dynamic occurs within autobiographical performance in general and she states: 'In a society almost obsessed with self-revelation [such work] makes for interesting alliances and strange readings' (MacDonald 1995: 193).

It appears that the audience for autobiographical performance is looking to make an authentic connection with the material it is presented with. This is problematised by the fact that such perform-ances are often a mixture of truth and lies and personal material is usually indistinguishable from the fiction. This authentic tone may prove seductive to audience members who, in the context of a confessional culture, want to believe that all they are told is real and this may backfire on the performers themselves. Third Angel, for example, was once confronted by an audience member who angrily stated 'You lied to me', despite the fact she had been aware that she was attending a performance (Third Angel 2004). In this way autobiographical performance work engages in complex negotiations with reality and fiction. This dynamic may itself be foregrounded within performance events. For example, in *Where From Here*, the female performer, having given her account of events throughout the piece, is left alone in the box set and delivers a monologue which begins 'I am a liar'. This charged moment highlights the performative quality of the work and heightens the audience members' critical awareness by asking them to re-evaluate all they have been told throughout the piece.

The concern to separate out reality from fiction relates to a desire to assess the skill of the performers, in that audience members desire to ascertain whether people are 'being themselves' or performing – a division that such work deliberately seeks to blur. In autobiographical performance there is always a play between what is truthful and what is make-believe. This reflects the processes of everyday life in that everyday performance may also embroider truth. On another level, however, such practice raises questions as to what constitutes art and where it differs from everyday life. The practice of non-acting can be traced back to the work of the modernist avant-garde and the anti-art movement where the negation of skill was seen to challenge and open up the limits of art practice. In this way the validation of personal stories through their framing in performance continues to develop a strand in radical art practice.

In conclusion, autobiographical performance can be seen to be a contemporary practice in the non-acting tradition of the modernist avant-garde. Like the avant-garde, the work raises questions about the relationship between truth and fiction and art and life as well as problematising the roles of the performer and audience member. Autobiographical performance relates to the current cultural climate, yet practitioners engage in autobiographical performance for a variety of reasons and this mode of working offers up particular methodo-logical issues and formal conventions. The practitioners discussed in this chapter have all created work involving a complex fusion of truth and fiction. In performance they are involved in a presentation of self which is a heightened form of an everyday persona. They also all seek to engage their audience in an active reception of the work, a mode of witnessing that acknowledges the vibrancy of personal stories that are played out in a public arena.

SIX

NARRATIVES OF COMMUNITY

Concepts of community

Drama practitioners have long recognised that devised theatre is a good vehicle for shaping communities and challenging social injustice. Collaborations between professional theatre practitioners and community-based participants are often intended to improve the lives of the participants, to extend cultural democracy and contribute to the process of social change. Because devised performance emphasises participatory working methods, it has often been regarded as an effective and flexible way to move from the individualism of autobiographical narratives to more collective forms of community participation and social identification. The community arts movement is indebted to the aesthetic strategies of political activists and theatre-makers that were documented in Chapter Four as well as to innovations in educational theatre that encouraged members of diverse communities to explore and represent their collective and personal identities. The efficacy of much community-based theatre is built on the understanding that participating in drama enables participants' own narratives to be represented, reframed, rewritten and re-interpreted in ways which challenge cultural orthodoxies. It is a way of thinking about social change which relies on two highly contested concepts – community and narrative – both of which are complexly nuanced. This chapter offers an investigation of the role of devised theatre in representing and interrogating narratives of community.

Although the concept of community is generally regarded in positive terms – Raymond Williams famously described it as a 'warmly persuasive word' (Williams 1992: 95) – the actual experience of belonging has become increasingly problematic, particularly in societies where there is a history of diaspora and migrant populations. Idealised pictures of homogeneous local communities as the bedrock of a stable society are not only highly sentimental, but they also provide an inadequate account of the complicated network of social relations in which many people now live. Furthermore, as Iris Marion Young argues from a philosophical perspective, local communities not only bind people together, but they can also act as a powerful means of exclusion, separating 'us' from 'them'. This sometimes has the effect of keeping people 'in their places' by entrapping the poor, and confining women to the sphere of the domestic and creating hostile environments for migrant populations (Young 1990: 300–303). Although it is important to acknowledge that many people rely on their locality for day-to-day companionship, for a sense of well-being and for systems of support, straightforward narratives of community based on the ideal of homogeneous local identities, shared histories and ideological unity are likely to be limited and limiting. It is not, as social theorists Benedict Anderson and Anthony Cohen point out, that such communities once existed but have now been lost or destroyed by social change. On the contrary, they argue, communities are formed when people imagine that they have common values, identities or characteristics (Anderson 1991) and through the symbolism of a collective cultural consciousness (Cohen 1985). Communities are sustained, therefore, by many different cultural practices – whether consciously or not – and are developed when people shape their autobiographical narratives in relation to their perceptions of the narratives of others. In Cohen's words, people consider community to be a 'resource and repository of meaning, a referent of their identity' (Cohen 1985: 118).

If communities are regarded as symbolic constructions, it suggests that how stories are told represents the different ways in which they are imagined. Theatre practitioners have often explicitly sought to tell stories from the point of view of their own collective identities, and to use performance to construct a strong sense of community. The British company Gay Sweatshop is a good example of such a company which, operating predominantly in the 1980s, sought both to offer a sense of shared identity to those who found themselves marginalised because of their sexuality and to change the attitudes of the prejudiced. The idea that narrative is both an instrument of self-understanding, a way of locating oneself in relation to others, and a mechanism of social change has been put forward by, among others, the phenomenologist Paul Ricoeur. Ricoeur argues that, because narrative reveals and constructs social and cultural values, narrative theory lies 'at the crossroads of the theory of action and moral theory'. He identifies the social and ethical significance of storytelling. 'Telling a story,' Ricoeur suggests, 'is deploying an imaginary space for thought experiments in which moral judgement operates in hypothetical mode' (Ricoeur 1992: 170). Narrative theory, in this configuration, lies between prescription and description, between fiction and reality. Or, to put it another way, narrative inhabits a space between how life is usually constructed and perceived, and how it might be reconstructed and re-imagined for the future.

Changing conceptions of community and narrative reflect a renewed interest in acknowledging the messiness of lived experience. This recognises the ethical possibilities found through multiple forms of identification with others, rather than those simply inscribed in dominant or conventional social narratives. Narratives of community and selfhood are not closed or self-sufficient social units but flexible and dynamic social practices, and this means that the experience of belonging to a community always represents a partial account of experience, a fragmented narrative. Vered Amit expands this way of thinking by suggesting that any one individual is likely to form allegiances with many different communities or social groups:

> The essential contingency of community, its participants' sense that it is fragile, changing, partial and only one of a number of competing attachments or alternative possibilities for affiliation means that it can never be all enveloping or entirely blinkering. Community is never the world entire, it is only ever one of a number of recognised possibilities.
>
> (Amit 2002: 18)

The idea that community represents 'a number of recognised possibilities' links it securely to phenomenological theories of narrative: both emphasise that interpretations of experience are provisional, incomplete and contingent on time and context. It raises questions about how narratives of selfhood and community are continually produced and reproduced through interaction with others. It is a way of thinking about community as a cultural practice, and suggests that the reciprocity between participants in performance enables them to negotiate their way through the competing attachments and the different narratives and values of the various communities to which they belong.

The similarities between theories of narrative and conceptions of community suggest that building communities is a creative endeavour and an imaginative process, in which the process of narration provides a level of social coherence – albeit temporary – and a way of representing events which makes them meaningful within a particular community and for a known audience. Telling stories in drama has a part to play in this imaginative process, providing participants with the opportunity to question how narratives of community are performed and embodied, and how they might be disturbed or re-interpreted. In order to explore this further, this chapter will focus on forms of devised performance in which practitioners aim to make theatre *with* community participants, rather than devising plays *for* them. Eugene van Erven succinctly describes community-based theatre as having:

> an emphasis on local and/or personal stories (rather than pre-written scripts) that are first processed through improvisation and then collectively shaped into theatre under the guidance either of outside professional artists . . . or of local amateur artists
>
> (van Erven 2001: 2)

The examples that follow in this chapter all illuminate this way of working, each offering an illustration of how community participants actively contribute to the process of making performances. This chapter will explore how theatre is used in community contexts to reflect and reframe autobiographical stories into community narratives, how performance might mediate public debate and encourage critical dialogue. It is a process that is intended to challenge expectations about what or whom is included in any given community, and where their boundaries may lie.

Imaginary spaces: from autobiographical stories to community narratives

Communities are widely regarded as a cultural resource for social change, a view which is predicated on the assumption that, as imaginary spaces, communities have the potential to mediate between the everyday and autobiographical narratives of individuals and more formal and established structures of power. In her study of cultural intervention through community participation, Marjorie Mayo observes that participation in drama provides a welcome alternative to 'top-down' forms of development because it is orientated towards facilitating the participants' vision of social change rather than furthering centralised agendas (Mayo 2000: 179–180). This is consistent with the praxis and pedagogies of the Brazilian educator Paulo Freire which have had a profound impact on theatre practitioners working in community contexts, not least because of his influence on the theatre director and fellow countryman Augusto Boal, who turned Freire's liberatory pedagogy into a practical politics for performance-making. Freire's work became widely recognised in the second half of the twentieth century, and he is particularly associated with furthering a revolutionary 'pedagogy of the oppressed' which encourages members of the community to reflect on their experiences as individuals and to use their ideas to imagine new ways of being and develop new forms of social action. He describes this process as an 'an act of knowing', in which participants re-order, reshape and re-evaluate the stories and knowledge they already possess to gain new insights into their own situations (Freire 2002: 31).

The relationship between autobiography and performance which was discussed in the previous chapter demonstrates how professional practitioners use devised performance to investigate performative constructions of selfhood. The representation of lived experience is also the focus of attention in much community-based theatre, albeit differently inflected according to the contexts and situations of the participants. For those following Freire, the exploration of autobio-graphical narratives is an explicitly political process. Freire is critical of what he describes as 'banking' systems of education in which the 'oppressed' were regarded as empty vessels waiting to be filled with officially sanctioned forms of knowledge (Freire 2002). His pedagogy of the oppressed is a way of thinking about learning which intends to reverse this dialectic, and his praxis seeks to value participants' own narratives as central to the process of social emancipation. Freire argues that the oppressed internalise their oppressors' view of them as lazy and unproductive – a view which Boal later personifies as a malign 'cop in the head' – and he believes that these negative narratives of selfhood need to be challenged if society is to be transformed into a more equitable place. Devised performance is one of the cultural strategies that contribute to this process by encouraging individual participants to reflect on their experiences by finding connections with others, a process which is intended to construct new social identities and revitalised communities. Actual changes in people's material circum-stances are difficult to effect, although this remains an objective for many community activists who work in performance-making.

The arsenal of games and exercises developed by Augusto Boal through his work with disadvantaged communities across the world provides a range of drama activities with which to examine how narratives of power are internalised, constructed and sustained (Boal 1992). One cultural strategy that invites participants to relocate autobiographical narratives in community contexts is known as *Reflect*, and although not Boalian, it is illustrative of the kind of approach that is widely circulated among community activists and theatre practitioners working in grassroots theatre. *Reflect* explicitly takes Freire's description of praxis as a synthesis of 'reflection and action upon the world in order to transform it' as its starting point (Freire 2002: 5). Designed for use in development education, *Reflect* facilitators invite community participants to represent their autobiographical experiences in the form of graphics. For example, they may map locations that have particular significance for them, or construct calendars showing rainfall or presenting charts to show how workloads are divided along gendered lines (www.actionaid.org). These graphics are constructed collaboratively, often on the ground, using locally available materials such as sticks and stones, seeds and grasses. The emphasis at this stage in the process is on dialogue and discussion rather than on any specific end product, and the images created by the group are designed to encourage participants to narrate their experiences. As its name suggests, this process involves them in reflecting on their everyday lives and their sharing insights into their daily patterns and – to use Bourdieu's phrase – their cultural *habitus*.

Where *Reflect* is used to develop adult literacy – a major Freirean objective – facilitators build on these group discussions and use these improvised graphics to develop more permanent teaching aids that have local relevance for the learners. When this work is translated into performance, the physicality offers additional opportunities for participants to develop an embodied understanding of their stories by representing them visually. This collaborative process both invites the group to interpret autobiographical narratives and offers participants the opportunity to locate and relocate themselves in relation to the multiple communities to which they belong. For example, a group of refugees might create a global map on the floor and mark the places where they felt most at home with a small paper heart. Tearing the heart in pieces, they might reposition the fragments on the map to symbolise where they felt they had left their hearts behind on the journey from their home countries to the places in which they now live. This simple act of mapping has the potential to generate a wealth of material to which further layers might be added during the devising process. By physically acting out each other's stories, and embodying each other's experiences, autobiographical narratives become integrated into the experiences of the group.

The devising process associated with *Reflect* is designed to be consistently domestic and vernacular, charting familiar landscapes and reflecting on personal experiences. This is an example of Freirean praxis not only because it relies on the personal knowledge and stories of the participants, but also because the process invites critical dialogue between them. Freire himself describes this form of learning as a 'creative process' precisely because it is dialogic and communitarian:

> Knowledge emerges only through invention and reinvention, through the restless, impatient, continuing, hopeful inquiry human beings pursue in the world, with the world, and with each other.
>
> (Freire 2002: 68)

It is an approach which is intended to resituate autobiographical knowledge, locating it firmly within the imagined spaces of communities rather than in the authority of official institutions. It is designed to reframe personal narratives, recognising that it is only through the continual process of invention and reinvention that new meanings and insights emerge. It is a way of thinking that has considerable appeal to practitioners working in community contexts, where the process of shaping and narrating autobiographical experiences into devised performance is intended to encourage collaboration, a collective act of imagination and interpretation.

Paul Ricoeur suggests that narrative enables us to negotiate the gap between 'description and prescription' or, to put it another way, between how things are and how they might be (Ricoeur 1992: 152). When allied to the efficacy of community, this suggests that performed narratives have a significant part to play in effecting social change by enabling participants to experiment with different ways of navigating the imaginative space between the real and the possible. The political potential of this negotiation has been interestingly addressed by the British theatre company Cardboard Citizens which was founded by Boal's English translator Adrian Jackson in 1991. Cardboard Citizens describes itself as 'the homeless people's theatre company', and its work is primarily centred on making theatre with and by homeless and ex-homeless people (www.cardboardcitizens.org.uk). What is particularly interesting about this company is that the actors have themselves experienced homelessness, a position which not only gives them credibility with challenging audiences, but also affords them a degree of shared understanding with the diverse members of homeless communities in Britain. Terry O'Leary, now an experienced facilitator and practitioner with Cardboard Citizens (a Joker, in Boal's terms), said that her first encounter with the company was when she went to a performance in the hostel where she was staying intending to disrupt it because she thought it would be a lot of 'noncy actors' doing a play *about* homeless issues. Once she realised that the actors had themselves previously been homeless, the work gained credibility for her (O'Leary 2004).

Finding points of connection between the actors' and audiences' autobiographical narratives and those presented dramatically is, according to O'Leary, integral to the efficacy of Cardboard Citizens' work with homeless communities. By seeing their own situations reflected on stage, there is the potential for audience members to recognise that it is possible to effect change in situations and to escape from cycles of behaviour in which they feel trapped. As Joker, she describes her role as providing 'a bridge between the real world outside and the imaginary world of the play' and recognises that, for this community group, seeing theatre that acknowledges the reality of their social circumstances often has powerful personal resonances. Cardboard Citizens' production, *The Man With Size Twelve Feet* (2002), captured the moment of uncertainty in the aftermath of the terrorist attacks on the World Trade Center on 11 September 2001 by exploring the related themes of social isolation and addiction within the context of global politics. In an interview about her work with this production O'Leary describes the importance of audience identification with the narratives represented on stage:

> Lots of audience members come up afterwards and say it was 'really real'. Real in the sense that the acting wasn't stagey, the situations that we portray are accurate. A lot of crack-heads come up and ask us 'where's that crack house? I'm sure I've been there'.
>
> (O'Leary 2004)

Not only does the play position the audience to recognise and identify with the protagonist's situation, it also, crucially, puts them in the position of experts. In this play, one of the reasons why the protagonist fails to change his life and his circumstances is because he has inadequate information about where to access support for his addictions. Because in this community audience members know some of this information, the forum at the end of the performance offers them an opportunity to share their knowledge. O'Leary analyses how this exchange is prompted:

> It all fails spectacularly for our main character because of lack of information, and hopefully our audience will feel passionate enough because of society being unjust, the unfairness of the situation, and they will step up and offer information. Swapping information is really important.
>
> (O'Leary 2004)

By creating an information gap, the audience is actively encouraged to take on the protagonist's role, and provide possible and imaginative solutions to situations that are recognised as 'real'. The company's work is, importantly, not confined to their audiences' identification with the fictional world of the performance. Theatre may act as a powerful medium of communication, but access to actual information and practical sources of support to the members of the homeless community is also integral to the company's politics and praxis.

Communities are built on reciprocity, common struggles and shared activities, however fluid, contingent and visceral they may be. Efficacy in community-based theatre depends on some level of shared understanding and experience which, following Amit's analysis of community as 'fragile, changing [and] partial', recognises that the shift from autobiographical to community narratives is dependent on inhabiting the kind of imaginative space offered by performance-making. It is a process which involves community-based participants and audience members challenging what Boal has described as the 'finished visions' of the world, which are often misrepresented as fixed and unchangeable narratives.

Memory and community narratives: authenticity and metaphor

The application of Freire's radical praxis to community contexts suggests that the process of bringing people together to share and question common experiences not only has the political effect of ensuring that marginalised voices are heard, but it also has clear psychological and social benefits for the participants. To use Freire's phraseology, this process develops critical consciousness, whereby participants are able to reassess their sense of self-worth from different perspectives. In the previous chapter it was noted that, when performers draw on their own experiences in devising, the work often emphasises how the boundaries between truth and fiction are blurred. Theatre that is devised in community situations may be similarly concerned with the representation of memory, and participants are invited to recognise that autobiographical narratives have social, communitarian and historical significance as well as personal relevance.

Theatre director Jatinder Verma aptly describes memory as 'a seductive, tricksy devil which does not always need actual experience to form a feature of the imagination' (Verma 1998: 128). Conceptually, memory contests the boundaries between truth and invention, and this means that one of the questions that faces performance-makers who devise work based on oral histories is concerned with authenticity. Good stories have performative qualities; they are embellished, change over time and are retold to suit the storytellers' perceptions of themselves in relation to their audiences. This is not, however, simply capricious or devious. The writer and critic Carolyn Steedman describes memory as 'an agent of social formation' where interpretations of the past enable people to shape, affirm or rewrite their identities in relation to their understanding of their present circumstances and relationships with others (Steedman 1986: 5). Theatre historian Thomas Postlewait similarly argues that narrative does not provide a transparent representation of events; it is always interpretive:

> Narrative provides coherence, a process of emplotment which configures these actions into a meaningful, comprehensible interpretation.
> (Postlewait 1992: 361)

Taken together, the process of turning memories into enacted narratives, therefore, illustrates how people understand and feel about their present situations. Narrative makes experience knowable, enabling individuals to recognise and relocate themselves in the context of their immediate audience and the wider community. In this sense, all personal narratives are authentic when they are retold, though they may or may not be literally true.

The London-based organisation Age Exchange Theatre Trust is a good example of a company that has recognised that the triangulation of memory, narrative and community can contribute to the process of social awareness. The focus of Age Exchange's work is with elderly people and intergenerational arts, and the company's theatre-making is designed to recognise the significance of both older people's personal histories and their present experiences. The pioneering founder, Pam Schweitzer, was well known as a theatre in education practitioner during the 1970s and 80s, and the participatory practices she has developed to trigger memories and prompt reminiscence is indebted to this tradition. The Age Exchange Reminiscence Centre in Blackheath, London is designed to resemble a 1930s' shop, and functions not only as a community and information centre, but also as a museum of artefacts and objects which have been used within living memory. Visiting this centre is not like walking directly into the past, but the attention to detail evident in the artefacts and exhibits captures a very specific sense of history and place. It invites an imaginative response, and the experience of being in the space is an engaging performative experience.

In its work with reminiscence groups, the company uses many strategies to prompt memories. One of these devices is known as a 'reminiscence box'. These boxes contain genuine objects from the past or photographs that older people will remember, often based around an evocative theme – such as wartime evacuation, immigration, seaside holidays or visits to the doctors. Designed to be multi-sensory, these boxes offer tactile and visual reminders of past times. Handling authentic objects triggers somatic memories which in turn prompt stories – and there is a qualitative difference between feeling the weight and size of an old but once familiar coin, for example, and picking up a counterfeit. In the project undertaken in 2004–2005, *Making Memories Matter*, older people from seven European countries collaborated with artists to make their own memory boxes, to create 'life portraits' that toured galleries and museums across Europe. In other projects, such as the National Creative Ageing Project (2002–2005), performances were generated with older people acting as both participants and consultants, thereby recognising that 'reminiscence and creativity go hand in hand' (www.ageexchange.org.uk).

Age Exchange's practice recognises the significance of the body in reminiscence work, in terms of the somatic memories invoked by memory boxes, the aesthetic of performance and in older people's active engagement with creative practices. In his work with retired San

Figure 6.1 Age Exchange Reminiscence Centre, Blackheath, London.

Reproduced by permission of Age Exchange Theatre Trust. Photographer: Simon Purins.

Franciscan dancers, North American choreographer Jeff Friedman similarly observed that when they recounted their life histories, their memories were often expressed physically as well as in spoken language. He describes these somatic responses as the 'mega-gestus of remembering', a term he uses to invoke the elision between the enculturation of dancers' bodies and the authenticity of their memories (Friedman 2002: 163).

The work and philosophy of Age Exchange emphasises authenticity, both in the process of reminiscence and in its customary use of naturalism as a theatre form. Schweitzer comments that, in the devising process of the play *Many Happy Retirements* (1990–1991), it was considered important to capture the pensioners' idiom in the dialogue in order to ensure 'maximum identification and authenticity' (Schweitzer 1994: 70). It is significant that the concepts of authenticity and identification are linked. The literary critic Lubomir Dolezel points out that no language or other form of representation can faithfully re-create 'the actual world', although an incomplete and fictionalised 'possible world' can be constructed (Dolezel 1999: 253). For this community group, Schweitzer records that it is the familiarity of the naturalistic dialogue that represents the 'possible worlds' of the elderly participants in ways that they find most accessible. Her objective in this play is to represent the social experience of retirement in ways that enable people to recognise parallels between the fictionalised narratives on stage and their own personal circumstances. To facilitate the audience's empathetic responses, the devisers did not use auto-biographical stories verbatim, but they isolated recurring themes which they structured into theatrical shape. One section of the script demonstrates the newly retired John who, dressed in his suit, is finding it difficult to come to terms with his change of status and his place in the home:

> *(Phone rings. John dashes to answer it.)*
> John: Hello, Powell here. *(Disappointed and impatient)* No, she's out. Yes. Yes. I'll give her the message. Well, I am going to be based here from now on. Yes. Goodbye.
>
> (quoted in Schweitzer 1994: 74)

In performance this scene prompted the laughter of recognition among an audience of retired couples, who identified with both husband and wife. This process of identification and recognition is intended to be used productively; after seeing the performance, audiences are offered the opportunity to participate by giving the characters suggestions for how they might negotiate this difficult and major life event. As Elin Diamond points out, there is an ambiguity about recognising oneself in another's situation which can prompt change, and she comments that 'identifications produce and simultaneously destabilise identity' (Diamond 1997: 112).

An emphasis on encouraging authentic emotional responses to performance-making can be seen to shape form as well as content. The work of North American practitioner Anne Davies Basting, who is similarly concerned with the role of elders in the community, offers a contrast to the social realism of Age Exchange's reminiscence work. Basting's client group is people with Alzheimer's disease, whose memories are fading and whose ability to interpret social experiences is becoming diminished. Basting's answer is to develop creative story-telling projects which work with images and metaphor rather than personal reminiscence and oral history. As the participants find it troubling to share experiences, and have little recollection of their lives or the people they know, they become increasingly socially isolated and frustrated. She describes her working methods in the following terms:

> We stretch the boundaries of traditional reminiscence activities – common and effective tools for exercising memory – by telling participants that we are not interested in their memories. Rather than rehearse their pasts, together our storytelling groups make up *new* stories.
>
> (Basting 2001: 80)

By showing participants images that 'suggested a fantastical story', they built stories together which, however surreal, communicated feelings and touched on significant aspects of their lives. Basting analyses recurring themes in their stories of 'longing for freedom', 'acceptance', 'intimacy with family' or 'lovers'. Finding creative expression through analogy and metaphor offers the Alzheimer patients a safe space to narrate their feelings, a process which has enabled them to find affinity with other patients and a place in the wider community. For these participants, it was the poetics of metaphor rather than the immediacy of naturalism which created a sense of belonging. Basting's play, *Time Slips* (2000), presented a theatrical representation of how the world seems to change for people affected by Alzheimer's by interweaving the surreal stories invented by the storytelling groups in ways which captured their very real sense of bewilderment and frustration. The *Time Slips* Project has subsequently developed into a comprehensive programme that celebrates the creativity of people with dementia (www.timeslips.org).

The distinction between the social reality of reminiscence theatre and the fictional metaphors of creative storytelling is primarily a question of representation. Chicago practitioners Laura Wiley and David Feiner draw attention to the ways in which the dramaturgy of devised theatre can raise questions about the 'representational authority' of community-based performance (Wiley and Feiner 2001: 140). One of the central issues for community-based theatre practitioners is concerned with community self-representation, and how the dramaturgical processes of devising – research, generating material, improvisation, scripting, editing and rehearsing – might serve as particularly effective means of encouraging social interactions. Age Exchange, Cardboard Citizens and the *Time Slips* Creative Storytelling Project have found different ways of addressing this issue of how

to adapt the narratives of people for the stage. None of these practitioners speaks with a single authoritative voice, nor do they offer a
collective vision which might represent all community members.
Through their work they have found ways to invite participants to
reflect on their own narratives and invent new stories, a process
which shows that any representation of narratives in performance is
only ever a partial and provisional construction of an imagined
community.

SEVEN

ADAPTING FICTIONAL STORIES

Sharing stories

Within the realm of devised performance, numerous practitioners have used published fiction as a starting point for their work. Though many critics believe that adaptations are undertaken for economic purposes – guaranteeing large audiences for well-known stories – this form of working practice offers an opportunity for actors, directors and writers to experiment with pre-existing material and develop a theatrical mode which fulfils their own purpose, be it aesthetic, cultural or political. A fundamental aspect of this mode is the use of stage metaphor. This is highlighted by Phillip Pullman's experience of theatrical adaptation. In 2003 the Royal National Theatre, London, commissioned an adaptation of the youth cult novel series, *His Dark Materials*. Author Pullman played an important part in the process of the adaptation (undertaken by playwright Nicholas Wright), attending many rehearsals and planning sessions. From the outset Pullman realised that in turning fiction into a stage performance, 'it has to become metaphorical not literal' (Butler 2003: 36). A metaphorical meaning is one in which the subject matter is referred to in a manner that does not literally describe it. The Greek meaning of metaphor is 'to carry across', which implies the transfer from one frame to another. This is very apt for this form of performance-making. Pullman's observation highlights the fundamental shift that occurs in the transition from page to stage and the differences in the experience of reading a piece of fiction and staging a performance work.

There are many reasons why companies decide to adapt fiction, and the work of British touring theatre company, Shared Experience, captures one of these. Founding director Mike Alfreds comments that adapting fiction 'seemed the ideal starting point for creating theatre as I defined it for myself: the actor, the audience and the space they shared . . . and a story' (Alfreds 1979–1980: 6).

For Alfreds, working with a known story that could be shared with the audience provided the basis on which to develop an original creative vision. Indeed, the very name of the company, Shared Experience, highlights the centrality of the relationship between the performers and audience. Alfreds views the use of previously known material as a useful vehicle for communication in that he understands that stories can act as a binding force within a community of performers and spectators. The previous chapter has investigated the way in which sharing stories can help both to construct communities and to question the nature of what constitutes community. Structuralist anthropologist Claude Lévi-Strauss examines the way in which common stories and myths operate within a variety of societies. He states:

> Ritual . . . conjoins, for it brings about a union (one might even say communion in this context) or in any case an organic relation between two initially separate groups, one ideally emerging with the person of the officiated and the other with the collectivity of the faithful . . . and the 'game' consists of making all the participants pass to the winning side by means of events.
>
> (Lévi-Strauss 1966: 32)

These remarks can be applied to the performance of a story. The use of known material forms the ritual that brings together the 'officiant', the performers, and the 'faithful', the attendees. A performance event can be read as the 'game' that co-joins both sides. For Alfreds the sharing of a story by actors and audience is central to his vision of what theatre might be, and led to the establishment of Shared Experience's particular aesthetic.

The sharing of a common story has wider resonances. In his analysis of fairy tales, Russian formalist Vladimir Propp observes that such narratives are organised in tightly codified patterns which become recognisable to the reader (Propp 1968). This sense of familiarity is also to be found within the roles of the main characters that serve archetypal functions. An audience sharing in the telling of a narrative will experience these underlying structures. The work on archetypal narratives has been furthered by Bettelheim who examines the use of the archetypal and notes the psychoanalytic importance of fairy tales (Bettelheim 1976). He proposes that they are archetypal containers for desires and fears. Seen in this light, the sharing of a narrative offers a mechanism through which to explore underlying structures and emotional responses. Many of the processes that are used to devise fictions for the stage draw upon personal responses. For example, when Grotowski was working on *Apocalypsis* in 1968, he asked his performers to find texts that had particular significance for them in order to catalyse the devising process. Similarly David Edgar's adaptation of *Nicholas Nickleby* involved cast members selecting moments from the novel that held importance for them and presenting these within a workshop situation. It is clear that the use of fiction on stage offers the opportunity for the recognition and exploration of common narratives through the development of a metaphorical structure.

The reasons why a company should wish to share a known story with an audience go beyond those already indicated: economics, theatrical innovation, communality with audience, expression of personal identification, or exploration of underlying emotional or structural responses. Performance ensembles are frequently interested in changing the status of the original artefact. In transferring this work from the written page to the stage the function that it served is often re-examined, challenged or deliberately altered.

This chapter will examine three aspects that can be identified within stage adaptations: first, how metaphorical language is developed in the process of adapting a work from the page to the stage; second, how far metaphor can be authentic to an original artefact; last, the way in which the aesthetic of the stage is transformed into a flexible playground where the performers are responsible for sharing a 'fiction' with the audience.

From page to stage

The translation of a piece of fiction from the printed page into performance requires a number of alterations. In *The Semiotics of Theatre and Drama*, Keir Elam distinguishes between narrative and dramatic modes. He perceives that narrative schemes are orientated to the 'there and then' (an elsewhere, set in the past that has to be evoked for the reader). The dramatic mode is set in the 'here and now', a world shown to the audience (Elam 1980: 110–111).

The change from the diegetic system of 'there and then' to the mimetic one of 'here and now' is essentially about creating action from narration. In undertaking this adaptation, practitioners have discovered a number of devices through which to convey fiction on stage. In effect they have developed metaphorical means through which to carry the meaning from one medium across to another. The act of transferring fiction to the stage draws attention to how narratives are constructed. Within a novel the narrator usually relates fiction from either within or outside the story; the influence of this role is key, for the story is told from their viewpoint. Narratologist Gerard Genette refers to this as 'focalization'. In searching for the metaphor through which to stage fiction, practitioners need to decide what 'focalization' will be taken, in other words from whose point of view the narrative is told and the relationship that the characters or roles will have with the audience. French mime performer Barrault recalls that for his 1930s' adaptation of Faulkner's *As I Lay Dying* he worked from the point of view of the wild horse. His desire to create the metaphor to express that horse formed the centre of his adaptation.

Other aspects of structural theory are useful in helping identify how to adapt fiction for the stage. Since the early twentieth century structuralists have distinguished between the 'plot' (Russ: *sjuzhet*) and the 'story' (Russ: *fabula*). The story is defined as the chronological 'what happened next' way of telling a tale. Few writers reveal the story in this manner; instead they employ the use of a plot, a reordering of the events through which the story is told. Roland Barthes hypothesises that a narrative can be divided into a number of units that hold various functions. Some of these communicate a hinge point in the narrative, a moment that determines the next course of events: Barthes calls these 'cardinal functions'. Other units are fill-in or linking ones that he calls 'catalysers' (Barthes 1977: 93). In transferring narrative to the stage, practitioners frequently reorder the fictional use of the plot – this is partly so that a 'here and now' can be presented. Restructuring the plot means that units are reordered; and in order to fit a piece of fiction on stage it is often the 'catalysers' that are removed.

The work of Mike Alfreds demonstrates how these aspects of narratology are engaged with during the process of adaptation. His company's practice shows that in making the transformation from page to stage it had to consider the issue of focalization and examine the function of narrative units. During Shared Experience's work on *Arabian Nights* (1975) the company explored methods for presenting narratives on stage. Alfreds notes that three basic modes were discovered (Alfreds 1979: 11–12). The first placed the narrator outside of the action, which he admits is fairly sterile as it often results in a narrator standing downstage while the action unfolds centre stage. The second mode involved the narrator operating in the first person within the action. Here the actor had to straddle two time sequences (both the 'there and then' and the 'here and now'), which involved both participating in and commenting on the action. The third narrative mode allowed the actor to be both narrator and character simultaneously. Alfreds observes that this third option opened up a huge range of options for the actor. In Shared Experience's adaptation of *Bleak House* (1977) much narration was delivered while in character, a device which allowed for the text and mode of delivery to counterpoint each other. For example, a character may play a moment seriously but the text being narrated ridicules that projection. Alfreds describes these moments as 'very full' with '"Stanislavskian" identification and "Brechtian" distancing at one and the same time' (Alfreds 1979: 12), and notes that within *The First Arabian Night* project actors often created a moment of transformation through using these narrative ploys. A performer might start narrating an incident as themselves and gradually slide into playing the character. Thus the action was not literal but played with frameworks of time, characterisation and focalization.

Alfreds' experiments created narrators and characters with distinctive attitudes towards the narrative, and these shifting points of view created a variety of relationships with the audience. For example, the first mode, the use of a third-person detached narrator, allowed for a variety of attitudes towards the staged action depending on the spatial relationship between the narrator and the audience. Placed downstage the actor held a distant relationship with the material; from behind the audience the role was often intimate; behind the action it was more critical; placed among the action the narrator seemed to be a type of puppet master (Alfreds 1979: 11–12). The second mode, the first-person narrator, was 'obviously subjective and led to stories demanding intense audience identification' (Alfreds 1979: 12), which Alfreds suggests are fantasies, dreams, psychological stories and the like.

Shared Experience's work also utilised other aspects of narratology. An idea similar to that of Barthes's units was used in order to switch between narrative and dramatic modes. Firstly, what Alfreds describes as the 'trampoline' words were located within the text. These were the moments that operated as a springboard and aided transition from narration to dialogue. Alfreds lays out an example:

Say the actor has a text such as: "When the prince heard this much from his royal sire, he was moved by youthful folly to reply, 'Thou art great in age but small in wit'." In this example, the trampoline word is 'reply' . . . [the actor] uses the previous sentence of the narration as a sort of run up, knowing that when he gets to the word 'reply' he has to gather all his forces to take off into the action.

(Alfreds 1979: 15)

In Alfreds' example the word 'reply' is taken as the fulcrum that leads to the cardinal function: in this extract, the prince's answer. The information given beforehand is fill-in material. Similar examples can be found in the Arts Archives video, *Storytelling as Theatre*. Here a pair of student actors enacts the story of *Tom Thumb*. The piece is littered with the use of 'trampoline' words that enable the switch from one character to another or one mode to another (for example, from narration to enactment). When the ogre appears the narration runs, 'in from the door came an ogre'. The actors narrate the first five words and use this fill-in detail to prepare for the moment of switching into the ogre, when one student climbs on the shoulders of the other to create the metaphoric representation of the ogre. The use of the division of the text into clear working units shows that the act of adapting fiction for the stage in effect sensitises performers as to how a narrative is assembled. By unpicking the narrative the performers become creative storytellers with the ability to control and direct the narrative they are sharing. Watching the video on storytelling it is clear that the actors in *Tom Thumb* have ownership of their material; the division of the narrative into units is precise and their engagement with moments of direct address to the audience and physical representation of character and action are detailed and often personal. The actors switch between modes of physical representation and storytelling in a manner that is informed by improvisation. There is a sense that the story has been carved to share with the audience, and this places the spectator in a privileged position. Through this process a relationship between the teller and told is evolved.

Authenticity

Michael Fry outlines the problems that face an adapter:

There are two basic hurdles facing the would-be adaptor: does he [*sic*] stick closely to the original novel and risk over-literary, reverential and possibly protected play, or does he adapt it more liberally and risk changing its emphasis, rewriting some of the text and attracting the critical ire of the audience that knows and loves the book.

(Fry 1996: xii)

Though Fry's remarks are addressed at traditional playwriting, his comments highlight one of the most controversial aspects of adapting fiction: fidelity to the original source material. Reviewing Shared Experience's 1996 adaptation of *War and Peace* at the National Theatre, *Guardian* newspaper critic Michael Billington wittily titled his response 'War Crimes' (Billington 1996). He objected that the production missed the central concerns of the book; in his opinion the adaptation was a poor copy. But how can devised performance possibly adapt fiction to create an authentic replica? Or indeed should it? The format of the original, as a piece of narrative, and the copy, as a dramatic form, dictates that there will be a number of differences. The characteristics of these two modes mean that it is impossible for a stage version of a piece of fiction to be faithful, or authentic.

The Wooster Group's 1984 piece, *L.S.D. (. . . Just the High Points . . .)*, aptly demonstrates the problem of the issue of authenticity. In the piece the group borrowed from Arthur Miller's play *The Crucible*. However, Miller, aware that the group proposed to use sections of his play in a manner other than he intended, refused to give his permission for performance and threatened legal action. For Miller the use of fragments of his play constituted a parody of his work and he didn't want the play 'mangled that way' (Savran 1986: 102). Elizabeth Le Compte, the director of The Wooster Group, wanted to 'use irony and distancing techniques to cut through the intellectual and political heart of *The Crucible* . . . I want to put the audience in the position of examining their own relation to this material' (quoted in Savran 1986: 102). These essential differences mark out the status of Miller as a playwright and Le Compte as the director of an avant-garde perform-ance ensemble who is interested in highlighting the intellectual and political impulses behind a cultural text. Le Compte's belief in the creation of a text that has a multiplicity of meanings for an audience is shared by Mike Alfreds. During his work on storytelling he strove in 'pursuit of the belief that a performance has many levels of meaning and that the more aspects of a piece we could release, the more rewarding for the audience who were free to respond to those levels which attracted them, rather than having a single view imposed on them' (Alfreds 1979: 5). Alfreds seeks to create theatre work that allows for a multiplicity of spectator responses and not a fixed meaning. Both of these ensembles use what are frequently seen as traditionally 'closed' narratives to create what critic Umberto Eco calls an 'open work', where the audience is seen as bringing a vital element for the completion of a cultural form.

There are many examples when authenticity is forsaken in order that the original fiction is used to address political issues. Often established materials are deconstructed so that the inherent values contained within the original work are revealed. This is the case with experimental American company Split Britches. Its radical adaptation of Louisa M. Alcott's *Little Women*, a canonical text within the United States, used the limitations of the daughters in Civil War New England in the 1860s to explore contemporary issues of censorship. The group used the symbol of Louisa May, an abolitionist and suffragist, to explore pornography, illicit sexuality and morality. The question of how authenticity might upset theatrical and cultural values was raised by Antoine Vitez's 1975 adaptation of Louis Aragon's *Les Cloches de Bâle*. The production, entitled *Catherine*, involved a group of actors on stage reading out the novel while they ate dinner. Audience members were expecting a traditional adaptation of the novel and were upset at the lack of authenticity, not to the novel, but to their expectation of how a novel should be played on stage. As Bradby and Sparks report, Vitez retorted that his interest lay in finding material that offered resistance to theatrical practices (Bradby and Sparks 1997: 38).

The issue of authenticity can be not only addressed within the final products of adaptations but is also in evidence within the process of devising these pieces. The working practices of The Wooster Group further reveal its attitude towards authenticity. Le Compte has admitted that 'when I think of texts, I think of them in the way that Kurt Schwiters used to, in a collage' (quoted in Savran 1986: 106). Her working methods are much inspired by the practices of chance that composer John Cage has advanced. Le Compte admits that randomness is important in constructing her company's work; for her it is like 'throwing a handful of beans up in the air. And when they come down on the floor, I must make a dance around that pattern' (quoted in Savran 1986: 106). Le Compte's work brings together a range of materials which are all assigned equal significance. The work of The Wooster Group reflects the notion of the 'death of the author' which was propounded by Roland Barthes. Barthes claimed that literature was no longer the message of a single God-like author, but a place where multidimensional clashing meanings could be iterated. The manner in which The Wooster Group devises its performances and the selection of texts that it uses as sources creates this multiplicity of meaning.

In reference to The Wooster Group's show *To You, The Birdie! (Phèdre)* (2002), one critic remarked that the group had taken 'hammer, pliers and welding kit to [the] seventeenth century classic' (Hewison 2002: 17). *Birdie!* draws upon both fictional and factual texts. These included Racine's *Phèdre*, Euripides' *Hippolytus*, and the IBF (International Badminton Federation) Laws of Badminton. For Le Compte there can be no question of remaining 'authentic' to the material; she is aware that her theatre allows 'as many interpretations as possible to co-exist in the same time and the same space' (Savran 1986: 107). The bringing together of different sources allows the final performance piece to embody different meanings.

Birdie! takes the narrative of Phèdre's lust for her stepson Hippolytus as its impetus. But instead of Racine's feisty heroine, here Kate Valk is a commode-bound cripple who undergoes frequent colonic irrigations to rid herself of the Venusvirus. The Wooster Group places Venus within this myth although prefers not to realise the character through dramatic presence on stage, but instead as an invisible virus which infects its host. The title of the piece takes its name from the shuttle-cock used in badminton. The tensions of the Greek court are played out through the formality of a high-tech badminton court. Much of the text is spoken by one character through a delayed-action microphone in either a casual or heightened tone; a male performer speaks Phèdre's text. Action is shown through video playback: a giant screen is used to portray Venus; conversations between Hippolytus and his tutor, Thereamenes, are played with the lower half of their bodies on video screens. The use of these multimedia devices continually disrupts the image and insists that the spectator re-evaluate his or her position.

Birdie! demonstrates the company's dedication to task-led sequences. Each member has a distinctive set of 'choreographies' that he or she performs. This includes playing badminton, giving enemas, narrating at the microphone, and so on. Any sense of authenticity to the 'original' text is further undermined by the use of character within the production. The actors bring themselves to the roles they encom-pass. This technique means that, as Auslander notes, the performers occupy an ambiguous position on stage which is neither 'non-matrixed' nor 'characterisation' (Auslander 1985: 95). In other words, the actors neither perform as characters, nor do they act purely as themselves since a 'character' is present on stage. This is substantiated by Willem Dafoe,

Figure 7.1 To You, The Birdie! (Phèdre) pictured (left to right):
Frances McDormand, Kate Valk and (on video) Suzzy Roche.
Photograph: © Paula Court.

Reproduced by permission of The Wooster Group.

a core member of The Wooster Group and performer within *Birdie!*. He claims that when he played John Proctor in *L.S.D. (. . . Just the High Points . . .)* he knew nothing of the character. Instead he was 'just doing it' (Auslander 1985: 96). The performers can be seen to be inhabiting and playing with the text, but they are not authentic to any particular interpretation.

The set for *Birdie!* is a gigantic steel-framed box, a playground in which many things can happen. Glass screens slide on and off the central stage and allow video images to be relayed on a giant scale. The steel structure becomes the badminton court and has a formality that reflects Theseus's court, though reviewers found it had 'echoes of a hospital ward and a television studio' (Johns 2002: 23). This use of a flexible playing space is a feature that has become a mark of many other adaptations. The use of fragmented or multidimensional playing areas allows narratives on stage to be presented simultaneously, something that is impossible within a book, is rare within film and allows for different modes of reading among the audience. For example, one viewer may select to watch one scene, while another chooses something completely different.

The adapting playground

In his study on adaptations of Charles Dickens's novels for stage and screen, Christopher Innes remarks that the process of adaptation acted as 'a catalyst for stylistic innovation' (Innes 1993a: 78). He sees that the 'traditional, limited' manner of literal translations, popular in the nineteenth century, had been replaced by the aesthetics of twentieth-century adaptation. In David Edgar's *Nicholas Nickleby* for the Royal Shakespeare Company in 1980, the cast of forty-nine actors was present on stage throughout the performance often interjecting commentaries, providing narration, forming parts of the scenery (a stagecoach, walls of houses within a street, passers-by within a crowded street) and providing vocal sound effects to accompany each scene. Innes remarks that 'every aspect of the performance consciously emphasized theatrical pretence, making the medium of expression as much the subject of the drama as the story itself' (Innes 1993a: 70). Innes's comment suggests that contemporary adaptations demonstrate a self-reflexivity; they reveal their status as theatrical constructs. The conceits are apparent through the use of actors playing multiple roles, shifts from narrative (often direct address to the audience) to dramatic representation, and the stage depiction of epic time and space. Stage space within these adaptations resembles a metaphoric playground.

The notion of the stage as a playground is exemplified by the work of Théâtre de Complicité, formed in 1983 by a group of graduates of Jacques Lecoq's Parisian mime school. Since its conception over twenty years ago Complicité has performed devised physical comedy, highly physical interpretations of classic texts, and adaptations of European novels and, more latterly, devised multimedia performances. Its work displays a commitment to processes that place the creativity of the actor at the centre: 'their style of performance creates, through imagination and voice and body, an embodied alternative to clever innovations, technological tricks, and other spectacular effects' (Reinelt 2001: 374–375). Though director Simon McBurney and writer Mark Wheatley are named as the adapters of Bruno Schulz's stories *The Street of Crocodiles* (1992/99), the company is credited as devising the piece. This process is illuminated by McBurney and Wheatley's introduction to the play script where they detail a rehearsal period that included working with original dialogue, taking text directly from Schulz's writings, initiating improvisations, leading re-enactments of dreams and developing rhythms of nightmares (McBurney and Wheatley 1999: introduction). Actor Clive Mendus observes that it was a genuinely collaborative process in which fragments of text were brought by McBurney and Wheatley to the rehearsal room. Improvisations created by the actors then shaped the use of these textual snippets (Mendus 2000). Simon Murray comments upon this process captured in a profile of the company for the BBC2 *Late Show* (1992). He notes that the rehearsal sequence consists of physical play between the actors: some roll, stretch and push against each other; others lift and carry one another. Director McBurney commentates that: 'I will simply be trying to lead people from a game into an exercise – into another game, which leads into a scene . . . so they hardly know when they are in a scene or not in a scene' (quoted in Murray 2003: 103). At the root of their work on the adaptation of *The Street of Crocodiles* is a game.

Schulz's writings outline life in East Galicia (later to become Poland), from the late nineteenth century until his shooting by a Nazi officer in 1942. His texts have been compared to the expressionistic feel of that of Kafka, or the imaginary strangeness of Chagall's paintings. This is reflected within the piece that Complicité devised. *The Street of Crocodiles* has 'no explicit narrative' and 'it's more like a poem or a piece of music than a play' commented McBurney (Rosenthal 1999: 18). The first scene demonstrates the surreal nature of the piece: Joseph, the protagonist, summons up the past. His family emerge from the set, one walking perpendicularly down the wall, others emerging from behind a bookcase; another struggles out of a wet bucket that has caught the drips from the leaking roof, a shop assistant materialises from within a packing case of books. This intense physicalisation of transformation forms part of the 'stylistic innovation' that Complicité brings to its adaptations.

The creativity of the physical performances is matched by the imaginative use of props and set pieces. Books are transformed into a flock of flapping birds, chairs are used to make a scant forest, desks form a shop counter, coats emit the sound of their previous owner, a ledger takes on its own life, books domino off the high bookcases. Jonathan Romney reviewing the production observes that 'the reason Schulz's stories lend themselves so brilliantly to the stage is because they offer the sort of manifesto of theatre practice' (Romney 1999: 23). He equates the style to that purported by Artaud's treatises, a total theatre where new language is bred through the cohesion of sound, light, image.

Complicité's physical approach to adaptations means that it has advanced the aesthetic identified by Innes. The playground of its rehearsals translates to the adaptations that it devises. In Complicité's adaptations the story is told through the physical language of the actors, the fluidity of the performance space, and the transformability of objects. It utilises a language that is one of multiplicity. The use of fictional material provides theatre-makers with an opportunity to discover a language of multiplicity and excess.

In conclusion, it is evident that the translation from page to stage demands the development of metaphor; an engagement with the original artefact and its contextual detail and the translation of this to the performance medium. The process of this translation poses creative problems that often prompt stylistic innovation. Many of the performances that have been cited have found their places within the avant-garde work of their time. Adaptations are often valued for the dialogue that the sharing of a story (frequently a known story) creates between actor and audience. Many of the stylistic features of an adapted work result from having to place narrative on stage, and these facets, such as the use of direct address to the audience, can help to create a sense of *communitas* between performer and spectator. This sharing of a narrative can provide a pleasurable experience for the audience through the recognition of narrative structures. But the use of fiction on stage can open up other possibilities. Companies that work in this genre often seek to open up the texts to new interpretations. The cultural status of the source is challenged, often inverted or politicised. The process of staging a novel demonstrates that cultural objects are not stable artefacts but are malleable.

PART THREE

Places and Spaces

INTRODUCTION: PLACES AND SPACES

Cultural geographer Yi-Fu Tuan observes that a fundamental human activity is to 'attach meaning to and organise place and space' (Tuan 1977: 5). In his philosophical reflections on contemporary society he notes that humans have a particular aptitude for symbolisation and that their organisation of place and space is often endowed with the impulse to make concrete representation of values and beliefs. This section of the book engages with discourses surrounding issues of place and space and considers how they have been employed by theatre practitioners within the symbolic process of performance-making.

Space is a fundamental element of performance which frames and contains activity. The history of performance encompasses a range of theatre architecture – from Greek amphitheatre to black box studio – and each architectural format exemplifies a particular set of performance dynamics. For example, the proscenium arch theatre separates the audience from the actors and provides a 'picture frame' for the action on stage. Experimentation with performance form has often involved experimentation with performance space as innovation in the organisation of space allows for a negotiation of theatrical conventions and a tangible expression of a new perspective. For example, bringing the audience into the action of the playing-space engenders a different relationship with the spectators. Thus the reconfiguration of space can be understood as part of the negotiation of the boundaries of theatre and performance.

When developing devised performance, practitioners often use space as one of the ingredients in the creative process. Interacting with the space may provide a springboard for creative ideas; for example, a host site of an old Victorian workhouse may lead to an exploration of personal narratives relating to the institution. Or the space may function as a framework that draws together an eclectic range of artistic activity. For example, a series of images and songs may be brought together in a processional performance that takes place on the streets of a particular town. In organising space for their experimental practice, theatre practitioners have developed a range of space-making strategies that engage directly with the environment within which they are working. These include transforming a non-theatrical place (a suburban home, for example) into a theatrical space; taking up a residency within a place to create a performance work relating to that place; and working with the realities of a site but 'over-writing' with a fabricated narrative. Such artistic interventions serve to activate the performance site and facilitate a process of creative symbolisation which may relate to the belief system of a community or the artistic values of a particular company.

Site-related work has the constitution of the performance environment as a fundamental concern and an examination of such projects must consider the way in which the performance space interacts with the wider culture both in theory and in practice. In this section a range of theorists are employed to investigate the processes at work in the development of social space and how this impacts on the creation of performance spaces. The section makes reference to cultural theorist Henri Lefebvre who posits the notion of lived spaces and troubles the idea of the theatrical empty space by acknowledging that space is always full of social meaning. The work of Michel de Certeau is also significant for the analysis within this section. His study of the practices of everyday life raises issues about the organisation of social space. He makes a distinction between space and place, arguing that 'space is a practised place' (de Certeau 1984: 117). For de Certeau, place is a geographic location with particular rules and regulations while space is the product of the social interactions which happen within that place and, as such, has a much more fluid identity. This distinction provides a useful lens for the examination of site-related performance as it allows for a differentiation between the host site and the practices that take place within it, as well as an appreciation of the social space-making activities relating to a site which may be drawn on within a devising process.

The following chapters focus on different aspects of the devising process as it relates to the issues of space and place. Chapter Eight examines the creation of performance environments with a particular emphasis on the creation of theatrical landscapes within theatre buildings. It considers how devised performance may transfigure the place of the theatre into a theatrical space. Chapter Nine focusses on artists who make work outside theatre buildings and pays particular attention to practitioners' reflections on the social spaces within which they work. The chapter examines how site-related work may result in an expanded understanding of what constitutes performance. Chapter Ten centres on the relationship between identity and location and highlights the political dimension of place and space through a consideration of the cultural ramifications of spatial performance practices.

The examples covered in this section span a range of places, spaces and performance practices from an inclusive environmental project in Cornwall to subversive protest on the streets of New York City. The scope of the work within the following chapters is intended to gesture towards the myriad of methods that theatre practitioners have experimented with and the different forms of symbolic practice that have been employed in the construction of performance sites. The particular focus on place and space draws attention to the way in which site-related work may challenge the conventional boundaries of performance places and how such work may be enriched by a sensitivity to social space-making activity. Overall, this section acknowledges that the performance environment shapes the interaction between audience and performer and examines how experimentation with space and place may engender a new perspective on particular sites and an opportunity for different modes of audience interaction with the performance event.

EIGHT

MAKING PERFORMANCE SPACE/ CREATING ENVIRONMENTS

From place to space

This chapter concerns a series of performance-making practices that have sought to create a sense of environment within theatre and performance spaces. In doing this, practitioners have frequently employed processes developed from modern art and architectural fields in which collections of objects and materials from the external world have been brought into the arena of the performance space. This process has forced audiences to re-examine the nature of the place where the performative act occurs. In creating a living space or environment within the performance area attention is drawn to the ways in which the place of a building can be turned into a malleable space. In other words, the fixed 'place' of the performance building ('an organized world of meaning', Tuan 1977: 179) is transformed into a 'space', a continuous, moving entity capable of shifting to reflect those inhabiting it. In this light, place is seen as a static, arranged location, while space is unfixed, responsive and moulds itself to its occupants. It is apparent that theatre buildings are 'places' since they represent a fixed location in which culture and social meaning can be controlled and represented for an audience. But the act of performance-making can shift the place to create a space. By changing this fixed, organised, institutional 'place' into a 'space' there is an act of liberation. The dichotomy of these locations is noted by Tuan: place is experienced as security, while space represents freedom (Tuan 1977: 3). Practitioners who have overthrown the idea of theatre as a place seek to widen the boundaries of performance by opening up the space of the building and consequently question the 'rules' of performance.

This chapter is primarily concerned with what happens *within* performance spaces, as opposed to site-specific work, where a site other than the performance space informs the work. It is difficult to maintain a close guard on this boundary, though, as many of the practitioners move between working in theatre buildings and found sites:

> Some experimenters in environmental theatre invited the audience to enter the performance space, and become co-creators of illusion; others transferred the performance from a theatre to an appropriate 'authentic' found space, generating yet another level of pretence.
>
> (Wiles 2003: 237)

While this chapter will endeavour to focus upon work made for inside established performance spaces inevitably the discussion will also embrace practitioners working beyond these spaces.

The work of Richard Schechner in the 1960s demonstrates the way in which a performance space can be used to its full extent. He overcame a sense of place in order to create a malleable space that the actors and audience could share. The desire to 'create and use whole spaces' was central to the notion of 'environmental theatre' created by Schechner's The Performance Group (Schechner 1971: 379). Established in 1968 in a small garage in New York City, and much influenced by Kaprow's notion of the Happening, the company utilised every aspect of the fifteen- by seven-metre space. Schechner notes how productions in The Performing Garage eliminated the divide between actors and audience. For performances such as *Dionysus in '69* (1968), the staging comprised two tall towers which the audience sat on, up and around. The performers also used these towers, so that the integration of actor and spectator was complete. The photographs of the production show the space littered with the bodies of actors and audience. The space is cluttered and erratic: there is no division between actors and audience, and no regularity with which they are seated; they inhabit various differing levels of the space. The space is fully used – the actors and audience fill the entire environment and in doing so create a living state in which a performance can take place. It is interesting that Schechner uses the geographical analogy of the contrast between a new city and a pre-existing one to define his ideas of environmental theatre:

> The ground plan for a 'new city' is such that you can find your place at a glance by the numbers. Your place is identical to every other place,

except that some places are near and some far from centers of action. Environmental theatres appear more lived in.

(Schechner 1971: 391)

The manner in which the performers and spectators inhabited the space in *Dionysus in '69* demonstrated a sense of 'living in' the environment.

The performer was one of the chief components of Schechner's environmental theatre. It is from the performer's work that the design and use of the space must come. Schechner's exercises included asking the actors to find a personal safe space within the room, finding the outer boundaries of that personal space, and having the group make the smallest possible ball in the middle of the space. These group practical exercises are used since 'articulating a space means letting the space have its say' (Schechner 1971: 385). For Schechner the relationship between the space and the performers/audience is a visceral experience; one in which the inside of the body perceives the space rather than the head dictating an organised response. This response is 'haptic' (meaning 'to touch') in that the properties of the space seem to 'touch' the spectator and actors. This touching is haptic because it is not literal, but through the senses; a feeling of the space.

Though Schechner's work focussed upon the haptic sense of the performance space, other practitioners have drawn upon notions of working with environmental space as a 'living', socially defined arena. French theorist Henri Lefebvre advocates that all space is the product of a series of relationships and that there is no such thing as neutral or natural space. He suggests that 'space is social morphology: it is to lived experience what form itself is to the organism' (Lefebvre 1991: 93–94). According to Lefebvre we live spaces; space is not a neutral void, but always the product of our lived behaviour and codes.

The notion of creating 'lived in' spaces was present within the theatre at the turn of the century. The work of scenic designers Adolphe Appia and Edward Gordon Craig sought to emphasise the expressivity of the stage settings. Appia developed a series of ideas for 'rhythmic spaces' in which a collection of podiums, stairs and platforms would enhance the plasticity of the performers' bodies. He envisioned a 'living art' in which spectators formed part of a communal experience, and to this end his experiments abolished the proscenium arch. Craig similarly attempted to rid scenic design of its painted scenic effects and, like Appia, favoured three-dimensional architectural structures, such as large pillars which imbued the stage with a sense of environment and mood. His 1906 production of Ibsen's *Rosmersholm* for actress Eleonora Duse covered the entire stage with greenish-blue-painted sacking and installed a large barred window upstage. Isadora Duncan reports that the creation of a shadowy enclosed house was met with gasps from the audience as the curtain was raised (Braun 1982: 88).

The ideas of Craig and Appia found resonance within the latter parts of the twentieth century in the notion of 'found space', defined by Joyce McMillan as a move 'away from designated performance spaces to places with a life or history of their own' (McMillan 2005). Here the sense of architectural structures forming part of the scenography was pushed further. In 1974 director Peter Brook inhabited the nineteenth-century Bouffes du Nord theatre in Paris. He embraced the notion of the particularity of an environment. He stripped the interior of the Victorian theatre bare, exposing its 'wrinkles, pock-marks and signs of having passed through life' (Wiles 2003: 263). In doing this, Brook, in the terms of Tuan's analysis, transformed an institutional place into a living space. The closed particularity of the nineteenth-century place was opened up to find new freedom within a liberating 'space'. But it must be recognised that inhabiting a found space in this manner brings together the past social history of the building with the here and now. Present images are shaped by negotiating with the material remains of the past. Lefebvre suggests these found spaces are also 'lived in', and reflect the concerns of the time. Peter Brook's empty Victorian theatre resonates the exposed nineteenth-century social élitism, just as his installed benches show modern desire for egalitarianism. This inhabitation of found spaces raises serious questions about the mode of cultural representation that a modernday audience requires; it expresses the social values and trends of a space. As Joyce McMillan notes, '[i]f theatre in unique spaces, with their own specific history, answers a deep need to heal a breach with our physical and iconic past, what can we feel but a sense of artificiality and loss when confronted with the classic "empty space" of a conventional stage or studio' (McMillan 2005).

In the process of creating an environment within performance spaces, practitioners have often drawn upon art-based processes, and in particular that of transposing collected objects from the outside to the inside. The practice of transposing artefacts from an outside environment into a new space was formulated in the late 1960s by artist Robert Smithson who collected objects from their natural sites and placed them within a 'neutral' gallery. Smithson labelled the space that played host to the objects as 'site' (the original habitat) and the new,

Table 8.1 Qualities afforded to site and non-site spaces, according to Smithson

	Site	Non-site
1	Open limits	Closed limits
2	A series of points	An array of matter
3	Outer coordinates	Inner coordinates
4	Subtraction	Addition
5	Indeterminate (certainty)	Determinate (uncertainty)
6	Scattered (information)	Contained (information)
7	Reflection	Mirror
8	Edge	Centre
9	Some place (physical)	No place (abstract)
10	Many	One

Source: Quoted in Kaye 2000: 95.

unspecific gallery space as 'non-site'. As Kaye points out, the non-site asserts its antithetical relationship to the site and 'establishes itself as a limiting mechanism . . . by exposing the limits and operation of the gallery itself' (Kaye 2000: 93). In other words, by placing real objects within a gallery or performance, the nature of the illusion of the display space is revealed. Smithson's work resulted in the development of a chart which set up a dialectical opposition between the qualities that are afforded to the site and non-site spaces.

The chart tabulates the site as an open series of points which are indeterminate, while the non-site is closed, contained, and a mirror of the reflection of the site. In transposing elements of one environment to another the issue of identity is exposed. While the objects are 'real' when they are in their home environment, they become 'false' when placed in a new one.

The work of Polish director and artist Tadeusz Kantor sought to devalue a sense of reality within his performances by manipulating space and objects. In 1944 a production of Wyspianski's *The Return of Odysseus* was staged within a room that had been blown apart by the Second World War. Kantor was aware that his audience served more as 'witnesses' than as a conventional audience. He described this piece as 'the first environmental art' in which '[t]he audience was inside a work of art; surrounded by debris, different objects such as a broken wheel, decayed wooden boards, a stolen loudspeaker which was used to broadcast Homeric odes, etc' (Kobialka 1986: 182). His later productions such as *In A Small Country House* (1961) utilised a selection of objects that had been gathered together by coincidence. (Kantor later realised the similarity between this and Duchamp's 'ready-mades', although he was ignorant of this field of practice at the time.) In the 1960s, after a visit to New York, Kantor, like Schechner, was inspired by the Happenings. His work continued to explore the fragmentation of reality through using real objects on stage and manipulating the use of space. For Kantor, '[a] theatre and a stage could be a real space, a room of memory, a cemetery, storeroom, a room of imagination, a hyperspace, or a room' (Kobialka 1994: 3). His later work was preoccupied with the motif of 'emballage' (packing or wrapping); frequently his performance pieces involved the wrapping of objects and people. This exploration of veiling and revealing objects within a performance space further disturbed notions of what was real/copied and the authentic/inauthentic nature of representation.

The practices that reinscribe the environment within performance spaces are important for the way that they renegotiate a series of performance principles. First, the relationship between the audience and the space is reconstructed by utilising real artefacts from the outside and bringing them inside to the representational space of the theatre. Through doing this, notions of reality/replication/identity are challenged. Second, the use of environmental space privileges a sense of space as being 'lived in'. It is capable of being shaped by, and reflecting, human experience. Last, architectural qualities of the space are often enhanced within this genre of work. The performers and audience experience a sense of 'touching' the building, and are aware of how the space of the building itself can be viscerally experienced and reflected within the performance. This touching of space ignites a haptic relationship between the space and the inhabitants. Audience and performers 'feel' the space around them.

Authentic spaces

The exposure of self and identity through an engagement with outer landscapes translated into interior environments is central to the work of Pina Bausch. As Felciano suggests, '[l]ike an archaeologist, Bausch digs up what social conventions and our self-protecting mechanisms insist on hiding. She scratches into the soil of human nature and then assembles her artefacts' (Felciano 1996: 70).

Pina Bausch, since 1973 the director of dance theatre company Wuppertal Tanztheater, Germany, invariably transforms theatres into environmental spaces within her compositions. The theatre buildings that host her productions are usually stripped bare of any curtaining, leaving an open stage and exposing brick back walls. Against this she unexpectedly creates natural environments such as heaps of old leaves, layers of peat, a field of carnations, sand dunes, crumbling walls, a forest of redwoods, or crammed metropolitan spaces: cafes, living rooms, public spaces. Her collaborator and designer, Peter Pabst, notes that 'it is not really a set at all. But with the performers and what they are doing in it, it becomes a world where things are living' (Shank 1997: 83). Bausch's use of environments seeks to collapse many of the traditional expectations of dance. Her stages are obstacles for the dancers and her montages build in ways that are antithetical to traditional form. Her works use her own and her dancers', experiences and memories; movements are often individualised and everyday gestures and spoken language are included within the dance language. Her work spans the genres of dance and theatre; as David Price remarks, '[w]hat distinguishes Bausch . . . is her development of an art form based upon a binary opposition that does not reproduce an either/or dichotomy; instead Bausch's productions are *both* dance *and* theater' (Price 1990: 332).

Bausch's work involving dance and design is heavily influenced by a legacy of relationships which intertwined dance, objects and design. This started in the early nineteenth century with the free dances of Isadora Duncan, who explored movement and material through her scarf dances, and Löie Fuller, who experimented with light and fabric. In the 1920s Expressionist choreographer Mary Wigman explored dance and space through masks and non-Western influences, while later innovations such as those of 1960s' choreographer Alwin Nikolais worked with restrictive set and costumes and focussed on the dancers' attempts to overcome these limitations. Bausch's own work often concerns the link between the dancer and the environment. For example, she has created a series of works inspired by sites: *Viktor* in 1986 (Lisbon); *Tanzabend II* in 1991 (Madrid); *Palermo* in 1989 (Palermo); *Ein Traverspiel* in 1994 (Vienna) and *Nur Du* in 1996 (American West). Bausch's performance work is enigmatic, as are her processes. She rarely gives interviews and seems reluctant to concretise her work by transcribing it into language, preferring to comment that 'I try to find what I can't say in words' (quoted in Cody 1998: 116).

The processes utilised in the creating of *Nur Du* demonstrate the way in which Bausch articulates the dialectic between Smithson's notion of the site and non-site. As Yvette Biró remarks, in *Nur Du* 'California becomes the site of the discovering adventure, and its multicultural music, the rhythm of this western landscape and lifestyle, shapes its dense fabric' (Biró 1998: 68). Her working methods are based on observation, improvisation and lengthy discussion. In 1996, in preparation for this piece, Bausch's dancers spent three weeks in West Coast America. Bausch claimed that during this time her dancers moved around the places 'with open eyes, open ears and our feelings' (quoted in Daly 1996). Much of the research took place between 11p.m. and 3a.m. going to social gatherings, and in particular dance clubs, observing nuances of life before taking these back into the rehearsal room for further interrogation. Laura Farabough recalls that a night spent with Bausch at San Francisco clubs brought about the creation of Jan and Regina, who appear in *Nur Du* cooking on a stove and dancing (Farabough 1997: 12).

The material that formed Bausch's music (which includes current popular music, that from the 1950s and 1960s and Latin American rhythms) and movement collage of social behaviour was drawn from company observations of the site that had commissioned the work. Other scenes within the piece showed the throwaway, media-based lifestyle of West Coast North America: a woman appears with clothing made from disposable food containers; women are recreated in the image of Hollywood movie stars and deliver one-liners; there is a cheerleader scene and another monologue on baseball. These fragments of West Coast American life are projected through the relationship between the performers' movements, voices and gestures and the landscape created on stage. But this relationship is far from simple. The environment does not merely stimulate a response within the dancer; instead there is an ironic distortion. As Cody notes, 'Bausch self-consciously uses mimesis as a grotesque form of mimicry and "undermines the referents' authority"' (Cody 1998: 121). Though the dancers' gestures may seem to belong to the environment, they are in fact an ironic representation of both it and the figures they observe during preparations for the piece. These images all seek to disturb notions of identity. As a critic observed, 'the work is less preoccupied with a sense of place than displacement' (Segal 1996). Like Smithson's work, the outside artefacts are used inside the theatre to force the audience to re-examine ideas much in the same way that Brecht's *Verfremdungseffekt* sought to distort the optical lens.

The use of the monumental redwood trees, whose trunks formed the environmental staging, was another way in which material from the site found its way back into the performance space. The felling of these trees for the performances was deemed by many as wasteful, but Cody points out that:

> Bausch's necessary cruelty extends to her use of 'real' nature, torn from its organic root and bluntly placed in the artificial enclosure of a theatre. This gesture – the mythical rendering of a catastrophic, global displacement – is in and of itself her most powerful metaphor for the fragmentation of our condition through the cultural representation of organic bodies.
>
> (Cody 1998: 127)

The displacement of the trees from their site and the placing of them in a non-site operated as a reflection on the fragmentation of identity. As Susan Kozel points out, 'when these natural elements are transferred to a theatrical context they confuse certain crucial categories: natural versus artificiality; reality versus theatre' (Kozel 1997: 106).

Inhabited spaces

Schechner's notion that environmental theatre works through creating a sense of 'living in' raises issues as to how a space may be inhabited. Many of Polish director Grotowski's productions created a sense of a living environment through utilising a mode of witnessing. This was established by Grotowski's practice in productions like *Dr Faustus* (1963), with the audience seated alongside the actors at the table where the action took place. Grotowski's aim in this was to create a sense of communion between the 'holy actor' and the spectator, in much the same way that participating in a religious ceremony might. In this style of performance there is a sense that a 'lived moment' has been placed on stage; that the present and past, and inside and outside can collide. For a moment the spectators from the outside join in a living moment with the actors who inhabit the inside space of the performance environment.

This creation of a 'lived-in' space is something that British performance company Reckless Sleepers has frequently undertaken. Reckless Sleepers was formed in Nottingham in 1989 to experiment within combined arts practices. Its work has included durational pieces, sound installations, exhibitions and outdoor performance.

In 2003 the company was commissioned to create a piece around the theme of the Last Supper. Its research process meant investigating ideas of 'eating your words', literally filling the mouth with texts and not being able to speak because it is too full of words. Another avenue they pursued was people's last meals, by reading the last chapters of biographies and researching the requests for last meals by prisoners on death row.

The research culminated in a performance piece in which thirty-nine members of the audience are invited to dinner. Before entering the 'dining room' they are given a number, a table number and an incident number. They are shown to a place at one of three long tables adorned with white tablecloths, fully set for dinner under a large chandelier. Three performers speak the last words of famous people, before eating them up (they are written on rice paper, often engulfed during a fascinating struggle by the performer to gorge themselves on their words). Every so often a chef appears and calls a number, and then a silver platter is delivered to a member of the audience. The dishes range from chocolate cake to liver, onion and cottage cheese (the last meal requested by prisoner Lennie White before he was executed in 1997). Lyn Gardner comments upon the way that the show 'gives voice to the voiceless', since it documents the last words of those that have died. Sometimes these are real people, at others the imagined words of those obliterated by the Hiroshima bomb (Gardner 2004). This sense of evoking the invisible is increased through a number of devices, including the director's encouragement of 'non-performing', achieved through the style of reportage and down-playing of the emotion in these scenes, as well as incidents such as deliberately reading the text from a script, and emphasising the game-playing that occurs within the piece through phrases when the performers seem to address the audience as themselves such as 'I don't know how to say this'. Indeed, the whole status of the performers is ambiguous. Are the actors themselves? (They are named as such in the script.) Are they invented personas? Are they momentarily representations of the people whose words they speak?

When the piece was performed at the Glasgow Tramway in 2005 the sense of 'inhabiting' the space was very strong. The Tramway, an old tramshed on the edge of Glasgow city, was used as a found theatre space for Peter Brook's *Mahabharata*, and played an incongruous host for the *The Last Supper*. The Tramway with its exposed brick, ducting, girders and concrete floor is a quintessential industrial space. The chandelier and long dining tables, which by the end of the

Figure 8.1 Reckless Sleepers: *The Last Supper*. Photographer: Mole
        Wetherall.

Reproduced by permission of Restless Sleepers.

performance are cluttered with wine and food, sit oddly in the space.
And yet this incongruity heightens the sense of the irony of the
inhabitation of the space. Somehow the industrial surrounds of the
space frame the sumptuous dinner table further.

The Last Supper creates a sense of the invisible inhabiting the
space and in this manner, fiction and fact are shown to be equally
unreliable, and the notion of history as a stable entity is banished.
This sense of dislocation and instability is reflected in moments in the
show when different endings are played out, for example the death of
Che Guevara is enacted in three different versions. Director Mole
Wetherell comments on *The Last Supper*, 'I'm not so sure that you
could call this piece a history play, as I'm not really convinced that I
really understand what that is? It does reference parts of history'
(www.reckless-sleepers.co.uk). The piece, in rearticulating last words,
evokes a sense of the past inhabiting the present and this effect is
increased by transporting an elaborate banquet setting into a performance space.

Architectural spaces and the haptic

Yi-Fu Tuan in *Space and Place: The Perspective of Experience* argues that: '[c]ompleted, the building or architectural complex now stands as an environment capable of affecting the people who live in it. Manmade space can refine human feeling and perception' (Tuan 1977: 102). This concept of the space informing and shaping a performative experience has been evident in much of the work already discussed, and no more so than in the notion of 'found space', as seen in the work of Brook and Mnouchkine. But architectural space informs practice-making processes in ways that are difficult to quantify. For the British company Station House Opera, the use of architecture is central to its work. In a series of performances involving breezeblocks the company provoked issues regarding 'the relationships between found and constructed architectures, objects, narratives and performance systems and processes' (Kaye 2000: 164). These pieces culminated with *Bastille Days* (1989) where a breezeblock sculpture containing 8000 concrete blocks was assembled and dismantled over nine days by a company of fifteen people. These blocks represented the French Revolution and demonstrated, as Tuan remarked, that 'architecture can educate people's awareness and concept of reality' (Tuan 1977: 110).

Tuan postulates that '[a]rchitectural space reveals and instructs' (Tuan 1977: 114); he draws upon the example of the cathedral in the Middle Ages where the building itself and the various different places within the space (such as the altar, the pictures in the stained glass windows, the pulpit) became a symbol for the values it projected. In other words, aspects of architecture were didactic tools through which to instruct the laity on religious matters. This use of space – whereby the building and the image it represents are combined into one – is present within much 'found space' practice. Since its formation in 1995 Scottish theatre company Grid Iron has worked extensively with utilising spaces in order to host its devised work, adaptations and self-commissioned plays. The company has used unusual locations as theatre spaces (department stores, underground dungeons and vaults) and found the unusual within theatre buildings. For example, in 1999 it used the foyer, alleys and car park of Glasgow Citizens' Theatre rather than the auditorium. For the first three years of the company's life a 'home' was provided by the Edinburgh Festival. Each year the company chose a site that reopened the dynamic of actor/audience boundaries. It is also used to moving house – work premiered at the Edinburgh Fringe Festival will then often tour nationally and sometimes to conventional theatres, and for this reason, its work is described by director Ben Harrison not as site-specific but 'site sensitive' (Harrison 2005).

In 2003, in a piece reminiscent of Kantor's work, the company chose to work in a derelict Georgian house, previously divided into small bedsits. *Those Eyes, That Mouth* was a devised piece for one actor and one musician. The piece was inspired by research into films by Buñuel and Polanski, paintings by Edward Hopper and writings of Milan Kundera among others. The performance explored a woman caught by her own mind within the house; the production probed the inner tribulations of a woman obsessed with Vermeer's painting the *Girl with a Pearl Earring*. As one reviewer noted, the sense of the place was imperative to the experience of the play: 'The smell of plaster hangs in the air, the walls drip emotion, despair seeps from the floorboards and the telephone always rings' (Gardner 2003). The house provided an intimate location, whereby the audience could experience the smallest detail. A route through the house started downstairs with audience members being ushered between scenes; gradually the piece trailed upstairs. In a bedroom a scene of unrequited love was explored through the creation on the bed of an idyllic garden with a tiny lawn, picnic hamper and babbling spring where the woman waited for her absent lover to arrive. This moment provided a sharp contrast between the hope of the imagined and the grim reality of bedsit land within a decaying house.

By stripping the house in Abercromby Place back to its bare walls and creating small mirages of habitation (such as the garden in the bedroom), Grid Iron plays on the relationship between the spectator's senses and the environment. The architecture of the building is exploited in order to excavate the theme of the performance. In particular, *Those Eyes, That Mouth* reaches out to the visual and haptic senses, which is clear from Lyn Gardner's review where she remarks that 'the walls drip emotion, despair seeps from the floorboards'; she can almost see and touch the feelings evoked by the building. In utilising the architecture to enable spectators to 'touch' the emotions of the woman, Grid Iron explores the way in which touch and vision are linked to spatial awareness and evoke the work of nineteenth-century Austrian psychologist Ernst Weber who advocated that '[t]he touch organs, like the visual organs, have localization-sense ... we therefore owe our accurate perception of spatial relationships to both senses' (quoted in Prytherch 2005: 2).

The work of Grid Iron brings together many of the concerns that have been raised within this chapter. Working primarily within Scotland has created a sense of the 'lived-in' habitation of the architectures and landscapes of Scotland. The interplay between environment and art is exceptionally strong and although this chapter has been mainly concerned with the creation of interior landscapes, it is worth recognising the importance of the exterior in forming many of our perceptions. Sculptor Barbara Hepworth notes how the physical environment educated her visual and haptic senses:

> All my early memories are of forms and shapes and textures. Moving through and over the West Riding landscape with my father in his car, the hills were sculptures; the roads defined as the form. Above all, there was the sensation of moving physically over the contours of fullnesses and concavities, through hollows and over peaks – feeling, touching, seeing, through the mind and hand and eye. The sensation has never left me. I, the sculptor, *am* the landscape.
>
> (quoted in Prytherch 2005: 2)

NINE

THE PLACE OF
THE ARTIST

Revisioning place

At the beginning of his influential book *The Empty Space* theatre practitioner Peter Brook famously announced that 'I can take any empty space and call it a bare stage' (Brook 1972: 11). Brook was interested in work that might take place beyond the conventions of the proscenium arch theatre and looked to experiment with different performance sites. This chapter will address artists who choose to create performances outside theatre buildings and develop work that responds to the environment. It proposes that artists predominantly respond to a place from the perspective of an outsider and considers the problems and possibilities that this affords to the creative encounter. At the core of the enquiry is an examination of the place of the artist both literally in terms of the locations that they inhabit and philosophically and psychologically in terms of the social functions the artist may perform.

Kaprow's early Happenings were contemporary with Brook's experimentation with the empty space. Kaprow was influenced by Cage's performances at Black Mountain College which were produced by residents at the college and were designed to be events that arose organically from the life of the community. At Black Mountain College people had a real familiarity with the space that was being worked with yet they were invited to experience the environment from a new perspective due to the performance that was enacted within it. Kaprow developed this work beyond a self-contained community to create Happenings that involved members of the public. Kaprow was excited about expanding the realm of performance and the scope of the performance space. He sought to disrupt the Aristotelian unities of place, time and action within performance and suggested that 'the Happening should be dispersed over several widely spaced, sometimes moving and changing locales. Finally, all around the globe' (Kaprow 1993: 62). Kaprow believed in the organic connection between art and its environment. *Fluids* (1967), for example, saw him building structures from ice in twenty sites around Los Angeles and leaving them to melt. Members of the public would come across the piece(s) as they journeyed through the city and were free to interact with them as they wished. Behind the piece was the notion that the 'quasi-architectural structures' of the ice blocks would activate the place for the spectator, encouraging them to see the site from a new perspective as the structures transformed the environment before transforming themselves into puddles of water (Schechner 1988: 8).

Happenings can be seen as marking an emerging interest in work that, as Kaye suggests, 'may articulate exchanges between the work of art and the places in which its meanings are defined' (Kaye 2000: 1). In such work place becomes an important element within the artistic encounter and there is recognition that a space is not empty but full of meaning. What becomes important is not just the geographical place in which the work is sited but also the social practices that are engendered as part of the space-making processes of the particular site that an artist may observe, articulate and manipulate.

More recently Marc Augé's interrogation of the 'non-places' of supermodernity can be seen to provide a critical climate for the reactivation of localised places within a globalised climate. Augé's anthropological study makes a distinction between socially loaded 'places' which are rich in history and 'non-places' which he sees as soulless, alienating spaces which are only of functional value – such as motorways and airports. Through this critical lens devised performances can be understood as responding to a need to develop 'places' that promote social interaction. This chapter is concerned with the way in which performance pieces interact with the cultural environments they occupy and, as such, opens up understandings of the relationship between performance and the environment.

Within contemporary performance, site-related work has become an established practice where an artist's intervention offers spectators new perspectives upon a particular site or set of sites. The following extract from *A Decade of Forced Entertainment* is a metaphorical indication of how practitioners may approach site-related material:

They drew a map of the country and marked on it the events of the last ten years – political and industrial conflict, ecological disasters, showbiz marriages and celebrity divorces.

(Etchells 1999: 30)

Forced Entertainment, like many other contemporary devising companies, directly engages with site and the issue of social space-making within everyday life and includes observations on this activity within its work. This practice can be understood in terms of Walter Benjamin's appropriation of Baudelaire's notion of the flâneur who walks through the city in a way that is attuned to the special beauty of the cityscape. Benjamin's model of the flâneur is a figure who reads the city through an inhabitation of its spaces and an appreciation of the accumulated social practices they represent. This flâneur is able to hold a critical position of 'relaxed expertise' when reflecting on social practice (Gilloch 2002: 232). In this chapter this model of the professional observer of spaces will be applied to the site-related deviser. Such artists may be seen as in a sense professional strangers who are able to bring to bear their sensibilities on the places and spaces they visit. The strangers' perspective may result in the space itself appearing strange to the spectators as the visiting artist offers up new understandings of the location and practices within the site. This process of making strange enables the artist to relate to the site in a way that may educate, inspire and politicise the audience.

Inhabiting space

Lone Twin's work begins with an interest in place and space. It is a British company which describes itself as 'making performance which deals playfully with travel, context and orientation' (www.lonetwin. com). Interestingly for a company focussed on place, it does not have a permanent base. Instead the two artists who are at the core of the company (Gary Winters and Gregg Whelan) live at opposite ends of the UK and come together to create work which often is developed on the road. The company commonly creates site-related work and, like many of the earlier Happenings, the work is constructed so that the performers interact with the people who inhabit a particular place. One of the first pieces that the company made was *Totem* (1998). The piece began with a commission from Colchester Arts Centre and Firstsite Gallery to make a piece 'about Colchester'. Starting from a creative response to a recent freak tornado that had happened in East Anglia, the company decided to work with the idea of returning things back into place and developed a piece where, from 21 March until 27 March 1998, the performers carried a pole as the crow flies between two buildings which took them through Colchester town centre (2005). As they undertook their task, the artists interacted with members of the public and collected stories and images. The company members note that the physical labour that they undertake within a place gives them a clear function within that setting and relate that to de Certeau's theorisation of a subject's agency arising through 'ways of operating' within a space (de Certeau 1984: xix). Lone Twin states:

> Our models are everyday, pragmatic . . . Working gives us a sense of place and a way of operating, like when you live somewhere and you get to know it because you have tasks to carry out.
>
> (Lone Twin 2005)

In *Totem,* as in subsequent pieces, the physically gruelling effort expended by the performers drew attention to the actual process of labour inherent in the piece.

The idea of staging working practices for public observation arose from the principle of task-based performance within the Happenings movement and has been successfully employed by many contemporary practitioners. An indicative example is Gob Squad's *Work* (1995). The piece was performed in an office building in the centre of Nottingham. The performance space was framed by other units that were functioning offices. The work was a durational performance that replicated the standard working week – nine to five, Monday to Friday. In the piece the performers 'performed' the activity of work. They turned up in suits and interacted with telephones, photocopiers and filing cabinets, yet, as they were approaching clerical work as artists, they sought to 'make strange' the activity. Thus they photocopied their faces and named the portraits – 'Me as the Queen Mum', for example – and they danced with the filing cabinets. The company documented the activity of the office space and understood it as performance. This was enhanced by the element of the show where they called people and interviewed them about their working life, interweaving the answers into the material of the show. Both Lone Twin's and Gob Squad's work demonstrates an anthropological approach to performance in that they see

Figure 9.1 Lone Twin: *SledgeHammer Songs*. (Pictured left to right) Gregg
Whelan, Gary Winters. Photographer: Team Brown.

Reproduced by permission of Lone Twin.

social practices as performance and the ability to reflect on these practices arises from the artists' perspective as outsiders. Thus, while others around them continued their daily routine, Gob Squad entered into a realm it does not normally inhabit. Although it observed many of the conventions of office etiquette, it also took artistic license with them and incorporated fantasy into its performance. So, for example, a door at the back of the office space Gob Squad inhabited opened to reveal a window into the hopes of careers that people dream of having and showcased figures dressed as spacemen, rock stars and other fantasy figures.

Artists may also clearly identify themselves as outsiders within a space. For example, for *Totem* Lone Twin negotiated the streets of Colchester while dressed as cowboys. The performers' costume and activity signalled their place as strangers yet also acted as a catalyst for the public to interact with them. The company always wears some kind of travellers' attire for its performance work which ranges from biking wear to rain coats. This apparel can be seen to communicate 'otherness' which pragmatically is important when working on the street as it draws the attention of the audience and, at another level, gestures towards the concerns of exploration and environment which are at the core of the company's work.

Lone Twin's piece *Walk With Me, Walk With Me, Will Somebody Please Walk With Me* (2002) is a performative lecture that reflects upon the company's site-related work and raises some key themes relating to this form of practice. De Certeau notes that 'to walk is to lack a space' and, within *Walk With Me*, Lone Twin negotiates the idea of the placelessness of the artist (de Certeau 1984: 103). Gregg states 'I am from somewhere else' and then Gary states 'I'm not from round here, I'm from .... [inserting the name of the place they are currently inhabiting]'. This troubles the notion of place in that the performer states that he is both from here and not from here, heightening an awareness of the possibility of being both a stranger and an inhabitant of a place. In this way Lone Twin consciously reflects upon the complexities of relating to a site through creating artwork within and about it.

Within the text of *Walk With Me* the company notes 'if you dress up funny . . . people will shout at you' and re-enacts moments based on events that have happened to it on the road. It acknowledges that local people are often mistrustful of two strangers who roam their streets but encounters may also hold a recognition of the potential that visitors may bring with them – an impulse confirmed by the fact that members of the public seem keen to share their stories with the company.

Lone Twin acknowledges its performers' status as migrant workers as being different to those who live in the places they travel to. The text of *Walk With Me* reflects on a piece entitled *The Days of the Sledgehammer Have Gone* where the artists carried out an eighteen-hour walk across two bridges in Konsvinger in Norway. They were joined by many local people during the duration of the piece, one of whom walked with them all night before going to work the next day. The artists reflect on the fact that, while they visited the city and carried out the labour of walking for paid employment, they were joined by people who engaged with the activity of walking during their leisure time. This reflection acknowledges the complex relationship that is always engendered between performers and audiences but which may be problematised by site-related work where local people may feel a sense of ownership of the site.

In *Walk With Me* the performers state that they are 'not from round here' but use that distance to make strange and observe what might otherwise not be seen. A critic for *The Stranger* in Seattle described Lone Twin as 'innocents abroad' and the company uses that perspective for artistic effect (Kiley 2004). In scoping out new territories the company remains sensitive to the stories that constitute that space. Lone Twin also looks to the particularities of a place and states that it 'learn[s] to speak its language through the stories that it tells' (Lone Twin 2005). Thus narratives the performers have heard are retold as part of the performance. They include the story of Burkhaard, a German man whom the company met in Denmark, who had fallen in love with a Danish woman and needed to gather words of love in Danish. Physical interactions that company members have on the street are framed as performance as well as the stories they have heard. *Walk With Me*, for example, includes a choreographed sequence of gestures which are condensed from an interaction with a woman who, on the night of England's football victory over Greece in the qualifying match for entry into the 2002 World Cup, described David Beckham's infamous penalty to Gary and Gregg. In this way, performative utterances are lifted from everyday life, framed as artistic practice and shown back to the community from whence they came. De Certeau states that '[s]tories thus carry out a labour that constantly transforms place into spaces or spaces into places' and devising companies like Lone Twin can be seen to be activating particular places by highlighting social practices within their work (de Certeau 1984: 118).

Reclaiming space

Contemporary public spaces present particular problems to the performance-maker. Augé develops de Certeau's notion of non-place and defines non-places as different from what he terms 'anthropological places' in that they 'cannot be defined as relational, or historical, or concerned with identity' (Augé 1995: 78). Augé identifies airports, railway stations, hotel chains, large retail stores and leisure parks as non-places that put 'the individual in contact only with another image of himself' (Augé 1995: 79). He argues that the non-place is a particularly contemporary phenomenon which promotes solitude rather than social relations and he suggests that the contemporary climate encourages people to travel through a landscape rather than inhabit it. He also notes an emphasis on commercial space within the contemporary city which leaves little space for non-economic social interaction. Some artists, such as the Space Highjackers, have taken up the experience of the non-place as a starting point for their site-related practice.

There are branches of the Space Hijackers in the UK, USA and Singapore. The UK division is part of The Laboratory of Insurrectionary Imagination which describes itself as 'a network of culturally and politically engaged artists and activists' who can be seen to be working in the Dadaist tradition of cultural guerrilla warfare (www.space hijackers.co.uk). The Space Highjackers are itinerant art activists and refer to themselves as anarchitects who are opposed to the hierarchy that is enforced by architects, planners and owners of space. They perceive that public space is being eroded and many of their recent projects have focussed on the lack of places to gather. They also 'oppose the blanding out and destruction of local culture in the name of global economic progress' (www.spacehijackers.co.uk). This can be seen to address Augé's issue of non-place and the lack of identity of commercial non-places. The Space Highjackers champion anthropological space in a globalised culture that may appear hostile to local identities. The Space Hijackers, whose moniker is a clear indication of their intent to steal/re-appropriate areas within the public arena, have been involved in a large number of insurrectionary projects employing guerrilla tactics and this chapter will focus on *The A–Z of Retail Trickery*.

As sociologist and cultural theorist Foucault notes, the negotiation of space is connected to power and there is a long tradition of people occupying places with political intentions. These range from sit-ins to military manoeuvres and all seek to highlight the forces of power at work within a social space. *The A–Z of Retail Trickery* took place on 31 May 2004 as part of the larger Urban Detour project which was curated by A2RT at the Bullring Centre in Birmingham, UK. The Bullring Centre was originally a Victorian marketplace that was developed as an 'innovative' shopping centre in the 1960s and then redeveloped in 2003 when it was launched as Europe's largest shopping centre. It covers over forty acres of the city centre and is home to a huge number of retail units, the large majority belonging to major high street brands. The idea behind the Space Hijackers' piece was to inhabit the retail outlets and create a promenade performance that considered how the retail chains attempt to construct the experience of shopping. The Space Hijackers state:

> Architecture is analogous to a type of language, buildings, and the layouts and components within them can act as a text, instructing users how they are intended to be used and affecting the ambience of the space. However users of space read this language in a distracted manner, the messages and signifiers within are therefore not consciously noted. We are too busy getting on with whatever business we are there for, to spend time laboriously deciphering the language of the space. It is because of this that companies can guide us around retail space and control our experience of that space.
>
> (www.spacehijackers.co.uk)

The A–Z of Retail Trickery was designed to encourage the audience to examine commercial space and to become aware of its social construction. The event highlighted the techniques that retailers employ, such as rounding ends of supermarket shelves for prime targeting; using the colour purple to promote a positive mental attitude; and carpeting some sections of the store while leaving others with vinyl passages, in order to control the movement of shoppers. The a–z (p for power display, for example) was not presented in alphabetical order but stops were initiated as the group of spectators was led through the spaces of the Bullring where different aspects of the constructed environment were highlighted. Just as retailers design spaces after watching CCTV footage of customers moving through retail environments, so the activists used the performance as surveillance of the retailers' behaviour.

Another company that engages with CCTV as an instrument of social control is the Surveillance Camera Players. Founded in 1996 they are fundamentally a pro-privacy group that sees CCTV as unable to offer any useful social function but to violate human rights. They are not professional actors but decided to use performance to mount a protest against the use of surveillance cameras in social spaces. They adapt relevant pieces of fiction – for example George Orwell's *1984* – and perform them directly in front of the cameras. They state that 'the action or message of this play should be clear, intelligible and relevant. Short is good; shorter is better' (www.notbored.org/the-scp.html). Most plays are around two minutes long but are repeated over a thirty- to sixty-minute performance period. Surveillance cameras do not pick up sound so the performances are silent but text is incorporated

Figure 9.2 The Surveillance Camera Players: *1984*. Performances are directed at surveillance cameras.

Reproduced by permission of Surveillance Camera Players.

through poster boards. They initially directed their performances at security officers and the police with unannounced performances in different sites, but now they advertise performances and members of the general public go to watch. Activity has spread beyond New York City and there are Surveillance Camera Players in cities from Arizona to Stockholm. On its website the company gives advice for others on how to stage performances providing scripts as well as organisational advice. Like the Space Highjackers, the company seeks to activate consciousness about the control of public space through performance in social sites.

The Space Highjackers and the Surveillance Camera Players may be seen as flâneurs, casting a critical gaze over the environment. Just as for Benjamin, the flâneur here is not an idle dandy, but someone who reads the city through engaging with its spaces and remembering its past. In A–Z the Space Highjackers clearly spoke as those who were familiar with the experience of the large retail units but the company also, perhaps, had a hankering for the Victorian market with its clearly delineated social transactions between trader and customer. Its performance work negotiated, rather than controlled, space as it moved though the constructed space of the shopping centre. The performers offered a perspective that caused audiences to stop and observe at particular places which traders may not have highlighted for attention and hurry past others which the retailers intended to be attractive. Likewise the Surveillance Camera Players embody a commitment to the free movement through social space. The Space Hijackers state that they attempt to 'create situations or place objects within architectural space that affect the way in which that space is then experienced' (www.spacehijackers.co.uk). They seek to reanimate and narrativise the space, and endeavour to 'create myths within space that then go on to become a part of that space' which works against the clinical solitude of the non-place.

This type of activity often brings the companies into conflict with authority. The Surveillance Camera Players' website advises participants not to be afraid of the police or security guards but to leave the area when asked to do so as the intention is to raise awareness rather than to enact civil disobedience. Security guards were called to attend to the Space Hijackers on 31 May 2004 and the group complied with the request to leave the Bullring Centre. The company actually continued with the performance on the street outside the shopping centre but the new location gave a different quality to the piece. Serra asserts that for site-related performance 'to move the work is to destroy the work' (Serra 1994: 194). In this case the work was not destroyed but considerably changed as the performer's presentation reverted to a lecture format rather than allowing audience members to experience and re-interpret the event for themselves. It also meant that the troubling of non-place became an ideological event rather than an actuality as, rather than holding a public meeting in the middle of a supermarket aisle, the company had to discuss from a distance what might have been found in that venue. Nevertheless, it did heighten the sense of displacement in the urban landscape and the eviction may well have become part of the mythology of the Bullring Centre site.

Transforming space

While there are ethical issues relating to occupying a place, there are also issues around being invited into a space. Yi-Fu Tuan acknowledges the important relationship between space and time and asks 'how long does it take to get to know a place?' (Tuan 1977: 183). This is an important question for site-related performance as artists may be allocated a short amount of time to research and develop a performance. This may only allow performers to gain a superficial appreciation of the site. However, as has been identified, there are also artistic opportunities in applying a stranger's perspective to a site. Tim Etchells, director of Forced Entertainment, poses a question which echoes Tuan but comes from an artist's perspective. He asks: '[h]ow long do you have to have lived somewhere until you are allowed to lie about it?' (Etchells 1996: 51). This question recognises that performers will blend fact and fiction and will shape the real material that they find in order to develop the creative project. Etchells' question was articulated in reference to a piece that Forced Entertainment produced in 1995 entitled *Nights in this City*. Unusually for the company this was a site-related work which took the form of a guided bus trip around Sheffield – a place that the performers knew well having been based there for eleven years. Fabrication was introduced in relation to the sites that the bus visited. Thus, for example, the audience was told:

> all the streets round here got names after famous football hooligans from history and all the buildings got names after ghosts and cleaning products and convicted kerb crawlers.
>
> (quoted in Kaye 2000: 15)

The piece took the audience around the city and told them invented stories, created from the essence of the site – the devisers had asked themselves questions such as '[i]f you had killed someone and had to dump the body where would you take it?' (quoted in Kaye 2000: 8). In this way the devising process was one of symbolisation, as places which suggested a certain atmosphere were identified as such and a 'truth of environment' was presented. This, however, was carefully blended with the actuality of the site. The event ended with an installation where the street index of the city was mapped out on the floor. This gave people the opportunity to identify where they lived and worked, and to introduce their real stories into the blend of reality and fabrication that had been offered to them by the company.

IOU Theatre offers another example of particular issues that arise within a process that seeks to interweave actuality with fiction. IOU has built a reputation for its site-related work. The company began with a commitment to open-air, public performances which they saw as democratising theatre practice and opposing élitist sensibilities. Buildings and landscapes continue to be important to the work, often acting as the inspiration for a show. The practitioners understand themselves to be imaginatively responding to the environment and their response as professional strangers works as a form of social agitation in that '[a]n audience will shake off its inertia when it experiences the surprise effect of space transformed' (Burt and Barker 1980: 72). Like Welfare State International, IOU Threatre understands creativity and imagination as important factors in consciousness-raising.

The Consulting Room was a collaboration between The Royal London Hospital, The Greenwich and Docklands International Festival and IOU Theatre and was performed on-site in the hospital on 9–11 July 1999. The company employed its usual working practice of employing 'the character of the place to help shape the piece, so that [the] performance can crystallize around it' but making a piece in collaboration with a hospital site raised particular problems for the company (Burt and Barker 1980: 74). The company began with an awareness that a hospital is loaded with particular norms and conventions. Foucault examines the discourse of medicine and the way in which the hospital building spacialises norms and values. He notes, for example, that the classificatory gaze of Western medicine demands that patients are grouped according to illness so that the clinician may observe them together as sets of symptoms. The division of the hospital space into orthopaedic wards and oncology wards, for example, is, for

Foucault, an expression of the power of the medical establishment that sees sick people as their illnesses rather than individuals. Foucault argues that the medical narrative rather than the patient's perspective is given precedence within the hospital (Foucault 1997: 78). IOU Theatre adopted this critical perspective and wished to address what it saw as an inequality. The company was interested in re-establishing individual narratives that inhabit the hospital space and used the creative means to facilitate that process. With consent, IOU used patient narratives within the performance and recordings of individuals' stories were broadcast to the audience via specially constructed drip bags that were held to the ear.

The company was also aware that a hospital is a contested space. It is marginal in that it houses sickness – a place between health and death. IOU saw illness as a 'margin between life and death where mental and physical battles are fought' and perceived the hospital as an appropriate site to highlight and explore the social interactions that frame such struggles (Sobey 1999). IOU Theatre was interested in exploring the 'hidden processes' that take place within the hospital and examining the symbiotic relationship of patients and staff in a manner which it hoped would provide a 'fresh, imaginative take on the overwhelming complexities of the institution' (Sobey 1999). The company looked to employ its trademark extravagant images and costumes and, by igniting the imagination, it hoped that its audience would be able to look again at the hospital institution and come to a deeper understanding of the way it functions. The company constructed two 'sound gardens' either side of the Garden Square. The structures resembled a blend of military field hospital, whitewashed allotments and excavation site and certainly piqued the curiosity of the hospital community that had been allocated seventy-five free tickets to the show.

The performances themselves were a journey through a sterile and stylised medical environment and ran three times over three days. The company employed the theatrical nature of the hospital environment with its costumes of staff uniforms and medical props as a key aspect of the presentation although, in IOU's unique style, the strangeness of the hospital environment was exaggerated. Thus, for example, the performance environment included a machine that the *British Medical Journal* described as a 'contraption resembling a mis-marriage of washing machine and motorised umbrella [which] looks as terrifying to the medically trained eye as most of the medical equipment in daily use looks to patients' (Knight 1999). This commentary suggests that the artists' eyes offered a new perspective to an audience from the medical community, delivering a sense of the uncanny which matched the experience of non-medical audience members.

The research and development for the piece included a residency at the hospital that sensitised the company to the site and allowed it to observe the workings of the institution. During their residency the performers maintained a sense of themselves as expert outsiders, coming in to gather information and offer professional skills through workshops, but they also worked with their own experiences of illness which they mapped onto the data that they collected. The programme notes cited cultural critic Susan Sontag who, in her book *Illness as Metaphor,* argued for the existence of two parallel universes within society: the kingdom of the well and the kingdom of the sick. IOU Theatre embraced this metaphorical landscape and looked to make its existence concrete. The poetic symbolisation of space in its piece gestured towards the psychosocial experience of illness and the audience was witness to fantastical sights such as levitating beds which served to illustrate an out-of-body experience.

The fact that the central Garden Square of the hospital was taken over by the performance was significant. People moving through the site were confronted by the performance and invited to experience the hospital in a new way. There was a troubling of the relationship between audience and performer as all were participants within the event. As part of the performance, audience members' names were called and they were invited to enter a waiting room before being led through a labyrinth of plastic sheeting. Rather than being passive spectators the piece encouraged the audience to participate in a new negotiation of the site.

Responses to the piece were varied and reflected a spectrum of interest as the 'indigenous' hospital community of East-End Londoners mixed with the visiting festival-goers who had obtained tickets through an external box office. In this case audience members, who represented a spectrum of class and ethnicity as well as medical interest, came together through their relationship to the environment. David Wheeler, artistic director of IOU Theatre, confessed that on first arriving at the site he had wondered whether it was appropriate to be occupying the real working space of a hospital with a piece about a fictional institution. He felt, however, that feedback from staff members describing how they had been encouraged to look at their work from a different perspective validated the work. Burt claims that work by the company encourages an audience to 're-examin[e] their own mythologies' which may prove to be a radical encounter (Burt and Barker 1980: 76).

In conclusion, de Certeau saw the need for 'therapeutics for deteriorating social relations' in late Western capitalism and it could be argued that artists may be able to fulfil this function (de Certeau 1984: xxiv). Through inhabiting social space and employing particular practices, the artists described in this chapter seek to engage and invigorate the people who inhabit the places that they visit. The artists use their professional skills, as well as their personal experiences, to create work that both investigates and activates social space. Lone Twin articulates a common desire to find a place of communion with its audience and describes how *Walk With Me* was structured so that 'everyone would end up in the same place' (Lone Twin 2005). Using a site as a literal gathering ground is fundamental in site-related performance but Lone Twin's work demonstrates how this meeting point may also be metaphorical. The tactic of working with lived experience as primary material for devising is common to all the artists discussed in this chapter and highlights how a particular focus on the interplay between place and social space draws into question the relationship between the audience and the performers as it recognises the framing of actual experience.

TEN

BETWEEN ROUTES AND ROOTS

Performance, Place and Diaspora

The significance of place

It is striking that, in this period of globalisation and cyber space, theatre practitioners are interested in rethinking how people relate to landscape and place. Spatial relationships have always been integral to performance-making; the configuration of performance spaces and their effects on actor–audience exchanges have been richly and variously investigated by practitioners across history and cultures. Spatial metaphors, however, are being used increasingly to describe the ways in which social identities are formed in this diasporic and globalised world. As time and space become compressed, there is recognition that contemporary perceptions of identity are formed by identifying with, and travelling between, different locations and multiple places. Metaphors of place and space – borders, margins, mappings, translocation, dislocation and so on – are frequently used as a critical device to explain how ideas of community and selfhood are experienced and understood. At a time when people are increasingly geographically mobile, either through choice or through enforced displacement, this metaphor is often associated with a political awareness of location in which 'sites' of power are 'mapped'.

Within this social climate, performance has acquired significance in framing and reframing places and spaces as the changing routes and roots of communities, and individuals are negotiated, questioned and explored. This emphasis on interrogating the significance of location and dislocation in performance represents a departure from the conventions of place developed in the community theatre of the 1960s and 1970s. This movement was, as Baz Kershaw identifies, frequently orientated towards representing local history as a means of under-mining hierarchies of class. Processes of theatre-making at this time often actively set out to question official versions of history in Marxist terms by retelling local stories from the perspectives of the working classes. In the work of theatre-makers such as Peter Cheesman and Graham Woodruff in England, for example, local geography and topography were significant as a backdrop to the dramatic action. The landscape provided a familiar setting for the dramatic action in which, as Kershaw documents, 'the town witnesses the reincarnation of its ancestors' (Kershaw 1992: 193–194). The historical and political significance of place is well illustrated in the work of Telford Com-munity Arts, where, from 1974 to 1990, theatre activists worked in the community to devise collectively authored plays that represented industrial history from the perspective of the working classes. Marxist theatre-maker Graham Woodruff describes one such play, *Who Built the Bridge Anyway?* (1979), in which the story of building the world-famous iron bridge in Shropshire was juxtaposed against contemporary experiences of factory work in order to 'demystify traditional and established versions of history' using well-known local landmarks as a focus (Woodruff 2004: 33).

In early community-based performance there was an assumption that devised performances would address relatively homogeneous audiences that were already familiar with local landscapes and were historically rooted to the place of performance. In the United States, as the civil rights movement gained force, community-based theatre companies such as Roadside recognised the political and economic divisiveness of mainstream theatre. Jan Cohen-Cruz analyses Roadside's first production in 1976, *Red Fox/Second Hanging,* which sought to tell the local histories of the Appalachia people using the oral tradition of storytelling and other indigenous forms of performance. In terms that echo the reception of English community plays of the same period, Cohen-Cruz records that the Appalachian people were 'witnessing its own history from its own class perspective' for the first time (Cohen-Cruz 2005: 53). The methodology Roadside uses to engage local audiences in performance-making has been documented by artistic director Dudley Cocke, who describes convivial evenings spent sharing and celebrating local music, and narratives of place often provided the starting point for devising a performance (Cocke 2004: 165–173). Cocke also notes that the company has recognised the cultural complexity of community and, since 1984, it has collaborated with

Native American artists in New Mexico creating bilingual plays that acknowledge the political significance of intercultural dialogue.

The emphasis on localism in community theatre has done much to challenge the idea that there was one official narrative of history, and although early experiments were primarily concerned with issues of class representation, community-based devised performance has become increasingly concerned with the combination of the local with the global. In the work that is the subject of this chapter, performance devised and applied to specific locations and audiences reflects contemporary unease with fixed inscriptions of both place and identity. Recognising that it is possible to have emotional attachments and a sense of belonging to more than one place at once, contemporary devisers have sought to develop performative practices that invite audiences to re-envision and re-imagine familiar places and recognise the multiplicity of meanings they carry. Methodologically, this means that companies and performers often work with the dynamic of performance site, and investigating its layered meanings becomes part of the process of production. Kneehigh Theatre in England, for instance, has responded to the local–global nexus both by re-examining its Cornish roots and by developing collaborations with performers whose work takes place in very different settings and situations from its own. For example, its adaptation of the Cornish folktale *Tristan & Yseult* in 2004–2005 was developed into a theatrical experiment in responding to place through the Three Island Collaboration between England, Malta and Cyprus. As the production travelled to these three countries, company members and local performers worked together on the play, developing and recycling it in new ways that drew upon indigenous forms of aesthetic expression, and engaged with the political concerns of the place of performance. Such strategies not only recognise the performers' cultural and material roots, but also acknowledge the impact of their artistic and performative routes on the process of devising and the reception of production.

Contemporary devisers have been effective in challenging the perception that communities are place-bound, while also acknowledging the significance and creative opportunities presented by working with the personal and historical associations inherent in specific sites, locations and spaces. Not only does this way of thinking about performance-making refute the modernist perception that theatre is a neutral space, but also it recognises that communities are plural and always in process. All places of performance, therefore, are multiply inscribed with cultural memories and variously significant to both performers and audiences. Marvin Carlson's insight that everything in theatre has always been haunted has particular relevance here. He suggests that the postmodern concern with recycling, although newly and self-consciously configured, has long theatrical antecedents:

> The retelling of stories already told, the reenactment of events already enacted, the reexperience of emotions already experienced, these are and have always been central concerns of the theatre at all times and places, but closely allied to these concerns are the particular production dynamics of theatre: the stories it chooses to tell, the bodies and other physical materials it utilizes to tell them, and the places they are told.
>
> (Carlson 2003: 3)

In relation to performance space, Carlson acknowledges that both conventional theatre buildings and other places of public performance (he cites factories, marketplaces and cathedrals as examples of extra-theatrical performance spaces) are marked by the traces of their other purposes and haunted by the ghosts of those who have used them in the past. In their study of the relationship between theatre and archaeology, Mike Pearson and Michael Shanks describe this aspect of performance as a balance between 'the host and the ghost', a negotiation between the contemporary and the historical in which 'no single story is being told' (Pearson and Shanks 2001: 96).

In devised theatre that aims for community involvement, the image of ghosts and hosts has particular resonance. Recognising that there is a multiplicity of stories invoked by places of performance, whether in or outside theatre buildings, indicates the significance of place to present relationships as well as to cultural histories. Social anthropologist Tim Ingold argues that life is perceived environmentally and experientially, and people are understood through the journeys they choose to make as well as their ancestral inheritance. Drawing on Deleuze and Guattari's concept of the rhizome, he suggests that people might be understood through a network of trails and routes they follow and through their connections with others rather than solely by their cultural and familial roots:

> Every position in the total network of trails or life-lines is an emplace-ment . . . places are understood as nodes of the endless comings and goings of people, each characterised by its particular assemblage of relations, and connected to others both socially and physically.
>
> (Ingold 2000: 145)

This way of thinking about identity formation fits well with a conceptual understanding of how the local and global are often complexly interwoven in people's life journeys. The image of life as a trail or path accounts for both the specificity and porousness of cultural memory, and suggests how multiple attachments to different places are part of the process of personal change and development. Translated into performance, the walk or journey has been used by contemporary devisers to symbolise how different pathways in life might be re-imagined, framed and understood.

This chapter offers an investigation into some of the ways in which performance encourages community participants and audiences to engage with particular locations, sites and settings. It is concerned with the ways in which physical places and sites are framed and re-imagined, and how forms of performance that reference the popular and communitarian have the potential to disrupt the discipline of conventional theatre spaces. It is organised in three parts. The first section examines the symbolism of the walk; the second section explores the performative practices in sites of ecology and leisure, and the third investigates how theatre spaces and community places are used to represent concepts of transition and diaspora. Taken together, they investigate the ways in which devised theatre contributes to interrogating global routes and local roots in places of performance.

Walking the city

The idea that place is recognised experientially through travel and movement has led to performative experiments which cast new light on how places are perceived and understood. The process of reframing and re-imagining place through different performative gestures owes much to the ideas of Situationism, a movement of radical intellectuals and artists centred around Paris in the 1950s and 1960s. The Situationists were critical of the 'society of spectacle' that was developing at the time, in which people apparently satisfied their desires through a capitalist consumption of goods and 'style', but were actually becoming increasingly alienated from their creativity, emotions and the immediacy of their own environment. One response to the isolation of individuals inherent in this social spectacle was to develop a political theory of place and space, with the intention to subvert the ways in which places (specifically urban environments) have become constructed and performed in a society of mass consumerism.

The Situationists developed the concept of psychogeography, a theory which was intended to explore how the psychological effects of the environment might raise people's awareness about the emptiness of their lives. Guy Debord was a founding member of Situationist International, a group of avant-garde artists and intellectuals working in France in the 1950s and 60s who followed the Dadaists by advocating the integration of art and everyday life. This impulse, which has been described in more detail in Chapter Two, aimed to transform society sifted by capitalism into a creative and imaginative space. As part of this visionary project, Debord advocated the '*dérive*', a 'drift' in the form of a walk or journey through the city during which people would:

> drop their usual motives for movement and action, their relations, their work and leisure activities, and let themselves be drawn by the attractions of the terrain and the encounters they find there . . . From the *dérive* point of view cities have a psychological relief.
>
> (Debord 1996: 22)

For Debord, the *dérive* was a playful encounter with the city, a way of reinventing its social meanings and alerting the critical consciousness of participants to their situation by observing the political patterning of everyday life. It was intended as a cultural experiment that would enable people to avoid the psychological seduction inherent in the superficial glamour of the society of spectacle.

The legacy of the Situationists' revolutionary relationship with urban environments can be found in Michel de Certeau's philosophical work, *The Practice of Everyday Life* (1984). The activity of walking, he suggests, has the potential to disrupt the regulatory system of 'place' and transform it into a more optimistic and counter-cultural 'space'. Nick Kaye, writing about site-specific art, recognises the significance of this intellectual shift to contemporary performance:

> The walker can never resolve the multiple and conflicting spaces of the city into the place itself. The walker is thus always in the process of *acting out*, of performing the contingencies of a particular spatial practice, which, although subject to the place, can never wholly realise or be resolved into this underlying order.
>
> (Kaye 2000: 506)

The political impulse of the practice of such walks is, therefore, to disrupt settled orders and hierarchies and to explore new networks of possibility, new symbolisms and ways of being. The process is intentionally incomplete, ambiguous and performative.

The concept of walking as a subversive and transformative spatial practice is evident in the work of a group of contemporary artists–researchers known as Wrights & Sites, who are based in Exeter in England. As well as creating site-specific performances, Wrights & Sites have published a book entitled *An Exeter Mis-Guide* which invites readers to undertake imaginative walks and journeys around the city and to see Exeter as 'an animated art gallery' as a way of 'unbalancing municipal definitions of the city' (www.mis-guide.com). For example, they encourage readers to walk around the busy city on a Saturday before Christmas:

> Allow yourself to be stopped and diverted as often as possible. Accept these delays for whatever they seem to offer you.
>
> (Wrights & Sites 2003: 10)

In terms which invoke Situationism, another suggestion to explore the city is to:

> Go drifting with a child or children. Let the children choose your direction at each junction. Call it 'exploring'. Maybe take a notebook for them to write their thoughts in or for you to record them.
>
> (Wrights & Sites 2003: 40)

By disrupting routines or habitual ways of seeing, the strategy is a way of re-imagining the social order of the city into a more fluid and interactive space. The journeys proposed throughout the book are performative in that they invite people to reflect on the familiar and to observe themselves self-consciously as they play out new roles in different locations in the city. The experience of undertaking Wrights & Sites' walks around Exeter is that of following the instructions of an absent guide. It is an aesthetic strategy that invites participants to interact with the public space of the city privately, as individuals, rather than as part of a collective movement. Packaged to resemble popular tourist guides, the postmodern playfulness of the Wrights & Sites' publication has captured the popular imagination, and the formula has been reproduced for different cities and places as *A Mis-Guide to Anywhere*, launched in London in 2006.

The work of Walk & Squawk, a performance project based in Detroit, USA and South Africa, is built on an explicit policy of social intervention. Collaboration between artists in Africa and the US seeks to develop global understanding through cultural exchange. By collaborating on performative walks, the agenda for the inter-disciplinary Walking Project is stated in the following terms:

> By examining how changing patterns of movement can alter attitudes and perceptions; how people make their own paths; and the influences of culture, geography, language, economics and love, The Walking Project asks how and why people's paths cross and how taking a different path might alter a life.
>
> (www.walksquawk.org)

The participants in Walk & Squawks' *Walking Project*, running from 2003–2006, were members of different community groups, whose contributions were shaped in partnership with professional artists. The methodologies used by the company, such as storytelling, night dances, performance and jamming workshops, are part of the process of mapping how day-to-day activities and decisions shape the course of minds and lives. Walking, in this context, has both a metaphysical and a social dimension, and is specifically designed to encourage both local community involvement and global dialogue. The project is an active exploration of how the routes of the walk and the roots of the people who inhabit the places and spaces visited intersect, and how they are negotiated and represented.

Ecological journeys

Although Situationist-inspired walks have been primarily conceptual-ised as urban experiences, pressing ecological issues and environmental change have forced a reconsideration of how the 'natural' world is exploited as well as how the built environment is experienced. In his discussion of how landscape is perceived, Tim Ingold rejects sharp distinctions between the natural and the artificial, arguing that all places are dependent for their meanings on how people interact with them over time:

> A place owes its character to the experience it affords to those who spend time there – to the sights, sounds and indeed smells that constitute its specific ambience. And these, in turn, depend on the kind of activities in which the inhabitants engage.
>
> (Ingold 2000: 192)

Ingold coined the phrase 'taskscape' to describe the patterns of activities associated with living in different places. The taskscape does not denote a fixed landscape but suggests the network of activities, journeys, pathways and trails that enable people to relate to, and interact with, the world in which they dwell. Ingold's use of the term articulates his advocacy of a cultural ecology that takes account of the layers of symbolism people associate with their environment and their physical engagement with places through the senses. The term also recognises that people have a pragmatic relationship with places in which they carry out the practical activities of everyday life and work. The concept of the taskscape provides a useful theoretical lens through which to read a case study in which performance is used to mediate between the aesthetic and the practical, the symbolic and the everyday, the natural and the artificial.

The Eden Project is a centre for scientific and ecological research and education situated in Cornwall, England. It is a good example of a taskscape, as it models how people's pragmatic, temporal and symbolic relations with the environment might be understood. The Eden Project was established in 2000, with funding from the Millennium Landmark Trust, and has become a highly successful visitors' attraction. Richard Schechner's analysis of the theme park is apposite here; he describes the plethora of restored villages and similar themed amusement parks as 'large environmental theatres' because they offer a place in which 'performances, goods, services, and ideologies are displayed and exchanged' (Schechner 1985: 79). Describing itself as 'a living theatre of plants and people', the Eden Project occupies the site of a former china clay pit, and consists of a large area dominated by huge greenhouses resembling giant golfballs, known as biomes. Indoor biomes are artificially heated to cultivate plants from the humid tropics and from warm temperate climates, while the outdoor biome is an area in which plants grow that can survive in Cornwall.

The vision upon which the Eden Project was built recognises the connectivity of the local and the global in environmental change, described in the following terms by the founder, Tim Smit:

> Many human interests are touched by issues raised at Eden. Take the creation of the soil: the search for solutions to biodiversity loss, erosion, pollution and land degradation is our concern ... Eden should demonstrate the interconnectedness of the plant kingdom with all these elements in the creation of the conditions for life, and by implication

raise awareness that if any of these elements is damaged there will be an impact on the life support system.

(Smit 2001: 302)

Integral to the sustainability of the Eden Project is its commerciality, and it partly depends on visitors for its research programme. Eden, however, has a serious educational intent and this impulse towards recognising the relationship between human action and environmental change is evident throughout its artistic and scientific programming. Despite the invocation of paradise lost implied in the centre's name, Eden does not exploit a nostalgic vision of the past but seeks to represent possible futures.

The experience of visiting Eden, a 'living theatre', is profoundly performative, and it is this quality that means it has the potential to change visitors' attitudes and perceptions. Taking the trail down into the former clay pit, visitors are faced with a series of information boards that illustrate connections between everyday activities (driving, water use and electricity consumption, for example) and damage to the environment. Drawing attention to one's own role in climate change is part of a process of education and awareness-raising which is integral to the Eden Project, and the experience of walking within the biomes is designed to encourage an emotional identification with different global ecologies. The humid tropics biome, for example, offers an imaginative journey into tropical climates, with the damp heat, the texture and colour of the plants, the sounds of flowing water providing visitors with a sensuous and tactile engagement with the actual space of Eden and imagined tropical places. The experience of walking becomes physically tiring in the heat and humidity, and the process of journeying through the space underlines one's own embodied connectedness with the environment.

As a site, the Eden Project compresses global time and space. It is, for example, possible for visitors to cross from the humid tropics where bananas and cocoa grow to the citrus and olive groves of warm temperate climates simply by walking through the restaurant. Woven into the plant structure are artworks and other installations such as recreations of shops and houses, banana bicycles and sugar lorries. Juxtaposed against the living plants, these visual interventions offer a playful way of seeing the 'natural' world and how it is shaped by human activity. The WEEE man is a robotic figure designed by Paul Bonomini, and this typifies the use of wit and visual imagery to make a serious point about environmental change. The sculpture is:

made of scrap electrical and electronic equipment. It weighs 3.3 tonnes
and stands seven metres tall – representing the average amount of
e-products every single one of us throws away over a lifetime.

(www.edenproject.com)

The WEEE man has an educative purpose, to transform public opinion
about electronic waste. The experience of encountering the figure on
the walk through Eden is an act of recognition, enabling visitors to see
the wastefulness of disposing of refrigerators, computer mice, cookers
and other electrical goods.

On summer nights Eden pulses to music, and live bands from
different parts of the world entertain visitors alongside storytellers
and celebratory children's processions. As part of the 2005 *Jungle
Nights*, Eden performers devised a show entitled *The Forgotten Forest*,
a morality play for family audiences which posed questions about
deforestation. Drawing on the structure of traditional fairy stories, the
plot revolved around a greedy king who was tempted to destroy the
rainforest in order to make money, and dramatised the dilemmas faced
by the woodcutters in carrying out his orders. The relationship between
activity and interactivity in environmental issues was demonstrated in
this performance, where children and families offered advice to the
characters in order to change the course of the action. By presenting
this issue for discussion, audiences were invited to challenge the view
that environmental destruction is inevitable, and to take responsibility
for this process of change. The Eden Project's ethos and agenda are
clearly articulated in its artistic work, and it is significant in this context
that the organisation hosted *Africa Calling* (2005), a concert that
featured many African musicians on the same night as the Live 8
concerts were staged across the Western world with predominantly
rich, white musicians.

Ingold's description of taskscape as *activity* and *inter*activity is
particularly apposite in relation to visitors' experience of the Eden
Project, especially as he uses the term to demonstrate the reciprocal
relations between human action and other forms of life. The journey
through the biomes, the artwork and the performances positions
visitors as active participants in an ecological performance and
repositions them as agents for change with responsibility for creating
a sustainable global environment. The aesthetics of space at the Eden
Project troubles oppositions between the local and the global, between
the natural and the artificial, art and science and encourages visitors
to take an imaginative journey to an ethical place of possibilities.

Figure 10.1 The WEEE Man at the Eden Project. Photographer: Ben Foster.
Reproduced by permission of the Eden Project.

Devising diaspora

If life in the twenty-first century is characterised by movement, mobility, border crossings, dislocation and transnational migration, the language of diaspora gains a new currency. The word 'diaspora', as cultural theorist Avtar Brah points out, is associated with both emplacement and displacement from home, and thus raises questions about where home might be located as well as invoking 'images of multiple journeys' (Brah 1996: 181). She argues that contemporary conceptions of community occupy a diasporic space, a site of struggle in which composite identities and multiple emotional identifications are constructed, imagined, narrated and remembered. This section will explore how spatial metaphors associated with home, translocation and diaspora are represented through aesthetics of performance in two contrasting productions. Performance artist Rona Lee devised *The Encircling of a Shadow* (2001) in response to the Cornish coastline and sought to explore images of the Newlyn area as a place of transition. RIFCO is a South Asian theatre company based in Slough, west of London, and its production *The Deranged Marriage* (2004–2006) aimed to celebrate contemporary British Asian culture and experiences. Both performances invited community involvement and, in very different ways, translated metaphors of space and place into tangible artistic forms.

While Rona Lee's work may not conform to conventional definitions of devised theatre as collaboration between a company of performers, *The Encircling of a Shadow* offers a fascinating example of how an individual artist can trouble boundaries between the visual arts and community performance. *The Encircling of a Shadow* was devised in the sense that although it was initially envisioned and curated by an individual artist, it was developed and shaped in response to, and collaboration with, local performers and other community members. *The Encircling of a Shadow* was a series of works that explored the coastline of south Cornwall as a haunted place of transitions, where generations of people have set sail and been reunited. The use of multiple performance spaces and sites reflected the ephemeral quality of the work; a multimedia exhibition installed in an art gallery in Newlyn traced shadows of the place's history, and a community-based outdoor performance held at sunset overlooking the sea at Mount's Bay captured the experience of travel, mobility, work and loss evident in the liminal space of the fishing village. *The Encircling of a Shadow* offers an artistic illustration of Tim Ingold's concept of the 'taskscape' because it charts how the interweaving of social activity, work and 'the normal business of life' is integral to perceptions of landscape and environment (Ingold 2000: 192). Because the work itself was curated and performed in different sites, it also draws attention to distinctions between place and space, and the symbolic values attached to each.

In the white space of the art gallery, Newlyn school artist Walter Langley's *In a Cornish Fishing Village – Departure of the Fleet for the North* (1886) was displayed alongside a list of ninety names of local fishing boats registered in Penzance, about half the fleet. Artist Rona Lee chose to inscribe the wall with the names of boats that had been called after girls or women – Our Margaret, Jackie, Rose, Gemma – thereby emphasising the association between the feminine and home in the minds of the sailors. Each name was evocative of the family ties, friendships and lovers and, although some names belonged to those long dead, many of the boats' namesakes were alive and able to witness the work. Painted on the white gallery walls, these names blended the past with the present, providing a poignant context for the installation in the upstairs gallery. In the upper gallery, the projected image of the shadow of a woman was caught in the beam of a lighthouse lantern, and intermittently mingled and played with the visitors' own shadows on the gallery wall (www.rona-lee.co.uk/encircle.html). The sense of movement and the visitors' engagement with the installation in the gallery suggests, as Tim Ingold describes, that the visual arts have inherently performative qualities, particularly when they invite interaction (Ingold 2000: 198).

The Encircling of a Shadow hinted at the personal and community stories behind the women's names, suggesting histories of location and dislocation, migrancy, colonialism and kinship ties. Names represent both roots and routes, and it was this symbolism that brought together the gallery exhibition with the outdoor performance. By inscribing the women's names on a gallery wall, there was a sense of mapping the names, of releasing them from the privacy of an archive or the domesticity of the family and resituating them, temporarily, in a public space. At sunset on 25 May 2001 on Mounts Bay, volunteers from Porthcurno Submarine Telegraphy Museum used Morse code to signal the women's names out to sea, accompanied by songs performed by members of the Marazion Apollo Male Voice Choir. Capturing moments of transition in performance inscribes them with new meanings, and the act of sending light signals out to sea symbolised the ephemeral quality of living and working in this environment. Edward Casey describes this process as 'the double interleaving of body

Figure 10.2 The Encircling of a Shadow, Newlyn Art Gallery.
Photographer: Steve Tanner.

Reproduced by permission of Steve Tanner.

with place and place with body', in which places are perceived physically
and experienced through movement, as performative representations
(Casey 1998: 238).

The use of both a gallery and an outdoor site in *The Encircling of a
Shadow* project is illustrative of different ways of conceptualising place
and space as developed by de Certeau. The white walls of the gallery
apparently await artistic inscription, suggesting an abstract space,
whereas the more obvious codifications of a coastal village seem heavier
with historical patternings. This piece, however, played on this relationship between space and place, drawing attention to the symbolic,
transitional and ephemeral qualities of both gallery and coastline. The
shadows which haunted the gallery were also present in the beams of
light signalled out to sea, capturing what Marvin Carlson has described
as 'the spatial associations' inherent in the 'narratives of cultural
memory' (Carlson 2003: 136).

By contrast, RIFCO's production *The Deranged Marriage* was
devised for a conventional theatre space and uses the traditions of the
Bollywood musical to tell the story of a British Asian marriage. The
production was first developed in 2004 and revived for a tour of
regional theatres in 2005–2006. The plot revolves around an arranged

marriage between Sona and Rishi, and the narrative is structured around the various rituals associated with Hindu marriage ceremonies. The action pivots around the ladies' sangeet, where the bride and her friends gather to henna their hands and, on this occasion, to get drunk. At the last minute the nervous groom confesses to Sona that he is gay; the bride's widowed mother discovers that the groom's uncle is her long-lost lover and marries him. Emerging from the chaos of events there is a marriage ceremony and, after all, everyone can sing and dance as family honour is restored. Despite the absurdity and playfulness of the Bollywood-inspired plot, the theatrical space is used to locate the audiences as witnesses to, and participants in, a theatrical representation of a British Asian marriage. In some venues, the ticket was in the form of a wedding invitation and 'guests' were encouraged to mingle as samosas and juice were served by in-role actors during the interval. At key moments of crisis, the bride's relatives break the convention of the fourth wall by addressing the audience directly, expressing their embarrassment at sharing their family troubles in front of the town's mayor. Breaking the discipline of the theatrical space, they ask to have photographs taken with the mayor (a member of the audience) as a way of poking gentle fun at the status-seeking qualities of some of the characters. The play is unashamedly celebratory, populist and exhibits all the 'feel-good' factors associated with Bollywood musicals.

The Deranged Marriage articulates the political dimension of place and space because it negotiates between the idea of diasporic communities as a cultural resource for mediating change, and conventional perceptions of the arranged marriage as a marker of cultural stability. By gently subverting and displacing prejudicial views about arranged marriages this production relocates audiences as cultural participants in a more ambiguous and contested space. Much of the material for this production was generated in collaboration with British Asian communities and this research gave the play its spatial and local texture. During the research and development period the director Pravesh Kumar and members of the company worked with British Asian elders as well as culturally mixed groups of young people, and they learnt about the cultural practices of different marriage ceremonies that would be familiar to potential audiences. It was from this research that the idea of some element of audience participation evolved. Company members found that sharing stories with South Asian elders prompted a spontaneous celebration of Punjabi songs and dance, and they decided to capture this spirit of 'home' in performance. They also

Figure 10.3 The Deranged Marriage. Photographer: David Fisher. Writer and
    director: Pravesh Kumar. Sharona Sassoon (Pramila) and Sam
    Vincenti (Rishi).

Reproduced by permission of RIFCO.

wanted to offer some insights into Hindi traditions to non-Asian audience members. The role of Jenny, the English wife of an Asian character, acts as cultural interpreter both by asking questions about the marriage traditions and by voicing some common misconceptions about the social practices of the Punjabi community. At one stage she comments with surprise on the Westernisation of the younger female characters and her line 'I thought you Indian women drank nothing stronger than tea' generally met with robust laughter from British Asian audiences. This response was matched by a moment of frisson when Sona lit a cigarette, with audiences acknowledging that her habit would be met with stern disapproval. Because the production was devised in response to a period of research and development with members of the South Asian community living in Slough, the company was able to anticipate audience response and generate work that invited audiences to recognise the familiarity of cultural convention as well as offering gentle social commentary through playful mimicry.

It is evident that contemporary devised performance has developed innovative ways to explore the different routes and roots of contemporary communities and individuals. The concept of diaspora and the metaphor of the journey offers a way of theorising an alternative to fixed patternings of identity associated with deterministic categorisations of place and ethnicity. Avtar Brah argues that the rigid policing of cultural borders might be eroded and traversed when it is recognised that community identities are 'constituted within the crucible of the materiality of everyday life; in the everyday stories we tell ourselves individually and collectively' (Brah 1996: 183). The interplay between the aesthetic and the everyday, space and place, the local and the global recognises that performers and audiences identify with sites of performance in complex ways. In this light, the performer–audience relationship represents a continual process of negotiating and mapping a sense of location and dislocation. Spatial practices are, therefore, often reconfigured and unfixed in performance, and how place is conceived, lived and perceived becomes redefined.

PART FOUR

Performing Bodies

INTRODUCTION: PERFORMING BODIES

Body and culture

Writing about his practice, Asian performance trainer Tadashi Suzuki notes that 'Culture is the Body' (Suzuki 1995: 155). Suzuki's method stems from the contact made between the feet and the floor, in effect a series of exercises that involves stamping the ground. Through this contact with the earth the performer feels the engagement of their whole lower body and reaches Suzuki's objective 'to make the whole body *speak* even when one keeps silent' (Suzuki 1995: 155). Suzuki's practice extends beyond the notion that the semiotics of the body are able to speak as loudly as the voice. Embedded in his statement that 'Culture is the Body' is another concern regarding the body. For Suzuki, a cultured society is one where notice is taken of the body and it is integrated into the communication systems of that society. Suzuki outlines how much of the development of a progressive nation is due to the body: for example the use of seeing led to the development of the microscope and the telescope and the associated discoveries attached to those two inventions. This final section of *Making a Performance* will examine the way in which notions of the body have affected performance-making practices.

To some degree it is inevitable within the performance practices that everything 'begins and ends in the body' (Schechner 1994: 132). The workshop techniques that underpin devised work stem from investigations undertaken by performers, and whatever the focus of the work, the bodily presence of the performer is never disregarded and is frequently responsible for generating the performative score. But the story of the performer's body is only one dimension of the resonance that the body holds within performance work.

Since the 1970s the body has attracted much discussion from fields such as sociology, anthropology, cultural theory, feminism and, more recently, post-colonialism. The findings of these studies have resulted in an awareness of the importance and diversity of the body. These disciplines have analysed the functions of the metaphor of the body as well as considered how the notion of the body is shaped through cultural practice. Readings of the body have impacted upon the fields of performance, for example in his book *Acting (Re)considered*, practitioner and academic Phillip Zarrilli quotes from anthropologist John Blacking, 'there is no such thing as *the* human body, there are many kinds of body, which are fashioned by the different environments and expectations that societies have of their members' bodies' (Zarrilli 1995: 72). The collection of essays in this book shows a remarkable diversity in how the body is viewed: for example, as a neutral vessel in the ideas of Copeau; a politically shaped tool for Brecht; capable of transgressing gender in the work of Rachel Rosenthal; mirroring the blurring of real and fictitious acts in the work of The Wooster Group; or as the racially distinct bodies of Yellow Earth. The range of these practices shows some ways that culture, economics, biology, sociology and history shape the image of the body.

Body and identity

The chapters that follow unpack how the body is used within devised performance practices. Central to the discussion is the way that phenomenological thinking, such as that of theorist Maurice Merleau-Ponty, emphasises the importance of the lived experience of the body. This notion of the lived body stresses the primacy of the individual identity and experience of each body and favours the importance of physiological impulses over psychological ones. These notions are to be found within many of the following practices discussed here. Companies such as DV8 emphasise the individuality and identity of each differing body and celebrate that difference. The first chapter in this section explores how phenomenological approaches can be used in physical performance and concludes by examining how the notion of the extreme body is expressed within performance work.

More recent scientific and technological developments have allowed the development of virtual bodies which simulate living bodies. The existence of these remodelled bodies complicates Merleau-Ponty's emphasis on the importance of lived experience by confusing what we see as reality (which is the real body? which is the simulated one?) and what the experience of actuality is like (what is the difference between a simulated experience and a real one?). The final chapter, 'Virtual Bodies', looks at how the body is refashioned through both medical and mediatised methods. Building on an examination of modernist avant-garde interests in the mechanical, the chapter looks first at how technological developments in body reshaping have created a series of performative pieces that have cosmetically altered the body. The chapter later reflects on how virtual bodies have been created through technologically driven practices, and analyses the effect of the creation of 'non-live' events on the status of performance.

Taken together, these two chapters argue for the centrality of the body in current performative practices. The importance of the body due to advances in the training of the body and technological developments, is becoming increasingly dominant with devised theatre. This is partly because the nature of the work allows for such rich analysis, for as Elisabeth Grosz notes, 'it is only very recently that philosophical and feminist theory have developed terms complicated enough to do justice to the rich (and aporetically cultural and individual) complexity of bodies' (Grosz 1995: 2). While these chapters investigate and celebrate the body, they also question the idea of an empirical sense of the body. As Grosz's quotation implies, contemporary bodies are represented in devised performance through a dual celebration of the diversity of cultural bodies and the individuality of each particular corpus.

ELEVEN

THE SPEAKING BODY

Physical Theatres

Roots of Somatic Practice

Contemporary physical practices have been shaped by a number of different generic strands. Most notable among these are the influences of early twentieth-century dance, mime, theatre and circus practices. Scholar Elizabeth Dempster analyses the development of modern dance and suggests that traditional structures of movement were redefined at the beginning of the twentieth century to create 'new languages of physical expression' (Dempster 1998: 223). This expression was one which shunned the uniformity of balletic movement; as Dempster notes, dancers such as Isadora Duncan, Löie Fuller, Ruth St Denis and later Mary Wigman, Martha Graham and Doris Humphrey, though often inspired by ancient forms of dance, 'inherited no practice: the techniques and the choreographic forms they developed were maps and reflections of the possibilities and propensities of their own originating bodies' (Dempster 1998: 223). This emphasis on personal expression forms a distinctive feature of much devised physical work. It is often, though, and such is the case of the early innovators cited here, that the physical practices developed are inspired by other influences such as social, political or anthropological concerns. For example, the work of early modern dancers was created as a reaction to the climate of post-war conditions.

Lloyd Newson, director of the British physical theatre company DV8 founded in 1986, while drawing on the practices of Pina Bausch, engenders a rehearsal situation whereby the dancers question the processes and discover their own improvisational material. Through drawing upon the dancers' individual expression these practices subscribe to the notion of the 'experienced body', whereby the body is seen to contain a lived history. This concept of the importance of the 'lived-in' body finds resonance with the philosophical ideas of mid-twentieth-century thinker Maurice Merleau-Ponty. He states that '[o]ur own body is in the world as the heart is in the organism: it keeps the visible spectacle constantly alive' (Merleau-Ponty 2002: 235). Merleau-Ponty advocates the importance of the body in experiencing the world: 'by thus remaking contact with the body and with the world, we shall also rediscover ourself, since, perceiving as we do with our body, the body is a natural self and, as it were, the subject of perception' (Merleau-Ponty 2002: 239). This perceiving and experiencing body is central to the concerns of many physical performance-makers, and leads to an emphasis on the importance of the process of creating work rather than the product. This is embodied within much of the performance work identified within this chapter.

Lecturer and practitioner Dymphna Callery suggests that physical performance started as part of a shift away from Stanislavskian approaches to actor training and towards devising performance 'through the body' (Callery 2001: 4). Although this observation negates the impact of Stanislavsky's later work on physical actions, it identifies a paradigmatic shift engendered by the approaches of drama practitioners such as Grotowski, Meyerhold and Chaikin. Each of them saw the importance of somatic approaches. In fact, Lloyd Newson suggests that the concept of physical theatre originated with Grotowski's work (Newson 1997: 2). Certainly Grotowski's emphasis on the expressivity of the performer's body places his praxis as central to the development of a more somatically based theatre. His theatre treatise *Towards a Poor Theatre* sets out clearly that 'we consider the personal and scenic technique of the actor as the core of theatre art' (Grotowksi 1968: 15). This emphasis on the training of the performer through psychophysical responses, and the creation of a theatre that rested on the encounter between performer and spectator, rather than scenic devices, led to a new emphasis within theatre. The philosophical and cultural shifts responsible for creating this practice have been outlined in Chapter Three.

The rise of a physically based theatre also owes much to the twentieth-century development of the genre of mime. Though traditions of non-verbal entertainment can be found throughout Greek, Roman and medieval theatres, and the utilisation of mime techniques can be seen further in sixteenth-century commedia dell'arte, it is the French director and teacher Jacques Copeau who can be credited with

extending the focus on the somatic body. Copeau's insights focussed
on the use of the neutral body, which is of course a somewhat para-
doxical notion since it is difficult for anyone to lose their physical
idiosyncrasies. As Eldredge and Huston note of Copeau, '[t]he pursuit
of simplicity made him eliminate distractions, to create the still
ground against which a movement or a form could be seen' (Eldredge
and Huston 1995: 121). Copeau's legacy can be seen in the work of the
quartet of French mimes: Decroux (his pupil), Marceau, Barrault and
Lecoq. Marceau engaged in traditional white-face mime which was
totally silent and undertook what Kipnis defines as 'the art of recreating
the world by moving and positioning the human body' (Kipnis 1974:
4–5). Meanwhile Decroux pioneered a corporeal mime in which he
invoked the image of Prometheus, and strived for the body to be
trained in order to execute exercises with purity – often stopping mid-
performance to re-execute a sequence if it had been incorrectly
performed. As Sklar remarks, '[l]ike Prometheus chained to the cliff
. . . the Corporeal Mime actor expresses the contradiction between
what we are and what we would like to be' (Sklar 1995: 110). Both
Marceau and Decroux evoked a system of representation in which the
body was responsible for the semiotic exchange with the audience.
Writing on Lecoq's training methods, Simon Murray notes the way
that both Barrault and Lecoq 'chose to inhabit a more expansive
territory in which mime was redefined' (Murray 2003: 29). For Lecoq
this redefinition, produced through his inclusion of improvisation
workshops *autocaurs*, is evidenced in the work of his pupils, such
as Ariane Mnouchkine with her creative collective, Theatre de
Complicité's physical approach to text, and Steven Berkoff's mimetic
inspired modernday myths. As Murray points out, the redefinition
that Lecoq undertook was to make a 'major contribution to the rise of
. . . what is called "physical theatre"' (Murray 2003: 158).

A further reason why practitioners focus on the body within
performance is as a celebration of the physical capabilities of the body;
the athleticism of the body. As Sally Banes observes, a major strand
of analytic postmodern dance showcased the athletic body (Banes 1987:
xxi); the influence of this preoccupation was not limited to dance.
Performance created within this realm celebrates the physical ability
of the body through displaying the agility, flexibility, power and stamina
of the performer's body. Such performances often highlight a difference between the physical capability and limitations of the body;
a Promethean dilemma. For example, if a performer undertakes a very
dexterous activity, the audience is at the same time aware of the skill

and the limitations (it can't be repeated endlessly without exhausting the performer; the activity cannot be achieved consistently or with greater skill than has been initially shown). This concept of the disparity of the athletic body is one that has found resonance within post-modern performance companies such as Forced Entertainment and The Wooster Group. In Forced Entertainment's *Emmanuelle Enchanted* (1992) the performers reveal both the athleticism and frailty of the body. Each performer runs on the spot while holding various signs which label the persona they represent (for example, 'A BLOKE WHO'S BEEN SHOT', 'A GIRL WITH BOY'S EYES', 'SIGMUND FREUD'). But as the running progresses, the initial celebration of pace and energy gives way to physical exhaustion, and the audience witnesses the performers fight to keep performing: the tired, sweating bodies show the limits of such athleticism. A glimpse of this frailty is also central to the representation of persona within performance pieces like this. As the actor tires, the audience loses a sense of watching a rehearsed performance and instead sees the real characteristics of the actor themselves – their exhausted, unobliging body attempting to undergo a task.

Though Banes observes that this celebration of the athletic body is linked to postmodern dance of the 1980s, the notion is also to be found within the circus tradition. Here the physical virtuosity of the body celebrated in eighteenth-century circus and vaudeville acts has continued to be effective in recent 'new circus' performances. New circus developed in the late 1980s and is identified by Peta Tait as differing from traditional circus in that it promotes an emotional tone and is thus 'closer to theatre in its aesthetic and thematic purpose and unity' (Tait 2005: 120). Tait cites examples such as that of the archaic intimidation of the 1990s' shows by Archaos, or the romantic exuberance of Cirque du Soleil. However, the tradition of physical performance continued by new circus companies stretches beyond that of a display of athleticism; it also raises issues concerning the representation of the body. As Tait notes, '[c]ircus performance presents artistic and physical displays of skilful action by highly rehearsed bodies that also perfume cultural ideas: of identity, spectacle, danger, transgression – in sum, of circus' (Tait 2005: 6).

The presentation of the body within a circus tradition not only celebrates the potential of the body, but also disrupts notions of normalness. Circus performers show the margins of the capabilities of the body and this emphasises the corpus as freakish. This sense of freakishness can include over-extended flexibility, highly developed

strength, and extreme balance and coordination. But often the development of these attributes is in a manner that unhinges natural somatic
codes. As Tait observes, '[t]here is also an untold cultural history of
bodies that encompasses the light gracefulness of males and the steely
muscular strength of females' (Tait 2005: 1). In other words typical
gender attributes are reversed within circus. The circus practices display
the transgressive nature of bodies that are developed to the margins
of possibility. In having acts such as lithe male jugglers or women
acrobats with highly developed strength an act of transgression occurs.
The normal expectations for gender aesthetics are reinscribed. The
margins of what is regarded as masculinity and femininity are broken
and new codes invented.

The notion of a reinscribed body is also present within contemporary practices that seek to highlight the importance of different
bodies. For example, Yellow Earth, a London-based company for Asian
performers, seeks to highlight the East Asian body. Rather than
blending their bodies into a European company, they seek to emphasise
the separate nature of ethnic difference. For example in 2005 they
produced a version of Hans Christian Andersen's *The Nightingale* that
used the setting of the Emperor of China's court as a context through
which to foreground an idiom of Chinese physical styles. In 2006 their
version of Shakespeare's *King Lear* was performed in both Mandarin
and English. They relocated Lear's court to Shanghai and through the
use of aerial practices sought to reveal 'the miscommunication that
arises from migration and Lear's search for Taoist enlightenment'
(http://yellowearth.org). The specific difference of the bodies is used
here to highlight issues which pertain to migrant communities.

This chapter has hitherto largely avoided the term 'physical theatre',
instead choosing to analyse how aspects of a broader paradigm of
physical performance developed within contemporary practice. This
has been a deliberate ploy since there is much disagreement about the
categorisation and terminology involved in defining physical theatre.
Dymphna Callery argues that '[t]he characteristics of the genre are
many and varied. Indeed the term is virtually impossible to define'
(Callery 2001: 4). Her attempts to categorise the genre reveal the
difficulties in undertaking such an exercise. Callery lists five factors that
identify the genre: the actor as creator; collaborative working methods;
the work is somatically led; an open actor-audience relationship; and
importance of live-ness to the work. It is easy to see how many of these
criteria can be applied to work which falls outside the realm of physical
theatre, or indeed exclude other work that should be included in the

corpus. (Where, for example, does DV8's film work sit? Is it excluded because it isn't live?) Instead this chapter advocates that the transection of a number of practices within the genres of dance, theatre, mime and circus at the end of the twentieth century led to the development of a recognisable genre of physically based performance. Though these performances are identified here as being of a physical nature, the practices and processes that companies utilise are often very disparate and draw upon a range of strategies including choreographic impetus, improvisations and visual practices.

This chapter examines three facets of physical performance. First, it explores the formation of connections between body and mind; in other words, how a holistic sense of the body is achieved. Second, it examines the emphasis on the body as the prime centre for knowledge; an investigation of the experiencing body which shapes both the process and product of performance. Third, it looks at the extraordinary body, the manner in which everydayness can be transcended by pushing the body beyond normal expectation so that new forms of meaning can be generated.

The inside body

In examining the use of the body within physical performance it is helpful to look to at critical analysis undertaken by Elizabeth Grosz. Her book *Volatile Bodies: Towards a Corporeal Feminism* is divided into two major approaches: those that prioritise the 'inside out' or those that stem from the 'outside in'. In order to examine the notion of 'inside out', Grosz utilises approaches taken from psychoanalysis, neurophysiology and phenomenology. While the division between inside and outside approaches forms the organisation of the book, she is aware of the limitations that such a dualistic stance may take (and indeed the historical limitations of the philosophy instigated by Descartes). She wisely advocates that 'different conceptual frameworks must also be devised to be able to talk of the body outside or in excess of binary pairs' (Grosz 1994: 24). In order to achieve this she creates a third approach in which she suggests how an investigation into the sexed body can avoid mere binary opposition. Drawing on the work of philosopher Baruch Spinoza, Grosz notes the importance of the belief in the integrated body: 'Spinoza is committed to the notion of the body as total and holistic, a completed and integrated system' (Grosz 1994: 13). Indeed, Grosz investigates how the sense of a whole body image is of paramount importance to human experience.

This thesis is supported by neurological evidence which provides further examples of the way in which the body imagines itself as whole. For example, patients who suffer amputations often report having sensations emanate from their missing limb; a type of phantom limb is imagined in order to fulfil the patient's image of their unified body. The maintenance of their body image as a whole entity is psychologically imprinted within their mind. This example shows a fundamental connection between physiognomy and psychology.

The notion of the holistic, unified body has shaped much physical performance practice. This is evidenced by the number of practitioners who have looked to Eastern theatre and martial arts practices in order to establish body–mind connections. Many twentieth-century directors such as Grotowski, Copeau and Meyerhold found much of use within Eastern theatre practices. And this fascination has continued well into the twenty-first century, through the work of practitioners like Phillip Zarrilli and Eugenio Barba. Odin Teatret formed by Barba in 1964 and based in Denmark has travelled to Europe, South America and Asia. Writing in his seminal book *Beyond Floating Islands*, Barba advises the actor that '[w]hatever you do, do it with your whole self' (Barba 1986: 52). Speaking specifically of the influence of Indian Kathakali, Barba notes how the importance of the exercises for his actors was not in reproducing the physical skill of the dancers, but in developing the 'personal attitude' of the actor through emotional and logical training (Barba 1986: 58). In other words, through utilising the training of Eastern theatre, Barba found that actors were able to reach a body–mind integration.

The emphasis on the inner body is important to the work of the Joe Goode Performance Group, a dance and installation company founded in San Francisco in 1986. The focus of the company is to make dances on 'human scales'; by this choreographer Goode means locating the 'unglamorized body', the vulnerable, intimate sense of being (www. joegoode.org). He achieves this by examining people who operate beyond the mainstream, and creating characters who live on the margins of society for his dance theatre pieces. Goode reports that the inner body is also activated by bringing together 'telling with the body (where I have been, where does my longing reside) with that of the voice (this is how I see the world)' (www.joegoode.org). Between 2003 and 2005 the company created a triptych of pieces exploring the inner lives of ordinary people, and how the external projection of these can seem so unimportant. The tri-part exploration began with *Folk* in 2003, which looked at rural existence, followed by *grace* (2004) which examined the inner mind, while *Hometown* (2005), a multimedia work, used Bay area teenagers to explore urban life. As critic Ann Murphy observes, 'Goode makes theatre that shows our surfaces while targeting our souls' (Murphy 2004: 1).

In *grace* (2004) the company presents a collection of moments of 'small awakenings notable for their insignificance' (Murphy 2004: 2). One such moment is that of an obsessive housewife who worries over crumbs being dropped on the floor, and nags her husband to squeeze the cleaning sponge thoroughly, only to glimpse a fleeting image of another woman moving gracefully slowly outside her window. Knotted up with jealousy, she declares, 'If I walked like her, wouldn't it hurt? Wouldn't I cry? Wouldn't I turn into dirt, or sand, or just die?'. The bringing together of text, movement and image are accomplished with a 'Zen-like economy' (Murphy 2004: 3). The observation in this review is apt, for Goode's style is born of his interest in Buddhist mediation – the bringing together of body and mind in this manner allows him to create works like *grace*. This is reflected in Goode's statement about the piece: 'I prefer to think of it as an absence, an empty space that opens up inside of us and let's [*sic*] us see nakedly, clearly' (www.joegoode.org). Indeed, this is a facet of his work that is notable from earlier performances. In *What the Body Knows* (2001), a dancer holds a bowl of breakfast cereal while his partner, sitting across the table, admits that her real hunger is for love. The two then escape into a fantasy-like moment in which they enact, through dance and acrobatic forms, a breath-taking duet; at moments they flit dangerously across the table, at others the dancers execute cleverly choreographed lifts and seem to hang in the air. These dance theatre pieces offer an insight into the inner lives of the characters created on stage for the audience and simultaneously provide an escape for Goode through his creation of the work. Writing on the company's website he confesses that:

> The dance theater pieces that I make are literally places I can go. Each one is a place of solace, a respite from the isolation and the feeling that I'm a disengaged observer. When I'm making art I am engaged. I am busy in the laboratory blending language and movement, alchemizing human gestures into dance, I forget that I'm outside and so I'm not.
>
> (www.joegoode.org)

This bringing together of the inside and the outside occurs through two processes. The first of these is through the exploration of the characterisations that take place in rehearsals. Though Goode presents the dancers with a 'physical score' of the performance (based on vignettes tried out in workshops), he recounts that a later stage of the process involves the actors investigating their characterisations so that 'a whole set of movements and relationships unfold and I use these to develop the text' – a device which allows the text to emerge 'out of the actor's own being' (www.joegoode.org). The second part of co-joining inside and outside concerns occurs when Goode crafts together the inner worlds that his company portrays with the outside environment as he sees it. In this manner, internal and external resources are joined.

The living body

The approaches taken by Lloyd Newson's 'physical theatre' company DV8 reflect Merleau-Ponty's notion of the experiencing body. This British company was named to reflect both the company's interest in video and film (Dance and Video 8) and, through the pun on 'deviate', its interest in resistant politics which underlies much of its work. Through investigating what Grosz refers to as the 'lived body', the company is able to draw upon the individual identities of the dancers in order to explore the relationship with the world. As Grosz points out, Merleau-Ponty's treatment of the body suggests:

> It is the condition and context through which I am able to have relations to objects. It is both immanent and transcendent. Insofar as I live the body, it is a phenomenon experienced by me and thus provides the very horizon and perspectival point which places me in the world and makes relations between me, other objects, and other subjects possible.
>
> (Grosz 1994: 86)

In this light, the body is a product of social and historical modes; it is able to both read and respond to the environment around it. Consequently this makes physical forms of representation an ideal mode through which to comment on and shape the world around us.

Newson deliberately works with dancers whose bodies are experienced and have histories. For example, *Bound to Please* (1997) included seventy-year-old Diana Payne-Myers in order to challenge the sense of uniformity which is inherent within much dance (expressed through the ideal of a corps de ballet). Indeed, much of Newson's work draws upon the notion of Merleau-Ponty's experienced body. It is through this that DV8 is able to explore contemporary issues and connect to the genuine concerns that the audience holds. In capturing a sense of the experienced body on stage, Newson asks that rather than creating beautiful shapes on stage, his dancers reveal and share something of their own identities.

The processes used by DV8 involve advance preparation and research as well as improvisation by the performers. Newson begins the research periods long before a work is shown publicly; for example, with *Enter Achilles* (1995) the initial stages were conducted two years in advance of the opening piece. Prior to the rehearsal period, Newson develops a structure for the piece (this is often done alongside one of the dancers) and collaborates with the set designer to build the set in advance so that the performers can live on it from the first day of rehearsal. The rehearsals are collaborative with Newson acting as a facilitator to enable the structure or 'dramaturgy' to be tested. In *Enter Achilles*, an examination of heterosexual male roles, each of the eight performers led a workshop and participated in research trips to pubs, clubs, strip joints and sex shops. Newson reveals, though, that the eventual starting point came one evening after rehearsal when the cast went to a pub and realised their communal identity actually arose from the fact they all drank pints of beer.

The obsession with the identity of the body is explored in *Just for Show* (2005). Here the company uses the format of the end-of-the-pier variety show and music videos to reveal modernday preoccupations with body image. A woman is pushed on stage in a supermarket trolley by a group of men, giving the impression that bodies can be bought from a shelf; bodies are also manipulated through yogic and gymnastic tricks, and often a dancer uses virtuoso acts to ensure that his or her body receives more attention from the spectators than their stage mate. At other moments bodies are projected onto so that their identity is changed, or shown to be completely fake with pretend designer-wear strapped onto the front of the body to create a façade, which is revealed as the dancer walks offstage with her back to the audience. Throughout the piece bodies are put on display; they are often dressed and redressed and, as Lyn Gardner remarks, this piece:

> constantly gives us little glimpses of what happens when the fourth wall is breached, the mask begins to slip and the veneer loses its gloss. It knows that illusion is a way of hiding the empty heart beneath and that

we behave like gaudy, glamorous butterflies because deep down we
realise we are no more than a handful of dust.

(Gardner 2005)

Just for Show shows the disparity between the external image and the
inner vulnerability of the body, and in doing this reveals the preoccupation of the living body with its image.

The extraordinary body

A number of physical performance practices are concerned not with
the inner identity and notion of the responsive bodies of the preceding
two sections, but with the way that ideas can be inscribed onto the
body. For Elizabeth Grosz this difference in attitude divides a sense of
the 'inside out' body and the 'outside in' body. The circus body
described in the introduction to this chapter provides an example
of the external, extraordinary body. It is a body that celebrates
the extraordinary and thereby separates itself from the normal, and in
doing so reveals the inscriptions placed by society that determine the
notion of 'normalness'. This is a point that is often expressed by
companies that are dedicated to the expression of racial difference, such
as the Dance Theatre of Harlem or Phoenix Dance in England. Foucault
in *Discipline and Punish* remarks how 'the body is . . . directly involved
in a political field: power relations have an immediate hold upon it;
they invest it, mark it, train it, torture it, force it to carry out tasks, to
perform ceremonies, to emit signs' (Foucault 1991: 26). Foucault
examines the way that power is exerted upon the body; in order to
punish crime, for example, a prisoner is incarcerated in jail and the
body is excluded from freely moving in society. In Foucault's example
bodies are identified as either ordinary (those that live among other
citizens) and extraordinary (those locked away in confined cells).

The intermixing of everyday normalness with the extraordinary is
a technique frequently used by Chicago-based performance collective, Goat Island. Formed in 1987, the company draws on dance,
theatre and visual arts practices and integrates both the ordinary and
extraordinary. It states on its website that 'we perform a personal
vocabulary of movement, both dance-like and pedestrian, that often
makes extreme demands on the audience' (www.goatislandperformance.
org). This notion was seen most effectively in its piece *The Sea and
Poison* (1998), where the company set out to discover the effects of
poison on the body. The impetus for the piece came during the tour

Figure 11.1 DV8: *Just for Show*. The identity of the body is altered through the projection of images. Photographer: Jane Joyce.

Reproduced by permission of DV8 Physical Theatre.

of their previous work when a company member was bitten by an insect in the Grand Canyon and experienced his whole arm go stiff; after six hours of a sweaty hard climb out of the canyon, the poison had been driven out. Other research into poisons within the body led the company to examine ritual dances such as the Tarantella performed in Italy to eradicate the poison of the tarantula spider and the choreographic epidemics called Saint Vitus' Dance experienced during famine in Italy. The company's work involved gathering a series of stories about poison and infection, and a book of diagrams of Scottish dances found when on tour to Glasgow. These disparate starting points reflect the eclectic research process undertaken by the company. Its methods are derived from visual arts practices where materials are selected by chance.

Goat Island's devising period usually lasts eighteen to twenty-four months during which time the collected material is investigated. For example, with *The Sea and Poison* one task undertaken was to create an impossible dance constructed from:

> a series of unperformable individual movements linked together by endlessly complex patterns and formulas, which challenge the limits of human ability, and as dance hover somewhere between musical composition and the clumsy marathon dance competitions of American depression years.
>
> (www.goatislandperformance.org)

Already embedded in the process was a sense of the ordinary (dance movements that can possibly be performed and the aesthetic of dance as graceful) set against the extraordinary (impossible combinations of steps; the clumsiness of marathon dancing). Sarah Jane Bailes notes how in rehearsal the company works from personal narrative, documentary footage, found images, observed and copied gestures, and fragments of text to create a network of associations (Bailes 2001: 3). This collection of material is one that frequently juxtaposes the everyday with that of the extraordinary. For example, at the beginning of *The Sea and Poison*, the empty space that contains the performance is soon filled by the performers engaging in repetitive jumping movements and gasping for breath to continue the arduous physical task. Although the jumping is an everyday action, its repetition becomes extraordinary and pushes beyond the limits of normality. Sections deal with deformity and devastation. White dust – like the fallout from a nuclear or chemical war – falls down onto bodies that become instantly aged and the performers enact frog-like movements that suggest mutations have occurred. In these moments a strangeness is signalled and the body is shown to be set aside from everydayness.

An engagement with the extraordinary body can be witnessed in the work of British Dance company CandoCo. This company was formed in London in 1991 and integrates both able and non-able bodied dancers. The company performs works commissioned from a range of choreographers and performance-makers so that the repertoire spreads from contemporary dance to physical theatre pieces, incorporating work that is created by the choreographer in a traditional manner and that which is collectively workshopped. In 2001 choreographer

Javier de Frutos worked with the company to make a piece based on a Tennessee Williams short story about a one-armed hustler who is condemned to death. De Frutos took the title for the piece, *I Hastened Through My Death Scene to Catch Your Last Act* (2001), from the words of Sarah Bernhardt (an amputee) to another actor. The image of the hustler is made by displaying the torso of a man on a box (built around his wheelchair). His muscular torso (developed from propelling his wheelchair) reflects the irony of his body; it is a doubly 'extraordinary' torso, first for its fine muscularity, and second for its location within a wheelchair.

Writing about another piece within CandoCo's 1991 programme, Jann Parry sees the company's work as providing a metaphor for dance. Doug Elkins' *Sunbyrne* draws on seaside and maritime imagery. Parry notes that Welly O'Brien sails though the air like a fish in water; only when she lands is it apparent that the dancer cannot

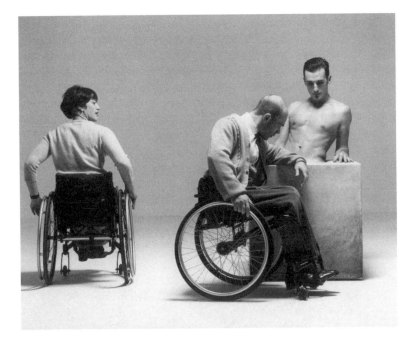

Figure 11.2 CandoCo: I Hastened Through my Death Scene to Catch your Last Act. The contrast between the musculature of the upper torso and the hidden wheelchair is striking.

walk. Parry suggests that this image of 'transfiguration' is what marks out the bodies of the dancers within Can*do*Co (Parry 2001). The presence of able and non-able bodies alongside each other on stage serves to trouble essential notions of identity and physical ability. As Judith Mackrell notes of the company's work: 'Can*do*Co reinvented the boundaries of dance by proving that virtuosity wasn't confined to the able bodied' (www.candoco.co.uk). This work shows how bodies can be transformed from seemingly limited to the unlimitless.

In conclusion, the development of physically based practices can be seen to stem from the collision of a number of performative practices. In focussing upon the body a number of issues are foregrounded; among these are the questions of identity, of the experience of the body, its fusion with the mind and the manner in which bodies are transgressive. Such transgressions occur when the everyday body is pushed beyond the usual limits. It is in this space that many interesting articulations can be discovered.

TWELVE

VIRTUAL BODIES

Multimedia performance

The late twentieth and early twenty-first centuries have seen a rise in performance that draws on and incorporates technologies that were new in the period. 'Multimedia' performance has become recognised as a distinct genre of work and companies such as The Builder's Association from New York are renowned for performances that blend live action, film, TV and computer-generated imagery. Such work is seen to be experimental, questioning the boundaries of performance practice and opening up new possibilities for staging and reception. This chapter explores work that interweaves technology and performance and examines the problems and possibilities that are inherent in this form of practice.

Technological performance can be traced back through the modernist avant-garde, who sought to exploit contemporary technology to enhance their performance work. The Futurists were particularly excited by the technological innovation that they witnessed within the early part of the twentieth century. They perceived the application of technology to performance as a vehicle for their radical artistic agenda which challenged bourgeois, Romantic theatre. The first Futurist manifesto outlines a vision of a new aesthetic:

> We will sing of the vibrant nightly fervour of arsenals and shipyards blazing with violent electric moons; greedy railway stations that devour smoke-plumed serpents; factories hung on clouds by the crooked lines of their smoke.
>
> (Apollonio 1973: 22)

Futurist innovations in performance both employed and emulated technology. Russolo's *Art of Noises* involved 'noise instruments' which were essentially mechanised boxes designed to simulate sounds such as the rumble of trains and trams and the roar of a crowd. While the *Art of Noises* sought to mechanise music, other Futurist experimentation focussed on the mechanisation of movement. Futurist ballets were performed by mechanical puppets and moving scenery and, where human performers were involved, their movements were conceived as robotic. For example, Marinetti advised that, for the *Dance of the Aviatrix*, the dancer's body should resemble the 'successive efforts of a plane trying to take off' (quoted in Goldberg 1995: 24). The Russian Futurist Foregger developed a new system of training for mechanical performance. He stated that 'we view the dancer's body as a machine and the volitional muscles as the machinist' (quoted in Goldberg 1995: 9). Meyerhold's biomechanics was another model of actor training which started from the principles of tailoring movement. Meyerhold's experiments in theatre reflected the theory of prototypal management consultant Taylor who proposed streamlining on the factory floor in the belief that greater productivity and effectiveness could be achieved through the elimination of all unnecessary movements by the worker (1911). Biomechanics can be seen to be an expression of a new attitude to the body as machine where energy flows are released and controlled for maximum efficacy. This, in turn, led to new forms of technologised performance practice which interacted with contemporary culture. Brecht, drawing on Piscator's employment of documentary film within his radical theatre practice, stated that film was a 'new gigantic actor that helped to narrate events' (quoted in Willett 1978: 78). Brecht embraced the new technology and was enthused by possibilities that film afforded in terms of being able to show events happening simultaneously in different places at the same time. Brecht followed Meyerhold by employing the cinematic terminology 'montage' to describe his epic theatre.

Many contemporary artists continue to be excited about the interface of human and machine in performance and the technological revolution of the late twentieth and early twenty-first centuries has provided a wealth of new tools for experimentation, particularly in relation to computing and electronics. Contemporary practice has seen a rise in multimedia performance that employs media such as film, digital art and virtual reality and their combination has often resulted in a critical exploration of form and content. In particular, work that incorporates new media brings into focus the ontology of theatre, which emphasises its liveness. Auslander has drawn attention to the question as to whether, if material within a production is prerecorded or virtual, a production may be considered a live performance. Auslander polarises theatre and the mass media and highlights the ephemeral nature of theatre and the importance of 'nowness' in live performance in contrast with the recorded and commodified nature of the mass media. Live performance places an emphasis on the relationship between the audience and the performer within the theatrical space. When elements of the performance are mediated through technology, the dynamics of this relationship can certainly be seen to shift. Performance theorist Jon McKenzie in his book *Perform or Else* identifies technological innovations in performance practice as a 'rebooting of the human performance paradigm' (McKenzie 1994: 90). This pioneering performance paradigm, with its range of technological tools, has the potential to explore aspects of performance practice in innovative ways that raise fresh questions about form and function. In his exploration of corporeality in contemporary performance, Henry Daniel suggests that the conscious application of technology within performance brings about a process of 're-cognition' which encourages the viewer to rethink their relationship to both the performance work and the technology itself (Daniel 2000: 68).

Multimedia activity offers a wealth of opportunities to expand artistic practice. It can be a truly experimental forum where artists are able to manipulate and re-present reality through sophisticated simulation. Innovations such as 'intelligent lighting', which can be programmed to respond to the movement of a performer's body, for example, enable performance-makers to explore their relationship with the performance space. Live video links that connect a network of performance spaces can also interrogate the nature of presence itself. Practitioners have also used technology to experiment with time and to disrupt the normal distinctions of past, present and future through techniques such as repetition and montage. Multimedia performance, therefore, both troubles and enhances the ontology of performance. This chapter seeks to examine the ways in which technology has affected the nature of performance in the twenty-first century, particularly in terms of the relationship between the visceral and the virtual, the process of simulation and the issue of interactivity.

The visceral and the virtual

Developments in contemporary performance practice have led to specialist journals like *Body, Space and Technology* that consider the interrelationship between technology and the flesh. The interaction between the visceral and the virtual remains a fundamental aspect within multimedia performance, in terms of both creation and reception. Despite technological advances and the new creative possibilities they engender, the body remains a fundamental aspect within the performance event. Birringer notes that:

> The crucial limit or out-line in the theatre . . . is, the actor's body – the source of action, the place of articulation, where language, history, the world outside [bodiliness] is incorporated, where something will be shown that the spectator can perceive in reciprocal relation to the scale of proportion offered by the body.
>
> (Birringer 1985: 228)

Even within the frame of a multimedia performance Birringer suggests that the performer's body remains an important nexus of signification and point of connection for the audience. Incorporating technology within performance does, however, offer up new possibilities for the representation and reception of the performer's body. In his examination of contemporary performance practice Causey outlines the prospect that 'the body of the performer is extended, challenged and reconfigured through technology' (Birringer 1985: 4). Within multimedia performance a body may be mediated through TV screens or via a web-site rather than existing as a visceral presence. This reconfiguration of the body demands adaptations in the decoding of performance and critics have taken up the notion of the cyborg as a point of reference when examining what has been termed 'digital flesh'. Feminist theorist Donna Haraway's cyborg manifesto suggests that the cyborg is 'a cybernetic organism, a hybrid of machine and organism, a creature of social reality as well as a creature of fiction' (Haraway 1991: 149). The cyborg can be understood as a metaphor as well as a living entity in that it articulates the blending of fact and fiction as well as flesh and machine that occurs in multimedia performance. This section will address the work of practitioners who are exploring the limits of the body within performance and consider how their hybrid, cyborg practice opens up the discussion of the relationship between the visceral and the virtual in multimedia performance.

Orlan is a French 'carnal artist' who works with the technology of cosmetic surgery. Her most celebrated project, *The Reincarnation of Saint Orlan*, was launched on 30 May 1990. Since that date Orlan has undergone nine surgical procedures – ranging from liposuction to facial implants – with a tenth operation mooted for an unknown future date. Orlan's project is centred on the interface between the visceral and the virtual as her series of surgeries are intended to reconstruct her own face in the likeness of representations of the feminine taken from celebrated works of art. The template for this work is a computer-generated image which Orlan constructed at the outset that melded iconographic features such as the forehead of the Mona Lisa, the mouth of Moreau's Europa and the eyes of Gerard's Psyche.

Orlan's work mimics both the form and content of cosmetic surgical practice and documents the physical changes her body undergoes. For forty-one days after the seventh operation-performance (until her face was completely healed), an installation was mounted in the Centre Georges Pompidou, Paris. Each day a photograph of Orlan, in her bruised, post-operative state, was taken and mounted in the gallery above one of Orlan's computer-generated images of idealised beauty. The intention behind this exhibition was, Orlan said, to explore 'a comparison between the self-portrait made by the computing machine and the self-portrait made by the body-machine' (Orlan 1996: 90). Orlan declares that her 'body-machine' has become a site for public debate, opening questions about the status of the body within contemporary culture as patriarchal notions of beauty are literally inscribed in her flesh. The artist further states that her intention is to 'mov[e] the bars of the cage' as she tests the limits of the body with experimentations that she describes as resisting nature (Orlan 1996: 91). Orlan says that she thinks the body is obsolete and that humans must find ways of adapting to the new technological climate in which they find themselves (Orlan 1996: 91). She sees the reshaping of her body as a model of cyborg practice that allows for the augmentation of the human form and comments that her work is similar in intent to that of Australian artist Stelarc.

Stelarc began working in 1960s on deprivation performances that tested the limits of the body. These works were often performed in relationship to technology and he employed weights and pulleys that were hooked into his flesh in order to suspend his body. Stelarc went on to develop his relationship with technology and create more sophisticated mechanisms for performance actions. In 1993 Stelarc worked on a stomach sculpture which was an electronic capsule which could open and close, extend and retract, had a flashing light and a beeping sound which was surgically inserted into his body. More recently, like Orlan, Stelarc has claimed that he is working with the obsolete body and that his process seeks to outline psychological limitations of the body and to augment it through technology. *The Virtual Arm* project (1992) is an example of this mode of work and involves a technological prosthesis which is wired to respond to Stelarc's body's muscular contractions. Stelarc is also working on the development of a third ear and is seeking the computer technology that can visualise it.

Stelarc's notion of the cyborg is not limited to the augmented body – the body that has prosthetic additions that expand its capabilities – he is also interested in the notion of a cyborg system where a multiplicity of bodies which are spacially separated but electronically connected can become a greater operational entity. Thus, for example, *Ping Body* – which was first presented as part of the *Fractual Flesh* event in Paris in 1995 – was a performance piece where Stelarc's body was wired to respond to electronic activity on the Internet. Gabriella Giannachi comments that in this work Stelarc's body became 'a barometer of Internet activity' (Giannachi 2004: 59). Artists are often measures of their times, and creative works allow an opportunity to explore social relations within shifting social climates. Orlan's work also examines audiences' relationship to technology and their contact with the media. Her seventh surgery (*Omnipresence* (1993)) was transmitted live via satellite to sites in New York, Paris, Toronto and Banff. Viewers in the various sites were encouraged to interact with the artist in real time as she remained conscious throughout the surgical procedures. This piece explored how technology may allow the public access to the 'sacred' space of the operating theatre as well as providing a means for a disparate group of people to be brought together – in this case around a performance event.

Stelarc and Orlan stage lectures about their work which demonstrate technology to the public. The most common format for Orlan is the video lecture discussing the scope of her project as well as screening images from her operations which raises the social, ethical and artistic issues surrounding her project. This manner of presentation, however, also highlights the relationship between the real and the mediated. At the Re-thinking the Avant-Garde conference in Coventry 1998, Orlan delivered a video lecture. She stood at a table reading from her notes while behind her footage of her seventh operation was projected. Orlan is a diminutive woman and her place at the front of the large lecture theatre made her seem even smaller, yet, at the same time, the audience was confronted by a huge image of her face on the screen. In reproducing herself Orlan allowed a dual perspective of her body from the social distance of a lecture audience and, at the same time, a view from the intimate distance of a lover – or a surgeon. This moment can be seen to destabilise the boundaries of distanced/intimate but also to trouble the relationship between the live and the mediated. Auslander argues that the audience's eye will be drawn to the mediated material, but, as Andrew Lavender points out, within multimedia performance the material on screen is only part of the performance which is made complete by the other elements of performance – that is, real space and bodies (Lavender 2002: 187). For the audience, the oscillation of attention between the live figure in front of it and the body on the screen presented an almost quantum reality as it existed in and between the two spaces of 'then' and 'now'. Spectators at Orlan's lecture were sensitised to the fact that the surgery they had witnessed in the video had permanently marked her body, now present at the front of the lecture theatre. This double image enabled the audience to reflect upon the creation of the version of Orlan they saw before them and raised further questions about the construction of selfhood and identity.

While Stelarc deals mostly with an exoskeleton, in Orlan's work the technological interventions are incorporated within her flesh. In this way Orlan's work relates to Baudrillard's notion of the simulacra in that reality and representation are problematised. For Baudrillard, the simulacra no longer equivocates or reproduces the real; the real is generated and reduplicated by and through simulation. Simulation is another key issue within multimedia performance as artists work to create pieces that incorporate virtual reality with live performance.

Virtual reality

The work of Blast Theory relates to the practice of Orlan and Stelarc in that it explores both the issue of simulation and possibilities for a mediated network of relationships within performance. The core members of Blast Theory met while working in The Renoir cinema in Bloomsbury Square and founded the collective in 1991. They describe themselves as artists who look for forms that can express the ideas that they are interested in. Not only has the company employed eclectic tools to make performance, but there has also been diversity in the shape of the performance events themselves. These have included installations, digital work, performance pieces and 'mixed-reality projects' (www.blasttheory.co.uk). The company describes its devising process as one of 'layering' and uses the metaphor of working with a range of elements which run on different 'tracks' (quoted in Stanier 2001). Yet its terminology 'mixed-reality' refers not only to the multimedia element of its work but also to the blend of art and life within its projects.

An example of Blast Theory's mixed-reality work is *Desert Rain* (2000), which raised questions about the nature of simulation in contemporary culture. One of the starting points for the project was the fact that a considerable amount of contemporary military training is undertaken via a simulator. Blast Theory was struck by an event within the 1991 Gulf War in which simulator-trained US soldiers mistook a civilian plane for an Iraqi fighter and, as a result, killed all 270 passengers. The company sought to engage with Baudrillard's contention that the Gulf War did not really happen and was merely a media exercise. It states, however, that the production was not designed to demonstrate this theory but to explore its cultural ramifications particularly in relation to the correlation between the real and the virtual (Baudrillaud 1994). Lyn Gardner describes *Desert Rain* as 'part performance, part installation and part computer game' (Gardner 2000). In groups of six, participants changed into waterproof clothing and attended a briefing where each individual was given a human target to locate. Players then entered separate, tent-like compartments facing a screen of water onto which a virtual desert landscape was projected. Using a foot-operated control panel they had to work to locate first their individual targets and then the exit within the allotted twenty minutes. When they came into contact with other players moving through the virtual landscape, they were able to communicate with them via headphones and a microphone.

Blast Theory's work is technically cutting-edge and for *Desert Rain* the company collaborated with the computer science department at the University of Nottingham. Yet the company is also playful and looks to use technology to subvert the passive role of the audience through encouraging interactivity. Indeed, instead of audience members, the participants in *Desert Rain* are identified as 'players'. Kaprow noted in relation to Happenings that '[r]eplacing artist with player as if adopting an alias, is a way of altering a fixed identity' and Blast Theory's work appears to draw on that dynamic (Kaprow 1993: 126). *Desert Rain*, however, does not seem to 'discharge and clari[fy] violence and un-reason' in the overt way in which Kaprow envisaged for play (Kaprow

1993: 121). The company's negotiation of issues appears more subtle and, while focussing on the politically sensitive subject of the Gulf War, the piece does not offer a clear political perspective, but grounds itself instead in the negotiation of simulation and reality posited by Baudrillard in his writing. The computer game element of the work subverts expectations in that, rather than seeking out a subject to kill as is the norm in the gaming world, the person is found so that their story can be told. After the first section of the piece, the players left their compartments and were taken, beyond the water screen and over a sand dune, to a three-dimensional mock-up of a hotel room which mirrored the environment in which they began the computer game. Here they were shown a video interview with the targets they searched for in the virtual environment, and this led them to witness a plethora of perspectives on the conflict. Clarke observes that:

> Here participants can engage, not only in the questions raised by the ethics of virtual reality and warfare, as presented within the Gulf War, but also question their own personal relationship to the events and the implicated role of the viewer/doer.
>
> (quoted in Blast Theory 2000: 6)

Responses to the performance emphasised the personal experience of the event rather than offering an examination of the political issues it raised. There does appear, however, to be a gesture towards political efficacy in the final action of the piece through an intervention with the items that people left in the antechamber when changing into their waterproof clothing. Gardner notes that:

> A few minutes, hours, or even weeks after experiencing Blast Theory's Desert Rain you could be rooting through your bag or pocket when you suddenly discover something you didn't know you had. It is a small plastic box that contains 100,000 grains of sand.
>
> (Gardner 2000)

The 100,000 grains of sand were given as signifiers of the estimated number of Iraqi dead during the 1991 Gulf War. Thus, while the characters within the video interviews gave a variety of responses to the question of the Iraqi casualties, the company appears to give a definitive signal of perspective in a final summation. Such a factual statement may indicate more of a resistance to Baudrillard's theories on the Gulf War than the company's material indicates, although it may be significant that the intervention took place on an individual basis after the collective experience of the piece had concluded.

Behind the technological wizardry that *Desert Rain* employs, there are some quite conventional theatrical ideas. In the company's documentation of the project the water screen is described as 'the equivalent of the fourth wall', a marker between a 'real world' and a performed virtuality (Blast Theory 2000: 10). Blast Theory company member Matt Adams comments that 'There's no real difference between the participants in *Desert Rain* believing in computer graphics and audiences at the theatre looking at an actor in a tinfoil crown and believing he is a king' (www.blasttheory.co.uk). Adams states that another aspect of the project is the way it creates bonds between strangers. This is interesting as participants were encouraged to interact with the piece on an individualistic rather than collective basis, with people receiving individual missions and zipped into separate cubicles. Indeed, Gardner comments that during the game she dashed for the exit of the virtual world, ignoring the other players' cries for help. This response was not uncommon although there were notable exceptions such as the group in Stockholm that wanted to work together to beat the record for completion. Such interventions, however, seem to work against the intention of the piece rather than enhancing it. Thus, the company describes its frustration with the fact that, after coming out of the cubicles, players wanted to spend time discussing their experiences with each other. The company comments that it altered the way in which this part of the performance was set up so that the players spent as little time together as possible. This isolation appears to be designed to intensify the raw 'reality' of the experience for the individual participant. The strategic lack of human contact amplifies what has often been described as the most striking element of the piece. Upon finding their target in the virtual world, a figure in a hooded jacket approached the player and held out a swipe card. Many participants assumed that this person was part of the simulated environment and cried out in surprise when they realised the figure was real.

Desert Rain demonstrates a desire to play between reality and fiction in a manner which harnesses emotional responses and instinctive impulses. While employing contemporary technology Blast Theory negotiates fundamental principles of human interaction and its shifting frames of reference appear to unsettle not only the parameters of performance but also those who participate. The responses of players in *Desert Rain* are indications of what may happen when the limits of the play-space become unclear. There was the participant who, unsettled by the isolation within the cubicle, had a debilitating panic attack, and there were also the players who, instead of returning their swipe cards into the outstretched hand of the figure in the hooded jacket, placed their own hands there. It appears that, whatever the artistic framework, the reality of human contact in the here and now remains important within the performance event.

Interactivity and the 'nowness' of theatre

There was a belief among theatre critics that multimedia performance would not be able to support the same direct mode of communication as live theatre and that the barriers it threw up between audience and performer would be insurmountable. This, however, has not proved to be so. Gob Squad, founded in 1994 and based in Berlin, Hamburg and Nottingham, is an example of a company which has 'use[d] technology as a tool . . . in establishing creative contact' (Gob Squad and Quiñones 2005: 114). There appears to be not only contact but also a sense of immediacy in Gob Squad's work. The intimacy that an image mediated on the screen might hold has already been referred to in this chapter and Auslander notes that television has colonised liveness in that the televisual mode is culturally perceived as an immediate medium which can take the viewer to breaking news and provide an instant window on the world (Auslander 1999: 13). Gob Squad makes use of this instantaneous quality of televisual media and blends it into the aesthetic of its live performance work in a way that proves both intimate and vibrant.

Room Service (Help Me Make it Through the Night) (2005) is a recent example of Gob Squad's work. The company outlines the logistics of the performance as follows:

Where: a hotel (a conference room for the audience, 4 identical hotel rooms for the performers)

Who: 2 women, 2 men

In the conference room: 300m of video cables, 700m of sound cables, 4 old computers; 4 big monitors; 1 telephone; 1 hotel bar; comfortable cushions to spend the night on

In the hotel rooms: 4 cameras; some costumes (7 coats, 12 suits, 14 dresses, 22 shirts, 8 nighties, 4 dressing gowns, 9 pairs of pyjamas, various bras, pants, ties); some props (9 wigs, 2 fake beards, 'Freddy

Krueger' mask, glow-in-the-dark hands, briefcase, business magazines, trashy novels, toothpaste); pop songs to sing; games to play; everything which comes with a hotel room; a phone call to call someone watching (and the hope that someone cares to answer)

(Gob Squad and Quiñones 2005: 113)

Gob Squad likes to make its work for spaces outside conventional theatres in order to open up the scope of performance. Thus a hotel was chosen for this project. One critic was particularly struck by the choice of venue in his own city and the opportunity to see inside a famous hotel. His response indicates the way in which voyeurism was played upon in the piece (Bhagat 2005). The conceit is that four people are returning to their hotel to spend the night and that they are each being watched by a surveillance camera. At one level, then, members of the audience are eavesdroppers who, via the screens in the conference

Figure 12.1 Gob Squad: video stills *Room Service (Help Me Make It Through The Night)*. Copyright © Gob Squad. Above left: Bastian Trost; above right: Johanna Freiburg; bottom left: Berit Stumpf; bottom right: Sean Patten.

room, can witness simultaneously the events in the four hotel rooms. Daniel notes that 'technologies place the individual spectator and performer in a much more complex situation', in that they can expand the possibilities of interaction and the event of *Room Service* offers a more sophisticated viewing experience than mere voyeurism (Daniel 2000: 61). Like Blast Theory, Gob Squad blends the conventional and the cutting edge in that the conference room has chairs laid out in an 'end-on' format, but facing four screens rather than a stage, and between the audience and the display screens is a phone. From the beginning of the piece the telephone is a symbol of communication between two worlds and sets up a kind of liminal space between the two areas of activity within the performance.

The company describes the work as 'a live interactive film' and this is interesting as the piece plays with televisual rather than filmic modes of interaction. It works in a quite different way to *It's Your Film* (1998) by Stan's Café which was a three-minute-long performance staged for an audience of one and used the cinematic language of long shots, close-ups, exteriors, interiors, cuts and dissolves. This piece was designed to look like a film while being performed live by two actors. In *Room Service*, however, the action is mediated via screens and it seems that its description as a 'live interactive film' is intended to sensitise the audience both to the way in which the production uses media technology and to the way in which it disrupts it. *Room Service* plugged into the televisual model of quiz shows, soap operas and reality TV, yet, as with other multimedia performances, it also played with those conventions. Causey notes that:

> The theatre, if it wishes to be responsive to the contemporary mediatized culture, needs to engage technologies that have helped occasion that culture.
>
> (Causey 2002: 182)

Companies such as Gob Squad seek to engage with pop culture and employ technology to inhabit and deconstruct the discourse of contemporary media. Thus, for example, in *Room Service*, the audience is witness to the development of stylised characters. Bastian (the performers within the piece are known to the audience by name) is witnessed creating the character of the cleaning lady and the audience sees him trying on costumes and describing the type of person he is going to play. This is juxtaposed with magazine-style montages which display personality traits of the different personas that the performers are presenting. This type of deconstructive practice which opens up the modes of performance echoes that of The Wooster Group which has been a pioneer in multimedia performance. A celebrated example of The Wooster Group's deconstructive practice is where in *L.S.D.* the audience is witness to Willem Defoe (also a film actor) placing glycerine in his eyes to simulate tears. Seeing the process of construction encourages the audience to reflect on the quality of the moment itself and offers up an element of uncertainty that troubles the conventional performer–audience contract. Gob Squad questions this relationship even further in that, as well as acknowledging the audience as witness, spectators are invited to become actively involved in the creation of the drama, for example, by giving advice on what the performers should wear.

The liveness of the event is emphasised in the presentation of *Room Service*. Although the performers in *Room Service* are physically separated from each other there are moments when they acknowledge their connection through choreographed sequences where their synchronised actions communicate a sense of togetherness. As well as the sense of communion between the performers, *Room Service* also engenders a connection between the audience and the company members which develops throughout the piece. This contradicts the expectation that spectators will remain distanced from mediated performers.

At the beginning of *Room Service* the performers direct their performance to camera and, like Orlan, build up intimacy through the use of close-up. The next level of interaction is when a call is made from one of the bedrooms to the conference room and a game of 'truth or dare' is initiated where telephone numbers flash up on the screen and audience members are invited to dial up the performer of their choice. This section clearly echoes a televisual convention but employs the technology available to create a new kind of theatrical event and offers an original twist on audience participation within live performance. The audience member takes up a position by the telephone, thereby becoming a performer in that they have to perform a truth or dare. The material he or she offers is then interwoven into the narrative of the performance event. The publicity for *Room Service* asks 'are you brave enough to cross over?' and the piece actually relies on the live interaction of the person who 'cares to answer'. Part of the performance involves an audience member literally 'crossing over' as they enter one of the rooms and appear on screen. In this way such multimedia performance can be seen to differ from film or television in that it relies on the presence of the audience to complete the event. Pieces such as *Room Service* can be seen to work in the tradition of the Happenings, making playful use of technology and using the 'ready-made' of the TV format to engage with an active audience.

Multimedia performance offers opportunities for enhanced modes of communication in that it offers the possibility of layering different levels of performance which are happening simultaneously. For example, while in *Room Service* there is communication within and without the conference room, in *Uncle Roy All Around You* (2003) by Blast Theory, live and online players communicate with one another and both sets of players and with Blast Theory performers. This notion of layering can also be applied to the element of time within multimedia performance. Birringer notes the way that time has been explored within such work. He says:

> Disjunctions between different time scales (filmic time, real time, musical time) . . . directly affect the way one perceives the actors temporally, separate from their bodies.
>
> (Birringer 1985: 229)

This disjunction can be identified as a significant element within multimedia performance as different times may be brought together within the performance moment. The Wooster Group, for example, has included material from its rehearsal period via TV monitors placed within the performance space. Other times and places have been created and introduced into the performance via technology; Forced Entertainment's piece *Some Confusions in the Law About Love* (1989) claimed it borrowed from 'bad TV movies' and included two characters – Mike and Dolores – who were supposedly interviewed 'live by satellite from Hawaii' and appeared on two monitors at the edges of the performance area (www.forcedentertainment.com). The use of recorded material may also be employed within multimedia performance to heighten an awareness of the process of creation and recreation. Blast Theory's production *10 Backwards* (1999), for example, was an exploration of déja-vu and combined live and pre-rendered mixes of video to represent a plethora of times and places. *Room Service* is a durational performance which draws direct attention to the element of time. The different time scales that Birringer outlines are interplayed as episodic moments are created and fade, and the fast pace of the televisual mode is played out against the real time of the durational performance which may last up to five hours. Within the performance there are pieces that are pre-set and have a televisual slickness while others involve improvisatory interaction with the audience and last as long as the participants want them to. This conflation of time scales serves to enhance and expand the live interaction, adding another dimension to the performance and the potential viewing pleasure of the audience.

In conclusion, far from putting theatre in crisis, the works discussed in this chapter suggest that contemporary performance-makers are employing new media to augment the theatrical event. It appears that new, hybrid forms of performance are developing which creatively engage with the current climate and reflect upon the advances in technology that seek to blend the visceral and the virtual. These works employ many well-established theatre conventions alongside technological innovation. This relies on the immediacy of the live event – its ontology – while also drawing on pre-recorded material.

Conclusion

THIRTEEN

SHIFTING BOUNDARIES
Concluding Thoughts

From devising histories to contemporary practices

During the course of this book, and most particularly in Part One, we have mapped some of the movements and shifts that led to the development of contemporary performance-making. The genealogy that is traced here is necessarily a partial and incomplete story, charting what Raymond Williams described as a 'selective tradition' rather than a comprehensive guide to how different performance practices developed (Williams 1962: 52). Furthermore, the process of creating a framework through which to analyse performance-making raises questions about how history is constructed. Walter Benjamin recognises that history-making is, in part, a risky and creative process:

> To articulate the past historically does not mean to recognize it 'the way it really was' . . . It means to seize hold of a memory as it flashes up at a moment of danger.
>
> (Benjamin 1999: 247)

In telling this story we have endeavoured to seize some of these memories, providing examples that illuminate how concepts of the performative have been created and challenged by processes of devising. This book captures moments when paradigm shifts have occurred from one mode of performance to another and when, in the words of the introduction to this book, these practices have 'expanded the language of performance'.

The structure of this study means that divisions have been made between different aspects of contemporary performance-making, with sections on narrative, site and place, and performing bodies providing the framework. The inevitable demarcations that occur here have resulted from the structural patterning that the book follows, and are intended to indicate broad classifications of devised work rather than lay down strict parameters. Indeed, many companies whose work is outlined within this book work fluidly across many of the areas that are covered. Forced Entertainment's work, for example, focusses on the athletic presence of the performer, often draws upon visual practices of collecting random objects, and sometimes works in specific sites to explore the centrality of place. Though this book has described work within certain categories, it is intended that it is used to open a dialogue across these boundaries.

The forms of performance-making that are discussed here track the processes through which artistic practice challenges cultural and social convention. What is also interesting to consider is the way these innovators influenced each other, and how a genealogy of devising performers emerges through these patterns of influence. The innovative work of The Wooster Group, for example, had a powerful impact on the work of both Forced Entertainment and Reckless Sleepers. Writing about business, Everett Rogers describes this process of innovation as an 'adoption curve', a term he uses to suggests how ideas are taken up and diffused after their invention (www.12manage.com/methods_rogers_innovation_adoption_curve.html). Applied to performance-making, diffusion theory suggests that the ideas of the innovators or inventors are initially taken up by 'early adopters', and subsequently find a more widespread forum as their value becomes recognised and the ideas become better known. This shift is evident both in the assimilation of the practices of innovative performance-makers into the work of a range of practitioners, and in the venues in which the work is performed. During the historical period discussed in this book, some particularly successful companies have moved from fringe theatres and festival circuits to mainstream theatre houses.

Relocating performance

Contemporary performance-makers have not only responded to the climate of global change by shifting the boundaries of performance and theatricality, but they have also re-imagined its cultural and social limits. At this early point in the twenty-first century, devised performance often hovers somewhat precariously between the packaged commodification of commercial theatre (even in its most avant-garde or experimental forms) and the radicalism and chaos of politicised performance.

Many devising companies display their work in an ever-widening international circuit. Rather than being confined to a particular theatre or buildings, most devising companies expect to tour their work. A good example of such an itinerant production is Theatre de Complicité's *Mnemonic*, which opened in July 1999 in Huddersfield. The production first toured to Cambridge, Newcastle, Oxford Play-house, the Salzburg Festival and the Riverside Studios in London. In 2001 the production was revived and toured to the National Theatre in London, Barcelona, Paris, and had a New York off-Broadway season. By 2002 the production had toured to Sarajevo, Greece, Germany, Poland and France, and was finally remounted at the Riverside Studios in London in 2003. This example not only indicates the potential longevity of such productions, but also demonstrates the thriving international touring circuit that enables companies to share their work with audiences in different countries.

As well as extending the shelf life of a production, touring can attract particular forms of funding. Work may be developed under the auspices of particular festivals or commissioned by specific venues. Lone Twin's piece *To The Dogs*, for example, was commissioned in 2004 by KunstenFestivalDesArts in Belgium and the company received further funding from the festival to develop its work, later touring the piece to Europe and North America. Some venues commission companies to make pieces of work, and it is not uncommon for more than one venue to co-commission work and thus share the cost. Working to a commission gives performance-makers the funding to develop a piece of work and also guarantees a venue in which to show-case the production. In their study of devised performance, Heddon and Milling point out that although festival and venue management have played an important role in funding the devising sector, they only fund on a project basis (Heddon and Milling 2006: 158). This has made it difficult for companies to sustain an ensemble working practice, forcing them instead to employ performers for particular productions and only allowing them to plan on a project-by-project basis.

Jen Harvie argues that the international touring market serves to dissipate the potential efficacy of devised performance. Reflecting on DV8's production *Can We Afford This* (2000), she suggests that a 'show's political impact [is] compromised when it [is] toured away from the contexts within which it [is] devised' (Harvie 2002: 68). She argues that, when productions are taken out of context, any political critique within devised performance is diluted and may be read in a generalised manner and without reference to the situation that prompted the devising process. By contrast, however, it is also possible to argue that, within a globalised culture, there are enough common-alities to allow performance to be read across national boundaries. Third Angel, for example, has found that its work is popular in both Germany and Portugal, suggesting that its success in different places reflects common cultural concerns. In *Where from Here* (2001), con-sumer culture provided a common reference point for the European tour, although it is interesting to note that attention to local nuances encouraged audiences to identify with the ideas represented. When arriving in a new place the company would check how 'IKEA' was pro-nounced as it had found that when the line was pronounced with the local inflection it always caused a laugh of recognition.

Companies sometimes even tour site-specific projects, which have traditionally been seen as one-off pieces developed for a particular place. For example the UK-based company Theatrerites premiered its production *Hospitalworks* (2005) at the Mayday University Hospital in Croydon and then recreated the piece at the Burgerhospital in Stuttgart. For this piece a generalised sense of hospital framed the activity on-site, which meant it did not rely on the particularities of the host hospital.

Straddling across boundaries, devised performance has the poten-tial to disrupt material, political, aesthetic and artistic conventions, as well as playing a central role in the landscape of experimental theatre that attracts increasingly wide audiences in mainstream theatre. These two ways of thinking about devising – the radical and the saleable – are not mutually exclusive nor binary opposites, but continually negotiated and re-negotiated by individual artists, performance-makers and by theatre companies.

Shifting bodies

One of the basic premises that underlies this book is the principle that devising matters. Devising performance is socially imaginative as well as culturally responsive, and articulates between the local and the global, the fictional and the real, the community and the individual, the social and the psychological. In these terms, devising performance has a significant part to play in redefining the ways in which debates about theatricality and performativity are enacted and in recognising how they are connected. Devised performance is an agency of both personal self-expression and community or civic activism, and these visions offer a means by which cultural exchange can be promoted. Devising is always a dialogic process, and questions about how far, and in what ways, the practices associated with collaboration are acts of cultural intervention as well as personal sharing remain one of the abiding themes of this form of performative creativity.

Performance always unfixes, and the processes of devising also allow for the kind of collective and collaborative action that has the potential to create a renewed sense of belonging in the participants and in audiences. The contemporary emphasis on performance and performativity has, however, both benign and more troubling consequences. On the one hand, as Baz Kershaw has argued, the development and spread of globalisation has been dependent on the performativity of Western societies at the end of the twentieth century (Kershaw 2006: 145). Conversely, the framing of everyday life as performance has also drawn attention to the paradoxes and contradictions inherent in an increasingly globalised world. Making a performance involves a process of critical reflexivity, and it is this attribute of performance that can encourage individual, community and national identities to be reformed and reshaped in ways that may be socially and artistically productive.

Devising performers have re-evaluated the aesthetic of performance with the consequence that the physicality of performance has been reconceptualised and revisioned. Emphasising the corporeal as well as the imaginative qualities of performance has inevitably and productively focussed attention on the performers' bodies, and has made the identity politics associated with movements such as feminism, anti-racism and disability rights tangible and visible. Writing about disability and performance, Peggy Phelan argues that performance has the capacity to 'transform one's worldview because it reorders the invisible and visible that frames our worlds' (Phelan 2005: 324). Many theatre companies whose work includes devised performance (Black Mime, Graeae, Nitro, Candoco and DV8) have actively challenged conventional aesthetics through altering perceptions of the body. These companies, and many others, have harnessed the popularity of devised performance to question the social and political readings of embodiment and to demonstrate how race, sexuality, ethnicity and ability might be re-presented.

Performance occupies a public space, and this means that it can be provocative and socially constructive. Contemporary constructions of the social body play on the interrelationship between the public and

Figure 13.1 Alison Lapper Pregnant. Artist: Marc Quinn. Photographer: Helen Nicholson.

the intimate, and it is this interconnectedness that seeks to redefine the cultural imagination both in everyday life and in the aesthetics of representation. A particularly interesting example of how the public space of artistic practice can be used to extend popular perceptions of the body is found in Marc Quinn's sculpture *Alison Lapper Pregnant*, which occupies the fourth plinth in London's Trafalgar square. *Alison Lapper Pregnant* is a marble portrait of a disabled artist sculpted when she was eight months pregnant, and is exhibited in juxtaposition to Imperial generals close to Nelson's Column, a famous London landmark. This piece of public art symbolises shifting attitudes about the body, an impulse that is also replayed in contemporary devised performance.

This public celebration of Alison Lapper's body in Trafalgar Square serves as an appropriate metaphor with which to conclude this book. The iconography of this sculpture implies changing concepts of beauty, and reasserts the feminine within a square that commemorates a sea battle fought to protect Britain's global economic interests. The sculpture performs its resistance to the dominant narratives of the nation state and, in the process, breaks political, social, historical and psychological boundaries. Applied to performance-making, this dynamic offers the potential to recognise the process of cultural change and exchange, not as a meeting point of fixed positions but as an aesthetic space where new identities might be formed. Performativity, poised as it is between activity and passivity, enables new social inscriptions and different ways of conceptualising the narratives of the body in space and place.

BIBLIOGRAPHY

Alfreds, M. (1979–1980) 'A Shared Experience: The Actor as Story-teller', *Theatre Papers*, Dartington, 3rd series.

Allen, D. (2000) *Performing Chekhov*, London: Routledge.

Amit, V. (ed.) (2002) *Realizing Community*, London: Routledge.

Anderson, B. (1991) *Imagined Communities* (second edition), London: Verso.

Anderson, L. (2001) *Autobiography*, London: Routledge.

—— (2003a) 'Artist Statement', *Barbican Programme*, London.

—— (2003b) *Happiness*, Barbican Theatre, London, 8 May.

Apollonio, U. (ed.) (1973) *Futurist Manifestos*, London: Thames and Hudson.

Artaud. A. (1977) *A Theatre and its Double*, trans. V. Corti, London: John Calder.

Augé, M. (1995) *Non-places: An Introduction to an Anthropology of Supermodernity*, London: Verso.

Auslander, P. (1985) 'Task and Vision: Willem Defoe in *L.S.D.*', *The Drama Review*, 29.2: 94–98.

—— (1997) *From Acting to Performance: Essays in Modernism and Postmodernism*, London: Routledge.

—— (1999) *Liveness*, London: Routledge.

Bailes, S. (2001) 'Moving Backward, Forwards Remembering: Goat Island Performance Group', *New Art Examiner* (July/August). Available online at www.goatisland performance.org/writing_moving%20backward.htm (accessed 24 August 2005).

Banes, S. (1987) *Terpsichore in Sneakers: Post-Modern Dance*, Middletown, CT: Wesleyan University Press.

Barba, E. (1986) *Beyond Floating Islands*, trans. J. Barba, New York: Theatre Communications Group.

Barker, C. (1977) *Theatre Games: A New Approach to Drama Training*, London: Methuen.

—— (2000) 'Joan Littlewood', in A. Hodge (ed.) *Twentieth Century Actor Training*, London: Routledge: 113–128.

Barker, C. and Gale, M.B. (2000) *British Theatre Between the Wars, 1918–1939*, Cambridge: Cambridge University Press.

Barker, H. (2005) *Death, The One and the Art of Theatre*, London: Routledge.

Barlett, N. (1999) 'What Moves: Pina Bausch', *Dance Theatre Journal*, 14.4: 4–7.

Barthes, R. (1977) *Image–Music–Text*, trans. S. Heath, London: Fontana.

Basting, A.D. (2001) 'God is a Talking Horse: Dementia and the Performance of Self', *The Drama Review*, 45.3: 78–94.

Baudrillard, J. (1994) *Simulacra and Simulation*, trans. S.F. Glaser, Ann Arbor, MI: University of Michigan.

—— (2004) *The Gulf War Did Not Take Place*, trans. P. Patton, London: Power Publications.

Beck, J. (1986) *The Life of the Theatre*, New York: Limelight Editions.

Benjamin, A. (1991) *Art, Mimesis and the Avant-Garde*, London: Routledge.

Benjamin, W. (1999) 'The Work of Art in the Age of Mechanical Reproduction' (1935) in *Illuminations*, London: Pimlico.

Betancourt, M. (2002) *Totentanz Transformation*. Available online at www.miami artexchange.com/pages/2002/05/betancourt_05 (accessed 27 July 2003).

Bettelheim, B. (1976) *The Uses of Enchantment: The Meaning and Importance of Fairy Tales*, London: Thames and Hudson.

Bhagat, A. (2005) 'Gob Squad's *Room Service*'. Available online at www.leftlion.co.uk (accessed 24 August 2005).

Billington, M. (1996) 'War Crimes', *Guardian*, 27 June.

Biró, Y. (1998) 'Heartbreaking Fragments, Magnificent Whole: Pina Bausch's New Minimyths', *Performing Arts Journal*, 20.2: 68–72.

Birringer, J. (1985) 'Postmodern Performance and Technology', *Performing Arts Journal*, 26/27: 221–233.

Blast Theory (eds) (2000) *Desert Rain*, London: Arts Council of England.

Blau, H. (1991) 'The Surpassing Body', *The Drama Review*, 35.2: 74–98.

Boal, A. (1979) *Theatre of the Oppressed*, London: Pluto Press.

—— (1992) *Games for Actors and Non-actors*, trans. A. Jackson, London: Routledge.

Bouchard, D.F. (ed.) (1977) *Language, Counter-memory, Practice: Selected Essays and Interviews with Michel Foucault*, Ithaca, New York: Cornell University Press.

Bradbury, M. and McFarlane, J. (1991) *Modernism: A Guide to European Literature 1890–1930*, Harmondsworth: Penguin.

Bradby, D., James, L. and Sharratt, B. (eds) (1980) *Performance and Politics in Popular Drama*, Cambridge: Cambridge University Press.

Bradby, D. and Sparks, A. (1997) *Mise on Scène: French Theatre Now*, London: Methuen.

Brah, A. (1996) *Cartographies of Diaspora*, London: Routledge.

Braun, E. (1982) *The Director and the Stage*, London: Methuen.

Brecht, B. (1964) *Brecht on Theatre*, John Willett (ed.), London: Methuen.

—— (1974) 'Against Georg Lukacs', trans. S. Hood, *New Left Review*, 84: 39–53.

Brook, P. (1972) *The Empty Space*, Harmondsworth: Penguin.

Burger, P. (1984) *Theory of the Avant Garde*, Minneapolis, MN: University of Minnesota Press.

Burt, S. and Barker, C. (1980) 'IOU and the New Vocabulary of Performance Art', *Theatre Quarterly*, 10.37: 70–94.

Butler, R. (2003) *The Art of Darkness: Staging the Phillip Pullman Trilogy*, London: Oberon Books.

Callery, D. (2001) *Through the Body*, London: Nick Hern Books.

Carlson, M. (2003) *The Haunted Stage: The Theatre as Memory Machine*, Ann Arbor, MI: University of Michigan Press.

Casey, E. (1998) *The Fate of Place: A Philosophical History*, Berkeley, CA: University of California Press.

Causey, M. (1999) 'The Screen Test of the Double: The Uncanny Performer in the Space of Technology', *Theatre Journal*, 51.4: 383–394.

—— (2002) 'A Theatre of Monsters: Live Performance in the age of Digital Media', in M. Delgado and C. Svich (eds) *Theatre in Crisis?: Performance Manifestos for a New Century*, Manchester: Manchester University Press: 179–183.

Chaikin, J. (1972) *The Presence of the Actor*, New York: Atheneum.

Chambers, C. (1989) *The Story of Unity Theatre*, London: Lawrence and Wishart.

Charnock, N. (1996) 'Nigel Charnock Was Here', in D. Tushingham (ed.) *Live 4: Freedom Machine*, London: Nick Hern Books: 24–32.

Cocke, D. (2004) 'Art in a Democracy', *The Drama Review*, 48.3: 165–173.

Cody, G. (1998) 'Woman, Man, Dog, Tree: Two Decades of Intimate and Monumental Bodies in Pina Bausch's Tanztheater', *The Drama Review*, 42.2: 115–131.

Cohen, A. (1985) *The Symbolic Construction of Community*, London: Tavistock Press.

Cohen-Cruz, J. (2002) 'The Motion of the Ocean: The Shifting Face of US Theater for Social Change since the 1960s', *Theater*, 31.3: 95–107.

—— (2005) *Local Acts: Community-Based Performance in the United States*, New Brunswick, NJ: Rutgers University Press.

Cohn, R. (1989) 'Ariane Mnouchkine: Playwright of a Collective', in E. Brater (ed.) *Feminine Focus: The New Women Playwrights*, New York: Oxford University Press: 53–63.

Coult, T. and Kershaw, B. (1990) *Engineers of the Imagination*, London: Methuen.

Daly, A. (1996) 'Pina Bausch Goes West to Prospect for Imagery', *New York Times*, 22 September.

Daniel, H. (2000) 'Re-cognizing Corporeality', in R. Mock (ed.) *Performing Processes: Creating Live Performance*, London: Intellect: 61–68.

Davis, J. (1993) 'The Play for England: The Royal Court adapts *The Playmaker*', in P. Reynolds (ed.) *Novel Images: Literature in Performance*, London: Routledge: 75–90.

Davis, R. (1975) *The San Francisco Mime Troupe: The First Ten Years*, Palo Alto, CA: Ramperts Press.

Dawson, A. (2002) 'The Mining Community and the Ageing Body: Towards a Phenomenology of Community?' in V. Amit (ed.) *Realizing Community*, London: Routledge: 21–37.

Debord, G. (1996) 'Theory of the Dérive', in L. Andreotti and X. Costa (eds) *Theory of the Dérive and other Situationist Writings on the City*, Barcelona: Museo d'Art Contemporani de Barcelona.

de Certeau, M. (1984) *The Practice of Everyday Life*, trans. S. Rendall, Berkeley, CA: University of California Press.

Deeney, J. (1998) 'Action and Reaction', in J. Deeney (ed.) *Writing Live*, London: New Playwrights Trust.

Deleuze, G. and Guattari, F. (1988) *A Thousand Plateaus: Capitalism and Schizophrenia*, trans. B. Massumi, London: Athlone Press.

Dempster, E. (1998) 'Women Writing the Body: Let's Watch a Little How she Dances', in A. Carter (ed.) *The Routledge Dance Studies Reader*, London and New York: Routledge: 223–229.

Derrida, J. (1987) *The Truth in Painting*, Chicago, IL: University of Chicago.

Diamond, E. (1997) *Unmaking Mimesis*, London: Routledge.

Dolan, J. (2005) *Utopia in Performance: Finding Hope at the Theatre*, Ann Arbor, MI: University of Michigan Press.

Dolezel, L. (1999) 'Fictional and Historical Narrative: Meeting the Postmodern Challenge', in D. Herman (ed.) *Narratologies: New Perspectives of Narrative Analysis*, Columbus, OH: Ohio State University Press: 247–273.

Drain, R. (ed.) (1995) *Twentieth Century Theatre: A Sourcebook*, London: Routledge.

Eagleton, T. (1983) *Literary Theory*, Oxford: Blackwell.

Edgar, D. (1988) *The Second Time as Farce*, London: Lawrence and Wishart.

Elam, K. (1980) *The Semiotics of Theatre and Drama*, London and New York: Methuen.

Eldredge, S. and Huston, H. (1995) 'Actor Training in the Neutral Mask', in P. Zarrilli (ed.) *Acting (Re)Considered*, London and New York: Routledge: 121–128.

Ervan, E. van (1988) *Radical People's Theatre*, Bloomington, IN: Indiana University Press.

Etchells, T. (1996) 'How Long Do you Have to Have Lived Somewhere Before you're Allowed to Lie about it?', in D. Tushingham (ed.) *Live 4: Freedom Machine*, London: Nick Hern Books: 51–58.

—— (1999) *Certain Fragments: Contemporary Performance and Forced Entertainment*, forward Peggy Phelan, London: Routledge.

Farabrough, L. (1997) 'Introduction: Casebook: Pina Bausch', *Theatre Forum*, 10: 61–62.

Felciano, R. (1996) 'Pina Bausch: The Voice from Germany', *Dance Magazine*, 70.10: 68–71.

Féral, J. (1989a) 'Mnouchkine's Workshop at Soleil', *The Drama Review*, 33.4: 77–87.

—— (1989b) 'Théâtre du Soleil – A Second Glance', *The Drama Review*, 33.4: 98–106.

—— (2002) 'Introduction', *Substance*, 31.2 & 3: 3–17.

Findlay, R. (1984) 'Grotowski's *Akropolis*: A Retrospective View', *Modern Drama*, 27.1: 1–20.

Foster, H. (2001) *The Return of the Real*, Cambridge, MA: Massachusetts Institute of Technology Press.

Foucault, M. (1991) *Discipline and Punish*, trans. A. Sheridan, Harmondsworth: Penguin.

—— (1997) *The Birth of the Clinic*, trans. A. Sheridan, London: Routledge.

Frank, A. (1995) *The Wounded Storyteller: Body, Illness and Ethics*, Chicago, IL: University of Chicago Press.

Freire, A.M.A. and Macedo, D. (eds) (2001) *The Paulo Freire Reader*, London: Continuum.

Friedman, J. (2002) 'Muscle Memory: Performing Embodied Knowledge', in R. Candida Smith (ed.) *Art and the Performance of Memory*, London: Routledge: 156–180.

Freire, P. (2002) *Pedagogy of the Oppressed*, trans. M.B. Ramos, London: Continuum.

Friedman, S. (1988) 'Women's Autobiographical Selves: Theory and Practice', in S. Benstock (ed.) *The Private Self: Theory and Practice of Women's Autobiographical Writings*, Chapel Hill, NC: University of North Carolina Press: 34–62.

Fry, M. (ed.) (1996) *Frontline Drama 4: Adapting Classics*, London: Methuen.

Fuchs, E. (1996) *The Death of Character: Perspectives on Theatre After Modernism*, Bloomington, IN: Indiana University Press.

Fumaroli, M. (1997) 'External Order, Internal Intimacy: Interview with Grotowski', in R. Schechner and L. Wolford (eds) *The Grotowski Sourcebook*, London and New York: Routledge.

Gale, M.B. (2000) 'Errant Nymphs: Women and the Inter-war Theatre' in C. Barker and M.B. Gale (eds) *British Theatre Between the Wars, 1918–1939*, Cambridge: Cambridge University Press: 113–134.

Gardner, L. (2000) 'Blood on the Sand', *Guardian*, 18 May.

—— (2003) 'Those Eyes, That Mouth', *Guardian*, 6 August.

—— (2004) 'The Last Supper', *Guardian*, 19 November.

—— (2005) 'Just for Show', *Guardian*, 14 November.

Giannachi, G. (2004) *Virtual Theatres*, London: Routledge.

Gibson, F. (1998) *Reminiscence and Recall*, London: Age Concern.

Gilloch, G. (2002) *Walter Benjamin: Critical Constellations*, Malden: Polity.

Gob Squad and A. Quiñones (eds) (2005) *The Making of a Memory: 10 Years of Gob Squad Remembered in Words and Pictures*, Berlin: Synwolt Verlag.

Goffman, E. (1976) *The Presentation of Self in Everyday Life*, Harmondsworth: Penguin.

Goldberg, R. (1995) *Performance Art: From Futurism to the Present*, London: Thames and Hudson.

Goodman, L. (1993). *Contemporary Feminist Theatres: To Each Her Own*, London: Routledge.

Gradinger, M. (1999) 'Pina Bausch', in M. Bremser (ed.) *Fifty Contemporary Choreographers*, London and New York: Routledge.

Graver, D. (1995) *The Aesthetics of Disturbance: Anti-art in Avant-garde Drama*, Ann Arbor, MI: University of Michigan Press.

Grosz, E. (1994) *Volatile Bodies: Towards a Corporeal Feminism*, Bloomington, IN: Indiana University Press.

—— (1995) *Space, Time and Perversion: Essays on the Politics of the Body*, London: Routledge.

Grotowski, J. (1968) 'An Interview', *Tulane Drama Review*, 13: 29–45.

—— (1975) *Towards a Poor Theatre*, London: Methuen. First published (1968) Denmark: Odin Teatrets Forlag.

Hanna, G. (ed.) (1991) *Monstrous Regiment: A Collective Celebration*, London: Nick Hern Books.

Haraway, D. (1991) *Simians, Cyborgs and Women: The Reinvention of Nature*, London: Free Association Books.

Harrison, B. (October 2005) Personal interview with Katie Normington. London.

Harrison, C. and Wood, P. (1992) (eds) *Art in Theory: 1900–1990*, Oxford: Basil Blackwell Press.

Harvie, J. (2002) 'DV8's *Can We Afford This*: The Cost of Devising on Site for Global Markets', *Theatre Research International*, 27.1: 68–77.

—— (2005) *Staging the UK*, Manchester: Manchester University Press.

Heathfield, A, Templeton, F. and Quick, A. (eds) (1997) *Shattered Anatomies: Traces of the Body in Performance*, Bristol: Arnolfini Live.

Heddon, D. (1998) 'What's in a Name . . .?', *Studies in Theatre Production*, 18: 49–57.

Heddon, D. and Milling, J. (2006) *Devising Performance: A Critical History*, Basingstoke: Palgrave Macmillan.

Hewison, R. (2002) 'Review of *To You, the Birdie! (Phèdre)*', *Sunday Times*, 19 May.

Himelstein, M.Y. (1963) *Drama was a Weapon: Left Wing Theatre in New York 1929–1941*, Westport, CT: Greenwood Press.

Hodge, A. (ed.) (2000) *Twentieth Century Actor Training*, London: Routledge.

Howell, J. (1999) 'Acting and Nonacting', in B. Marranca and G. Dasgupta (eds) *Conversations on Art and Performance*, Baltimore, MD: Johns Hopkins University Press: 394–409.

Huizinga, J. (1980) *Homo Ludens: A Study of the Play Element in Culture*, London: Routledge.

Hulton, D. (1998) 'Creative Actor (Empowering the Performer)', in C. McCullough (ed.) *Theatre Praxis: Teaching Drama Through Practice*, Basingstoke: Macmillan: 38–61.

—— (2000) 'Joseph Chaikin and Aspects of Actor Training', in A. Hodge (ed.) *Twentieth Century Actor Training*, London: Routledge: 151–173.

Ince, K. (2000) *Orlan: Millennial Female*, Oxford: Berg.

Ingold, T. (2000) *The Perception of the Environment: Essays in Livelihood, Dwelling and Skill*, London: Routledge.

Innes, C. (1993a) 'Adapting Dickens to the Modern Eye', in P. Reynolds (ed.) *Novel Images: Literature in Performance*, London: Routledge: 64–79.

—— (1993b) *Avant Garde Theatre 1892–1992*, London: Routledge.

Johns, I. (2002) 'Plenty of Muscle but Little Heart', *The Times*, 11 May.

Kaprow, A. (1993) *Essays on the Blurring of Art and Life*, J. Kelley (ed.), Berkeley, CA: University of California Press.

Kaye, N. (1996) *Art Into Theatre*, Amsterdam: Harwood.

—— (2000) *Site-Specific Art: Performance, Place and Documentation*, London: Routledge.

Kellman, A. (1976) 'Joseph Chaikin the Actor', *The Drama Review*, 20.3: 17–26.

Kelly, A. (2000) 'Third Angel: Class of '76', in A. Heathfield (ed.) *Small Acts: Performance, the Millennium and the Marking of Time*, London: Black Dog Publishing: 45–51.

Kermode, F. (1979) *The Genius of Secrecy: On the Interpretation of Narrative*, Cambridge, MA: Harvard University Press.

Kerr, W. (1997) 'Is G right – Did the Word Come Last?', in R. Schechner and L. Wolford (eds) *The Grotowski Sourcebook*, London and New York: Routledge: 152–56.

Kershaw, B. (1992) *The Politics of Performance: Radical Theatre as Cultural Intervention*, London: Routledge.

—— (1999) *The Radical in Performance: Between Brecht and Baudrillard*, London: Routledge.

—— (2006) 'Performance Studies and P-Chang's Ox: Towards a Paradoxology of Performance', *New Theatre Quarterly*, 22.1: 30–53.

Kiernander, A. (1990) 'The Role of Ariane Mnouchkine at the Théâtre du Soleil', *Modern Drama*, 33.3: 322–331.

Kiley, B. (2004) 'Arty out of Towners', *Seattle: The Stranger*. Available online at www.thestranger.com (accessed 9 July 2006).

Kipnis, C. (1974) *The Mime Book*, New York: Harper & Row.

Kirby, M. (1972) 'On Acting and Not-Acting', *The Drama Review*, 16.1: 3–15.

Knight, S. (1999) 'Performing Arts: The Consulting Room', *British Medical Journal*. Available online at www.bmj.com/cgi/content/full/319/7203/199/a (accessed 31 October 1999).

Kobialka, M. (1986) 'Let the Artists Die?: An Interview with Tadeusz Kantor', *The Drama Review*, 30.3: 177–183.

—— (1994) 'Forget Kantor', *Performing Arts Journal*, 16.2 (May): 1–17.

Kozel, S. (1997) ' "The Story is Told as History of the Body": Strategies of Mimesis in the Work of Irigaray and Bausch', in J.C. Desmond (ed.) *Meaning in Motion*, Durham, NC and London: Duke University Press.

Kristeva, J. (1982) *Powers of Horror: An Essay on Abjection*, trans. L. Roudiez, New York: Columbia University Press.

Kumiega, J. (1985) *The Theatre of Grotowski*, London and New York: Methuen.

Kwon, M. (2000) 'One Place After Another: Notes on Site Specificity', in E. Suderberg (ed.) *Space, Site, Intervention: Situating Installation Art*, London and Minneapolis, MN: University of Minnesota Press: 38–63.

Lamden, G. (2000) *Devising: A Handbook for Drama and Theatre Students*, London: Hodder & Stoughton.

Lasch, C. (1978) *The Culture of Narcissism: American Life in an Age of Diminishing Expectations*, New York: WW Norton & Co.

Lavender, A. (2002) 'The Moment of Realized Actuality', in M. Delgado and C. Svich (eds) *Theatre in Crisis?: Performance Manifestos for a New Century*, Manchester: Manchester University Press: 183–190.

Leask, J. (1995) 'The Silence of the Man: An Essay on Lloyd Newson's Physical Theatre', *Ballett International*, August/September. Available online at www.dv8.co.uk/press/interviews/silence.html (accessed 2 August 2005).

Lefebvre, H. (1991) *The Production of Space*, Oxford: Blackwell.

Lévi-Strauss, C. (1966) *The Savage Mind*, London: Weidenfield and Nicolson.

Littlewood, J. (1961) 'Goodbye Note from Joan', in *Encore*, October: 15–16.

Loizos, C. (1969) 'Play Behaviour in Higher Primates: A Review', in D. Morris (ed.) *Primate Ethnography*, Garden City, NY: Anchor Books: 156–178.

Lone Twin (July 2005) Personal interview with Emma Govan, Rindlesham.

McBurney, S. and Wheatley, M. (1999) *The Street of Crocodiles*, London: Methuen.

MacDonald, C. (1995) 'Assumed Identities: Feminism, Autobiography and Performance Art', in J. Swindells (ed.) *The Uses of Autobiography*, London: Routledge: 187–195.

McGrath, J. (1996) *A Good Night Out*, London: Nick Hern Books.

McKenzie, J. (1994) 'Virtual Reality: Performance, Immersion and the Thaw', *The Drama Review*, 38.4: 83–106.

—— (2001) *Perform or Else*, London: Routledge.

McMillan, J. (2005) 'Pride of Place or Threat to Old Mode of Performance', *The Scotsman*, 27 July. Available online at www.edinburghfestivals.co.uk/reviews.cfm (accessed 17 January 2006).

Mayo, M. (2000) *Cultures, Communities, Identities: Cultural Strategies for Participation and Empowerment*, Basingstoke: Palgrave.

Melzer, A. (1994) *Dada and Surrealist Performance*, Baltimore, MD: Johns Hopkins University Press.

Mendus, C. (January 2000) Interview with Katie Normington, London.

Merleau-Ponty, M. (2002) *Phenomenology of Perception*, trans. C. Smith, Oxford and New York: Routledge.

Murphy, A. (2004) 'Small Awakenings', *The DanceView Times*, 13 June. Available online at www.danceviewtimes.com/dvw/2004/spring/joegoode.html (accessed 5 January 2006).

Murray, S. (2003) *Jacques Lecoq*, London and New York: Routledge.

Nadan, C. (2003) 'Inside Forced Entertainment: The Route to *The Travels*', *Studies in Theatre Performance*, 22.3: 133–138.

Neelands, J. and Dobson, W. (2000) *Drama and Theatre Studies at AS/A Level*, London: Hodder & Stoughton.

Newson, L. (1997) 'DV8 . . . Ten Years on The Edge', interview with Mary Luckhurst. Available online at www.dv8.co.uk/press/interviews/tenyears.html (accessed 2 August 2005).

Oddey, A. (1994) *Devising Theatre: A Practical and Theoretical Handbook*, London: Routledge.

O'Leary, T. (2004) *Applied Theatre: Three Examples of Practice*, L. Keyworth (ed.) Palatine DVD.

Orlan (1996) 'Conference', in D. McCorquodale (ed.) *Orlan: This Is My Body . . . This is My Software*, London: Black Dog Publishing: 82–93.

Parry, J. (2001) 'So Then Hamlet Turned into Calvin Klein', *Observer*, 27 May.

Pasolli, R. (1970) *A Book on the Open Theatre*, New York: Avon Books.

Patterson, M. (1994) 'Brecht's Legacy', in P. Thomson and G. Sacks (eds) *The Cambridge Companion to Brecht*, Cambridge: Cambridge University Press.

Pearson, M. and Shanks, M. (2001) *Theatre/Archaeology*, London: Routledge.

Phelan, P. (2005) 'Reconsidering Identity Politics, Essentialism, and Dismodernism', in C. Sandhal and P. Auslander (eds) *Bodies in Commotion: Disability and Performance*, Ann Arbor, MI: University of Michigan Press: 319–326.

Poggioli, R. (1968) *Theory of the Avant-Garde*, Cambridge, MA: Harvard University Press.

Portelli, A. (1998) 'What Makes Oral History Different', in R. Perks and A. Thomson (eds) *The Oral History Reader*, London: Routledge: 63–74.

Postlewait, T. (1992) 'History, Hermeneutics, and Narrativity', in J.G. Reinelt and J.R. Roach (eds) *Critical Theory and Performance*, Ann Arbor, MI: University of Michigan Press: 356–368.

Price, D. (1990) 'The Politics of the Body in Pina Bausch's Tanztheater', *Theatre Journal*, 42.3: 322–331.

Propp, V. (1968) *The Morphology of the Folk Tale*, trans. L. Scott, Austin, TX: University of Texas Press.

Prytherch, D. (2005) 'So What is Haptics Anyway', *RTI Research Issues in Art and Design*. Available online at www.biad.uce.ac.uk/research/rti/iadm/issue 2/webber.htm (accessed 5 July 2005).

Puzyna, K. (1971) 'A Myth Vivisected: Grotowski's *Apocalpse*', *Tulane Drama Review*, 15.4: 36–46.

Reinelt, J. (2001) 'Performing Europe: Identity Formation for a "New" Europe', *Theatre Journal*, 53.3: 365–87.

—— (2002) 'The Politics of Discourse: Performativity meets Theatricality', *Substance*, 31.2&3: 201–215.

Renza, L. (1980) 'The Veto of the Imagination: A Theory of Autobiography', in J. Olney (ed.) *Autobiography: Essays Theoretical and Critical*, Princeton, NJ: Princeton University Press: 268–295.

Richter, H. (1997) *Dada: Art and Anti-art*, London: Thames and Hudson.

Ricoeur, P. (1984) *Time and Narrative*, Vol. 2. Chicago, IL: University of Chicago Press.

—— (1992) *Oneself as Another*, trans. K. Balmey, Chicago, IL: University of Chicago Press.

Rogers, E. (1995) *Diffusion of Innovation*, New York, Free Press.

Romney, J. (1999) 'End Zone: Even Tables and Chairs have souls', *Guardian*, 29 January.

Rosenthal, D. (1999) 'Crocodile Tears', *The Times*, 18 January.

Rudlin, J. (2000) 'Jacques Copeau: The Quest for Sincerity', in A. Hodge (ed.) *Twentieth Century Actor Training*, London: Routledge: 55–78.

Runkel, R. (1987) *Theatre Workshop: Its Philosophy, Plays, Processes and Productions*, unpublished PhD thesis, University of Texas, Austin.

Rush, M. (1999) *New Media in Late 20th Century Art*, London: Thames and Hudson.

Sainer, A. (1997) *The New Radical Theatre Notebook*, New York: Applause Books.

Samuel, R., (1994) *Theatres of Memory, Vol.1: Past and Present in Contemporary Culture*, London: Verso.

Samuel, R. McColl, E. and Cosgrove, S. (1985) *Theatres of the Left 1880–1935: Workers' Theatre Movements in Britain and America*, London: Routledge & Kegan Paul.

Sandford, M. (ed.) (1995) *Happenings and Other Acts*, London: Routledge.

Savran, D. (1986) *The Wooster Group: Breaking the Rules*, Ann Arbor, MI: UMI Research Press.

Schechner, R. (1971) 'On Environmental Design', *Educational Theatre Journal*, 23.4: 379–397.

—— (1985) *Between Theatre and Anthropology*, Philadelphia, PA: University of Philadelphia Press.

—— (1988) *Performance Theory*, London: Routledge.

—— (1994) *Environmental Theater*, New York: Applause.

—— (1997a) 'Exoduction', in R. Schechner and L. Wolford (eds) *The Grotowski Sourcebook*, London and New York: Routledge: 462–494.

—— (1997b) 'Introduction: The Laboratory Theatre in NY, 1969', in R. Schechner and L.Wolford (eds) *The Grotowski Sourcebook*, London and New York: Routledge: 114–117.

—— (1997c) 'Introduction to Theatre of Productions', in R. Schechner and L. Wolford (eds) *The Grotowski Sourcebook*, London and New York: Routledge: 23–27.

—— (2002) *Performance Studies: An Introduction*, London: Routledge.

Schechner, R. and Wolford, L. (1997) *The Grotowski Sourcebook*, London and New York: Routledge.

Schutzman, M. (1994) 'Canadian Roundtable: An Interview', in M. Schutzman and J. Cohen-Cruz (eds) *Playing Boal*, London: Routledge: 198–226.

Schweitzer, P. (1994) 'Many Happy Retirements', in M. Schutzman and J. Cohen-Cruz (eds) *Playing Boal*, London: Routledge: 64–80.

Segal, L. (1996) 'Review of Bausch's *Nur Du*', *Los Angeles Times*, 5 October.

Sennett, R. (1976) *The Fall of Public Man: On the Social Psychology of Capitalism*, New York: Vintage Books.

Serra, R. (1994) *Writings/Interviews*, Chicago, IL: Chicago University Press.

Seyd, R. (1975) 'The Theatre of Red Ladder', *New Edinburgh Review*, 30: 36–42.

Shank, T. (1982) *American Alternative Theatre*, London: Macmillan.

—— (1997) 'Design and Collaboration: An Interview with Peter Pabst', *Theatre Forum*, 10 (Winter/Spring): 81–83.

—— (2002) *Beyond the Boundaries: American Alternative Theatre*, Ann Arbor, MI: The University of Michigan Press.

Sklar, D. (1995) 'Etienne Decroux's Promethean Mime', in P. Zarrilli (ed.) *Acting (Re)Considered*, London and New York: Routledge: 108–120.

Smit, T. (2001) *Eden*, London: Bantam Press.

Sobey, R. (July 1999) Personal interview with Emma Govan, London.

Sontag, S. (1991) *Illness as Metaphor*, Harmondsworth: Penguin.

Stanier, P. (2001) 'Interview with Matt Adams of Blast Theory', *Live Art Magazine*. Available online at www.liveartmagazine.com/core/reviews (accessed 6 February 2001).

Steedman, C. (1986) *Landscape for a Good Woman*, London: Virago Press.

Stourac, R. and McCreery, K. (1986) *Theatre as a Weapon: Workers' Theatre in the Soviet Union, Germany and Great Britain, 1917–1934*, London: Routledge & Kegan Paul.

Surveillance Camera Players (2006) *We Know You Are Watching: Surveillance Camera Players 1996–2006*, New York: Factory School.

Suzuki, T. (1995) 'Culture is the Body', in P. Zarrilli (ed.) *Acting (Re)Considered*, London and New York: Routledge: 155–160.

Tait, P. (2005) *Circus Bodies*, London: Routledge.

Taylor, F. (1911) *The Principles of Scientific Management*, London: Harper and Brothers.

Theatre Alibi (1993) *Story Telling as Theatre*, Exeter: Arts Archives.

Third Angel (November 2001) *Where From Here*, Crucible Theatre, Sheffield.

—— (2003) *Class of '76*, Arnolfini, Bristol.

—— (2004) Personal interview with Emma Govan, Sheffield.

Tomkins, C. (1997) *Duchamp*, London: Chatto and Windus.

Toolan, M. (2001) *Narrative: A Critical Linguistic Introduction*, London: Routledge.

Tuan, Y. (1977) *Space and Place: The Perspective of Experience*, London: Edward Arnold.

Tytell, J. (1997) *The Living Theatre: Art, Exile and Outrage*, London: Methuen.

van Erven, E. (2001) *Community Theatre: Global Perspectives*, London: Routledge.

Verma, J. (1998) 'A Generation of Asian Theatre in England', in R. Boon and J. Plastow (eds) *Theatre Matters*, Cambridge: Cambridge University Press: 128–137.

White, H. (1987) *The Content of the Form: Narrative Discourse and Historical Representation*, London: Johns Hopkins University Press.

Wiles, D. (2003) *A Short History of Western Performance Space*, Cambridge: Cambridge University Press.

Wiley, L. and Feiner, D. (2001) 'Making a Scene: Representational Authority and Community-Centred Process of Script Development' in T. Nellhaus and S. Haedicke (eds) *Performing Democracy: International Perspectives on Community-based Performance*, Ann Arbor, MI: University of Michigan Press: 121–142.

Willett, J. (ed.) (1978) *Brecht on Theatre*, London: Methuen.

Williams, D. (ed.) (1999) *Collaborative Theatre: Théâtre du Soleil Sourcebook*, London and New York: Routledge.

Williams, R. (1961) *The Long Revolution*, Harmondsworth: Penguin Books.

—— (1962) *Communications*, London: Pelican.

—— (1983) *Keywords: A Vocabulary of Culture and Society*, London, Fontana.

—— (1992) *Culture and Society 1780–1950*, Harmondsworth: Penguin Books.

Wolford, L. (1997) 'Ariadne's Thread: Grotowski's Journey through the Theatre', in R. Schechner and L. Wolford (eds) *The Grotowski Sourcebook*, London and New York: Routledge.

Woodruff, G. (2004) 'Theatre at Telford Community Arts 1974–1990', *Research in Drama Education*, 9.1: 34–45.

Wrights & Sites (2003) *An Exeter Mis-Guide*, Exeter: Wrights & Sites Publications. Available online at www.12manage.com/methods_rogers_innovation_adoption_curve.html (10 July 2006)

Young, I.M. (1990) 'The Ideal of Community and the Politics of Difference', in L.J. Nicholson (ed.) *Feminism/Postmodernism*, London: Routledge: 300–323.

Zarrilli, P. (ed.) (1995) *Acting (Re)considered: A Theoretical and Practical Guide*, London: Routledge.

Websites

www.actionaid.org (12 July 2004)

www.ageexchange.org.uk (13 July 2006)

www.blasttheory.co.uk (3 May 2006)

www.candoco.co.uk (13 July 2006)

www.cardboardcitizens.org.uk (10 October 2006)

www.edenproject.com (11 July 2006)

www.forcedentertainment.com (29 June 2006)

www.goatislandperformance.org (24 August 2005)

www.gridiron.org.uk (14 July 2006)

www.joegoode.org (28 August 2005)

www.labofii.net/home/ (11 November 2005)

www.lonetwin.com (16 April 2006)

www.mis-guide.com (15 November 2005)

www.notbored.org/the-scp.html (7 December 2005)

www.reckless-sleepers.co.uk (25 May 2005)

www.rona-lee.co.uk/encircle.html (4 July 2006)

www.spacehijackers.co.uk (27 November 2005)

www.timeslips.org (12 June 2006)

www.walksquawk.org (20 June 2006)

www.yellowearth.org (14 March 2006)

INDEX

Devising Theatre
A Practical and Theoretical Handbook
ALISON ODDEY

Devising Theatre is a practical handbook that combines a critical analysis of contemporary devised theatre practice with descriptions of selected companies, and suggestions for any group devising theatre from scratch. It is the first book to propose a general theory of devised theatre.

After identifying the unique nature of this type of performance, the author examines how devised theatre is perceived by professional practitioners, and provides an historical overview illustrating how it has evolved since the 1960s. Alison Oddey examines the particular working practices and products of a number of professional companies, including a Reminiscence theatre for the elderly and a theatre-in-education group, and offers ideas and exercises for exploration and experimentation.

Pb: 978-0-415-04900-9